MORE PRAISE FOR *THE WORLD IS A WAITING LOVER*

"From colorful threads of personal experience, ancient myths, and modern stories, Trebbe Johnson weaves together a stunning tapestry of the Beloved, mortal and immortal. This candid narrative describes the passion and creativity that enriches life when one encounters the Beloved as soul-guide."

> — Nancy Qualls-Corbett, PhD, author of
> *The Sacred Prostitute* and *Awakening Woman*

" 'The Beloved beckons us into our own being,' writes Trebbe Johnson, and as she reveals her quest for Sacred Intimacy, she offers us myriad possibilities to allure, attract, and hold the human as well as the divine Beloved. An inspiring, courageous journey, inviting us to live passionately ever after."

> — Diane Wolkstein, author of *Treasures of the Heart:*
> *Holiday Stories That Reveal the Soul of Judaism*

"*The World Is a Waiting Lover* is a rich, vivacious treatise on spiritual longing and the allurement of a mystical engagement with life. Like the familiar curves of a once-forgotten lover — compelling and unveiled — these sensual, wisdom-drenched pages will remind you and guide you toward your heart's ancient passion and your soul's truest desire; a masterful blending of the personal and archetypal powers in action."

> — Frank MacEowen, author of *The Mist-Filled Path*

The World Is
a Waiting Lover

THE WORLD IS
A WAITING LOVER

Desire and the Quest for the Beloved

Trebbe Johnson
Foreword by Thomas Moore

NEW WORLD LIBRARY
NOVATO, CALIFORNIA

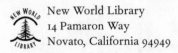 New World Library
14 Pamaron Way
Novato, California 94949

Parts of the section in chapter 2 about fear and limitation were first published as "The
Monster of Grim Prospects," *Parabola* 23, no. 3 (fall 1998), and sections of the story of
Psyche and Eros and the longing for rapture with the divine in chapters 8 and 9 are from
"Wedding Night with the God," *Parabola* 24, no. 4 (spring 2004).

Text design and typography by Tona Pearce Myers

Library of Congress Cataloging-in-Publication Data
Johnson, Trebbe.
The world is a waiting lover : desire and the quest for the beloved / Trebbe Johnson.
    p.   cm.
 Includes bibliographical references and index.
 ISBN 1-57731-479-4 (pbk. : alk. paper)
 1. Johnson, Trebbe 2. Love—Religious aspects. 3. Spiritual biography—United
States. I. Title.
BL73.J6455A3 2005
204'.092—dc22   2005017342

First printing, November 2005
ISBN-10: 1-57731-479-4
ISBN-13: 978-1-57731-479-X

 Printed in Canada on 100 percent postconsumer waste recycled paper

g A proud member of the Green Press Initiative

Distributed to the trade by Publishers Group West

10 9 8 7 6 5 4 3 2 1

For Andy — beloved

CONTENTS

FOREWORD

Love is the strangest thing: When you want it most, it isn't there. When you think you have it in place, well packaged and arranged for comfortable living, it falls apart, or a new love appears. It comes and goes. You sense it in its absence as much as in its presence. You need it, but sometimes you'd rather not have it with all its encumbrances.

In the well-known story of Eros and Psyche, the psyche as young woman enjoys some time sleeping with love in the dark. But, prodded to know who and what her lover, or love itself, is, she lights a lamp one night and accidentally spills some hot oil on her companion. He wakes up and leaves her.

Unconscious love is sweet and desirable, but it isn't enough. It gets us into big trouble. So we search and learn and analyze and hope to love freely and less blindly. But consciousness has a stinger, and love suffers from the effort to learn more about it.

Trebbe Johnson is like Psyche. She has looked at love and discovered that he has large, beautiful wings. She tracks him down as he flits from one place to another, always disguised, never what he seems to be, always pointing to another level.

Her writing is personal and mythic, social and mystical, concrete and confessional. It is honest and relentless in pursuit of the winged Eros that hovers behind every momentary attraction and persistent obsession. Few write about love and desire like this, understanding that they are not just human passion and not all about human relationship. She has written a *theology* of love, if we can understand theology to be a close study of a spirit.

But, as Psyche learned, when you try to be more conscious about love, it disappears, at least for a while. You have to be initiated, become more sophisticated about life, be a different person, and then love may return. We tend to write and use books as tools of enlightenment, so there is an inherent contradiction in writing and reading about love and desire. Somehow our explorations have to keep us in the dark even as they shed a little light.

Accordingly, Trebbe's book is full of rich stories, old and new, that don't give definitive answers to your questions but bring you a long way in your reflection. As you follow Trebbe's efforts not to act out her illusions, think about your own infatuations. How could you honor them and yet not act them out?

I think highly of illusions. They are the soul breaking through the mundane walls of our lives. They are essential, but they also deceive. The Greeks called Aphrodite, Love's mother, the Deceptive One, and you might realize the danger to your tranquility in reading this book. It is deceptively simple, deceptively enlightening. Love may seem rational, after all. But once you leave the book and get back into life, you will discover that you have been deceived once again.

The deception of the gods is different from human deception. It has its necessity and its value. Even though you may have learned from experience that love can be cruel, you try it again. Love has deceived you, sprinkled you with illusions, and yet you are more ready to respond to his arrows once again.

Your loves and desires, especially the complicated ones, show you who you are. As love forces you to reassess your values and identity, your heart is revealed, peeled away layer by layer, time after time. The more you have loved, the more complex you are, more interesting, maybe more lovable.

As you take up this excellent book on love and desire, read between the lines. Note the rich and valuable unconsciousness of the author. She has much to teach you precisely because she has been willing to stay with her illusions. In telling her captivating story, she is honest about the travels it has forced her to make. She tells you how she was caught in her own illusions. You may see some that she overlooks, and that could be a lesson to you: You can't be fully conscious about love, no matter how willingly you try to be. You do your best, and the slightest insight goes a long way.

Your attractions take you into the depths of your soul. Love is always poetic, always signifying more than appears to the naked eye. Your love of chocolate may hint at your desire for the sweet life. Your love of cars may suggest a desire to move on. Your love of nature may say something about the untamed wildness in your character.

Love is also dark. Psyche's sisters insist, rightly I think, that love is a dragon and a beast. Countless statues from the East show the lover as a fanged, grimacing, sharp-pointed partner. It is not only in our sweet loves that we glimpse our souls. Trebbe refers to her former bond with alcohol. This, too, is a love, a dark attachment, that has something of great value to reveal.

I was drawn to this book because it honors the poetics in life and love. Trebbe understands that there is always another step to take, another level to explore. I appreciate her ability to make traditional myths and stories so vivid and relevant, and to step beyond the obvious and the literal, to keep her illusions alive and productive. She demonstrates well how to weave an impossible love into life and allow it to be continually creative and livable. This is a rare sensitivity in a culture that craves final explanations and conclusions.

Like all good books, this one is seductive. Quite properly, the spirit of Aphrodite graces its pages. It entices you to fall into your own precious mystery, to let your spirit take flesh as you become a human being, and to let your ordinary life find its spiritual core. For your particular loves and desires, whether meaningful or senseless, make you who you are — unique, quirky, passionate, transcendent.

— Thomas Moore,
author of *Care of the Soul*

The Embrace of the God

Many mortal women have made love with Krishna. Long ago — some say the practice continues even today — the playful, sensuous god who, as a child, was often caught stealing butter from the neighbors' churns, would go among the villages of his hot, moist land and call to the women to join him in an afternoon of delight. Age mattered nothing to him, nor did looks or marital status. The god loved all women and wanted to be loved in return. And the women, if they had any erotic curiosity at all, answered the summons. Who would choose not to? And besides, little good comes to those who turn their back on the call of a god.

When Krishna's alluring invitation interrupted their attention to their tasks — or to their daydreaming in the midst of their tasks — these women awoke to a great possibility. They smelled perfumed skin and fresh mangoes. They heard bells tinkling and felt long grasses tickling their legs. They experienced the touch of the sun in their dark, secret places and recalled, suddenly, that something once had burned inside them, something precious and bright. They remembered that it had been quite a while since they had thought of this lost, elusive thing, longer still since they had tended it, and they experienced a small shiver of regret to think that, by their neglect, they might have allowed it to fade.

In the wake of the concern came a sense of relief, even joy. Perhaps the bright thing shone yet. Yes, it shone even now, and burned, and the quickening had to do with the call of Krishna. The women remembered then that they had a task to fulfill, not just in their homes but in the very cosmos itself. They recalled that the gods had always expected more of them than simply watching over the cattle or sweeping the floor or minding the babies or rubbing the aching feet of their husbands. A tantalizing and vital thing had to be done, and they, only they, could attend to it. Their bodies tingled with anticipation.

So the women answered the call. The *gopi*, the cowherd girl, left her animals browsing on the hillside. The obedient daughter paused in her weaving to listen intently. Then she stood, left the loom, and turned toward the doorway. The servant set the spoon in the cooking pot. The mother walked past her children playing among the spilt flowers under the jasmine bush. The elder withdrew her thoughts from the faraway hills and gathered up the hem of her sari. The dancer in the temple paused in the midst of a mudra. Off they went, all of them, to the flowering grove, where Krishna awaited them.

There the dance began. The women raised their eyes to the sky and twirled and laced their arms together and moved as winemakers pressing out the luscious juices of the cosmos. They danced with abandon, and Krishna danced among them, and at some point — they scarcely knew how to distinguish when it began — the god made love with them, each and every one, in the way they liked best. So intoxicating was Krishna's touch, so attentive his presence, that each woman felt herself to be the sole recipient of his passion. Each woman he made love to was, in that moment, beloved of the holy one and filled with him.

Then it ended. No one, after all, can remain for long in the embrace of a god. Waves of orgasm smoothed into ripples of contentment. Each woman fluttered down from her ecstasy and recalled her humanness.

The god, lighthearted, light-footed as ever, moved on. The women stood up and arranged their saris and made their way back to their cows and looms, their families and duties.

But they went transformed. From that day forth they listened with their whole being for the call of Krishna to summon them back into his embrace. The longing became a source of exquisite torment, for it formed in them a hole shaped like the divine one himself, and able to be filled only by him. And because the longing breached them so utterly, they found that they remained open and expectant, like a clay urn just before it is dipped into a rushing stream. All experiences and prayers and gestures that passed through them then molded to the longing that was shaped like their moment in Krishna's embrace and hence took on the outline of the holy. Every act these women undertook became imbued with sacred presence and readied them for their next encounter with the god. Thus began their lifelong thrall to soulful yearning. Thus did they walk into the world as into the arms of a waiting lover.

LET US BE REALISTIC. We are modern women and men. We lead demanding lives. We do not, most of us, tend cattle on the hillsides or weave our family's clothes, and if we do, we do a thousand other urgent things as well. Nor have most of us been trained in a spiritual tradition that enables us to recognize the call of the holy lover when it comes. Who, then, is the god that might beckon to us? What is the seductive force that will arouse us and remind us that we are shining beings with vital tasks to perform? What will carve into us the shape of what we most long for? It is the Beloved.

The Beloved is the elusive, alluring presence who has beguiled lovers in the myths of many cultures, from Persia to Sweden to the icy seas of the Arctic. Ecstatic mystics of the world's great religions have called out to their god as the Beloved they ached to know more intimately. According to Socrates, the erotic force that animated the soul was the semidivine partner, the daimon, who never forgot why his special mortal charge was born and who served only to keep that person on track while faithfully bearing his prayers to the gods. To Jung, the beloved Other who appears occasionally at night to clasp a dreamer in an embrace she wishes never to awaken from confirms one's wholeness as a human. The Beloved is our link to what we hold most sacred and long to be a part of, and, at the same time, it is our most intimate companion. The compelling force that lures us to where our soul most needs to go and emboldens us to get there as only we can do, the Beloved is the fuse between loving and being loved.

To walk toward the arms of the Beloved is to choose an erotic connection with life. Just out of reach, like a figure half-hidden in dappled sunlight, the Beloved beckons us into a passionate embrace with all we undertake, from the boldest first step to the simplest spontaneous response to some arising need. Unmappable, shape-shifting, always sidling out of our greedy embrace, only to lure us forth once again, the Beloved impels us to embark on a journey toward ecstatic engagement with people and places, ideas and acts. The Beloved is less an iconic image to be obeyed and to remain steadfast to than an invitation to accept with fascinated curiosity.

The World Is a Waiting Lover charts a quest rooted in the myths of many lands, fleshed out by mystics, cosmologists, psychologists, and poets and profoundly relevant to men and women today.[1] It is a personal story and, at the same time, it weaves a modern myth of its own — about the different guises (and occasional disguises) of the Beloved; the obstacles, mirages, enchantments, and treasures encountered on the search for that rare and rapturous embrace; and the human yearning to live with fearless authenticity. It is the story of women and men who have used the heartbreak of an unattainable love or a lifetime's indefinable longing for Spirit (or God or the great mystery) as an opportunity to define and form a bond with Eros. And it is an invitation for our time, when so many people are looking for some way to bring passion and meaning to their work, their relationships, their view of the future. It is a quest that often finds resolution, but never completion.

My own search for the Beloved began with a love affair that could not be realized. I was fifty years old when I fell in love with a young man who was assisting on a wilderness program I was leading. When he told me at the end of the trip that he loved me, I succumbed to a whirl of passionate desire that melted me like the hot summer days during which I moped for him.

I knew, almost from the start — though, frankly, I tried to deny it — that my longing betokened a plunge into something other than a relationship with this particular man. Curious, spellbound, I was compelled to explore a new frontier by tracking passion itself. And so I came to know the longing for ardor and oneness with myself and my world, which, as the myths make plain, is a very old and universal quest. It changed my life. It revived my postmenopausal sexuality and shifted the ground of my attitude toward my femininity. It deepened my relationships with my husband, my friends, my colleagues, and my clients. It emboldened me to offer programs, as well as ideas and approaches within those programs, in a more spontaneous, effusive manner, unafraid of being judged. Through my pursuit of the Beloved, I saw the world change around me: strangers in airports and restaurants ceased to be mere background figures and took on a shimmer of impenetrable mystery. I no longer saw distances between myself and people, ideas, and prospects without also envisioning the bridges that might link us. My heart, breached by longing, forgot how to close. The journey to the Beloved taught me how to walk into the world as into the arms of a waiting lover. It started with a mountain in southwestern Colorado that held a dream that, so it turned out, not just the dreamer but the dreamed of had need of.

CHAPTER ONE

The Leap of the Flame

THE SOUL'S LONGING TO THRIVE

Longing draws us toward what we have never known and will recognize instantly. We yearn to be a part of the world. We long to be at home wherever we go, to enjoy fearless, passionate relationships with the people we meet and the things we do. We yearn to express our true self, the essence of our being that has too long flickered inside us like a timid flame. We ache to move in joy, as a dancer does, or a musician in ecstatic dialogue with his instrument, as an athlete running for her life. We want that pitch of commitment. We want to smell and taste the world we're passing through, as we shape it with our hands, our being, our delight. We long to be embraced by wonder, to be imbued with the Mystery that pervades all things, to be swept off our feet by a world that falls in love with us, over and over, because we are who we are. We long to be welcomed by the world because we have something to offer that has been sorely needed for a very long time.

Every now and then we have heeded the longing and given license to the flaring of that flame: when we spoke up, despite our fear, in the face of an injustice, or raised our arms in exultation at the beauty of some wild landscape, or done some unrehearsed and generous thing. We have felt it when we set out to make something — a painting, a garden, a wooden spoon — and lost ourselves in a pool of unself-conscious enchantment. The flame of authentic passion leapt up even in the face of death, illness, or loss, when, huddled in a ball of unspeakable grief, we recognized ourselves as part of something eternal and undimmed, and felt fortified as a result. In these moments we glimpsed the possibility of living so intimately with our own possibilities that our blood and the world's huge, incomprehensible currents flowed as one.

Too often, just when those moments of brighter burning began to warm us, we've been tempted to quenched the flame. Such intensity seemed dangerous. As if chastised, we jerked ourselves back to the more familiar view that we are but puny and helpless things. How, we asked ourselves, as if to justify our tampering in potential greatness, could such passion survive in the world anyway? Living it, we would go crazy, would we not? We would die in exile, abandoned by all our friends. We would be ridiculed for our foolish presumption.

Each thing, Spinoza stated in his *Ethics*, "endeavors to persist in its own being."[1] Trout and paramecia, dinosaurs, oaks, and dandelions, polar bears, chimpanzees, human beings, and red-winged blackbirds — all busy themselves zealously in doing what they must do to thrive. Being alive is not just surviving and making do, it is living with zest and glory. Even a quartz crystal, "growing" in the dark earth at the rate of two millimeters a day, accretes each of its glassy molecules in a pattern of angles and planes distinctive to it alone. Life strives, wrote deep ecologist Arne Naess, to perfect itself. You could say that each entity on earth seeks union with some possibility of itself that it can hardly conceive yet to which it nevertheless moves resolutely closer.

I MYSELF HAVE HEARD THE VOICES OF BEINGS striving to persist in their own being as I've sat in circles of men and women who struggled to find words to express what has compelled them to undertake a vision quest. "Vision quest" is the name anthropologists of the nineteenth century assigned to a Native American rite of passage that has counterparts in cultures worldwide. It is the practice in which a seeker leaves the community behind and ventures alone into the wilderness to fast and pray for guidance, that she may return with some insight into the most personal, specific, and crucial way that she can practice her own self-perfection while contributing to the self-perfection of her people. The vision quest is a mythic journey. Battling demons (rain, heat, bugs, boredom, fear of the dark), accepting the wisdom of helpful allies (a hummingbird, a face in rock, a dream), facing old anxieties and deep longings, and emptying the heart, the seeker suffers spiritual death that she might be reborn into her higher, beckoning self.

Spiritual leaders of many traditions have sought — and found — God in wild nature. Jesus, after his baptism by John the Baptist, consigned himself to the desert and there toughed out temptation, fear, lust, and vainglory until he could accept at last that he was born to preach to his people a theology of forgiveness and love. Muhammad repeatedly climbed to a cave on Mount Hira for twenty-three years to meet with the angel, who transmitted the Koran to him in snatches of song so unforgettable that the human messenger could easily chant the verses to transcribers each time he went back down to Mecca. The resolute but not always patient Moses twice trudged up and down Mount Sinai to receive Jehovah's commandments. Sitting under the bodhi tree, the Buddha flailed at all the distractions of past and present lifetimes until he sank into the peace of nirvana and grasped the Four Noble Truths. King Minos of Crete, it is said, retreated to a cave on Mount Ida once every four years to review his rule with the gods and to take their counsel for the years ahead. The most recent narratives of the vision quest belong, of course, to the Plains people of North America, whose tradition of solitary fasting and prayer has remained unbroken (if severely challenged) for many generations. The selfless, sometimes apparently foolhardy paths of action (such as boldly prancing on a war-painted pony before an army of aimed rifles) that Crazy Horse, Sitting Bull, Black Elk, and other spiritual warriors took in an effort to protect their land and people from white control were often revealed to them while they fasted in a sacred spot.

The contemporary variation on the practice began in 1974, when Steven Foster and Meredith Little, two suicide-prevention hotline volunteers working in Marin County, California, began to meet after hours. As they were falling in love, they were also speculating on how a coming-of-age rite of passage might benefit the young people whose despair they attended to every day. They began to take teens, then adults, out into the California desert both knew well and to support them through the process of self-acceptance and even the first stirrings of sensible self-love. They consulted Native American elders and other indigenous spiritual leaders for advice and support. Often, those they had guided or "put out on the mountain" returned, begging to be taught how to introduce the work into their own communities. The Fosters started an organization called the School of Lost Borders that combined vision quests with the training to lead them, and people from all over the world came to learn. Currently about 150 people and small organizations offer wilderness rites of passage in the United States, and there are even more in Germany, Switzerland, South Africa, Russia, and other countries.

A seeker who embarks on a contemporary vision quest might be graced with any variation of the metaphysical experiences that enlightened her forebears: a moment of oneness with all creation, a clear understanding of the path that she must take, a poem or song emerging whole and perfect and searingly true, a healing, an acceptance of her whole self with all its marvelous, messy parts. Quite often it is not a single, blazing moment of truth that occurs, but a kind of layering: some ray of insight, which seems to be immediately and directly magnified by a natural event — a hummingbird hovers before the eyes, a boulder leaps down a mountain, a spruce branch grabs hold of an arm — which, in turn, illuminates another aspect of the self. "There was no difference between me and what was happening all around me," a schoolteacher from Michigan once told us upon her return to base camp. "I finally stopped trying to figure out what was me and what was outside of me, because I realized we were one."

On the wilderness rites of passage my co-guides and I lead, the group meets for a few days before each individual goes off to sit in solitude for three days and three nights. On the first evening of the journey, as twilight dims the borders between what is known and taken for granted and what is mysterious and unknowable except through soulful exploration, we form a circle and, one at a time, the questers tell a bit of their story. Almost always, what they say reflects their longing to feel the heat of that inner, too often timid, flame.

"My life is devoted to God, to spirit," says an Episcopal minister. "I know what I do is valued in the community. But I feel like I'm working from the organized body of the Church, rather than from my soul."

A successful songwriter admits, "I've got a reputation for writing hard, tough love songs, but somewhere inside of me there's another kind of song trying to get free. I want to know my own heart so I can write the songs that have never been sung."

A woman whose husband left her for another cries, "I feel as if I have no home, as if there is no place for me in the world. Maybe on the mountain I can find my true home, which I know is within me."

A physician says, "I've been a doctor for thirty years. What I really want is to become a healer."

A successful businesswoman weeps, "I have money, a beautiful house, prestige. But I have contributed nothing of value to the earth."

Such longing pierces the heart. Awakened, it hurts even more than when it is allowed to sleep undisturbed. Tears flow in this first circle, not only from the eyes of the speakers, but from the eyes of others as well, for everyone's ache for a life of meaning, authenticity, and passion is gouged deeper by each consecutive voice. They would do anything to find the antidote to this holy yearning. They would do anything to embrace the joyfully self-perfecting soul, the authentic nature that they were born with and that keeps titillating yet eluding them.

The year I turned fifty, I sat in one of those circles in a ranch house at the foot of a solitary peak in the San Juan Mountains of southern Colorado. As I listened to the voices of the people who had come on an

Animas Valley Institute (AVI) quest led by the Institute's cofounder Bill Plotkin and me, I congratulated myself on having attained, at least for the present, some relief from that fierce longing.[2] I was doing the work I loved. I was married to the man I loved. I was postmenopausal, my red hair was whitening, and even though I had begun to stop thinking of myself as a sexual being, I was fired with energy for bringing myself into the world. I looked forward to becoming less a hungry flame and more a lantern, steadily burning to guide the searches of others.

In any tale, such smugness is an invitation to the Fates to create a little chaos. On this particular vision quest Bill and I had welcomed as an apprentice guide a handsome thirty-five-year-old psychologist from the Puget Sound area. Lucas would gain experience in the practical and metaphysical aspects of leading a wilderness trip devoted to enhancing one's relationship with the soul, the unique and particular essence of the self, as he helped out with cooking, setting up base camp, counseling individual questers, and undertaking such random yet specialized odd jobs as digging the pit for the ceremonial fire of sacrifice, helping questers tie their tarps tight against thunderstorms, and drumming for ceremonies.

Five nights after that opening circle, after our group had climbed two thousand feet higher up the mountain known to the native Utes as Shandoka, "Storm-Gatherer," Lucas had a dream. The next morning he joined me in the circle of seven spruce trees we called our "kitchen," where I was boiling water for tea on a camp stove. Fifteen feet above our heads, roped to a sturdy pole wedged into the forks of two trees, and inaccessible, we hoped, to bears, dangled four industrial-strength garbage bags containing our food for eight days in the backcountry. The early-morning air was clear and cool. Lucas and I were alone; the questers had left the previous morning for their three-day solo, and Bill was catching up on his sleep. I made the tea. As we grasped the hot cups in our cold hands, Lucas told me his dream.

He was making his way up the mountain to a tiny cave that he had, in fact, noticed as the group backpacked up the trail and that was visible from the meadow where he and I had strung our tarps. What lay below had faded away. He concentrated only on the ascent. Standing in the opening to the cave, beckoning to him, was a woman he recognized as me. A long purple scarf, printed with stars and moons, was tied around her head. The cave was her domain. He realized that she was singing to him, and the song was an invitation to join her there. She was singing him up to the far depths of his own heights, and he felt an irresistible pull to be united with her. And so he climbed. It was a very powerful, vivid dream, he told me, and he had awakened knowing that he must undertake the actual journey that very morning.

"Who is the Trebbe of yourself?" I asked him, following the theory that every character in a dream represents some aspect of the dreamer.

"She's the older, wiser inner guide of myself. It's that energy of yours that I have to claim for myself up there. There is something about you as a guide that my soul needs."

He prepared well. When Bill got up, they peered through binoculars at the slope, an obstacle course of boulders that had crashed down from the summit, and discussed the most feasible route. In a daypack he stuffed warm clothing, rain gear, extra water, and some trail mix in case of emergency. He resolved to be back at base camp before the afternoon thunderstorms rolled in.

He asked if I would send him off. I went to my tarp in the meadow and got out the purple scarf printed with moons and stars, which I had, in fact, worn the previous morning during the final ceremony for the departing questers, when, one at a time, they had stated their intention for the solo and stepped over a ceremonial threshold of stones into the adventure awaiting them. Now I stood on the far side of the stream that separated base camp from the long, broad skirt of the mountain's slope and bid Lucas good-bye, offering words (symbolic, now forgotten) to the tune of his dream. I played the part of myself as a part of him that he needed to embody. In short, I invited him toward his own calling. We hugged, and he stepped over the stream and began the climb.

At first the slope rose gently, a grassy hill punctuated occasionally by enormous boulders and tiny spruces. Soon, however, the incline turned sharper. The grass disappeared as the rocks became more abundant, so the slope, from afar, presented a design of a gray hand reaching down and a green hand reaching up to interlace fingers. The steep upper third of the ascent was a tumble of rocks.

I watched Lucas's journey until he reached the rocks and became so high and small that he turned into a mere symbolic figure, a shadowy movement on a mission to something remote and alluring. Standing below, I was a mirror of his dream image of me. Instead of watching his face come toward me from the cave, I saw his back move away. In his dream, I was the soul guide, drawing him up toward my high precinct with an inviting song; in the waking world, I was a mentor, pushing him upward and away from me, closer to his life's next step. As he approached the cave, I started to feel that I was spying on something that was none of my business, so I turned and headed back to our base camp in the spruces.

What happened to Lucas in the cave that day is a story that belongs to him alone. Suffice it to say that he encountered something sacred there, which seemed to have been waiting for him, and that he returned to base camp transformed, with a vision of how he would bring his work into his community in a new way. The being-there is his. The dream, on the other hand, belongs irrevocably to both of us, because the ascent he made was only the beginning of what it ignited.

TWO DAYS LATER, we guides got up early to prepare breakfast for the returning fasters: an avocado half, followed by a stew of yams, carrots, onions, brown rice, and miso. Before long they started reappearing, making their way slowly across the meadow from the slopes below or through the trees from the uplands. They were thin, sweaty, dirty, unshaven. The eyes of most were radiant. Some wept when we hugged them. Some could not let go. A couple, not yet ready for the shock of company, broke away from the welcoming embrace as soon as possible and went to sit by themselves. They ate slowly and with concentration. In late morning we gathered in a circle and began to hear the stories.

The musician told us that on the third morning of his solo, he had awakened suddenly because he thought he heard drumming. He sat bolt upright, only to realize that the sound that had alerted him was the beating of his own heart. The rhythm pounded on. It seemed to him that all the land — trees, birds, clouds, the mountain itself — was drumming out some song for him. Because he had wanted to leave behind everything that might remind him of his past identity in the music world, he had taken no drum or rattle on his solo. Now, however, he felt the imperative to join in whatever it was that had to be played. He remembered his emergency whistle. Holding it up to his ear and shaking it, so the tiny ball inside served as a rattle, he joined the rhythm the place was giving him. Over the course of several hours, the rhythm occasionally peeled back to reveal a song, which he now sang for the group, accompanied by a big yellow whistle. It was a song about the mountain, about solitude, about the body being broken down and the heart filled. The man who had wanted to write songs from his heart had emerged with one that had begun, literally, with his own heartbeat.

On the day the questers had searched for their solo spot, the woman whose husband had left her for another had returned to base camp in tears. She who had hoped to discover on the mountain the refuge she longed for had not even been able to find what felt like the right place to spend three days. She had ended up claiming a site that would suffice, nothing more, and went off to it the following morning with glum resignation. That afternoon she was on her way back from the stone pile, a cairn midway between the spots of two fasters, where each quester places a stone once a day as a sign that they're all right, when she tripped and fell. It was the final insult. Her husband had left her, and not even a mountain could support her. She burst into tears, then giving herself over to grief and outrage, lay on the ground sobbing. Finally, she calmed down and sat up. And then she realized that the spot where she had landed was beautiful. She had a clear view of the mountain peak. There was level ground between two trees where she could tie her tarp. The stone that had tripped her would be her altar. This, then, was her rightful place. She moved her things, set up a new camp, and began to fall in love with the place that had brought her to it in so undignified a manner. On the altar she placed small stones representing her husband and his new girlfriend and prayed that she might accept what had happened and that her own life be strengthened and sacralized because of it. She gave thanks to the four directions. On the last evening, she held a marriage ceremony in which she wed her highest self.

During an all-night vigil, sitting in a circle of stones and facing east, the minister had a vision of herself as a dancer who could move gracefully between the light of spirit and the dark concerns of her parishioners. A man who had sacrificed his childhood to care for an ailing mother had awakened every night for three nights in a row to see a falling star he could wish on. Sitting for hours before a tree that held in a crook of its branches another toppled and dying tree, the doctor realized that what he needed to become a healer was not new skills but the compassion he had always been too busy to practice. What happened to each person was as rare, intimate, inevitable, and true as the conjunction of one place, replete with teachings in myriad forms, and one person whose very life depended on learning those lessons.

On a vision quest, all things — objects, inhabitants of the natural world, and the infinite components of the individual — take on a life of their own. A dead ponderosa pine grabs the attention of the one person — and no one else — who needs to learn from it, and then slowly reveals itself. Perhaps it shows its core, sliced by lightning, now pale and raw. Perhaps it shows survival skills: a black waste of wood enduring through all seasons. Perhaps a western bluebird alights on one of its wrecked boughs, demonstrating that grace lands where it is least expected. And as the tree reveals itself, it also, startlingly, reveals something of the self who is raptly looking at it. The trunk, blasted black, harks back to a terrible emotional burning. The bird is a holy messenger of forgiveness. "Every object, rightly seen," says Emerson, quoting his friend Samuel Taylor Coleridge, "unlocks a new faculty of the soul."[3] In this time of solitude, where the natural world is home, companion, teacher, muse, lover, and deity, the quester moves in and out of mystical rapture, in which everything about the self that must be heeded and transformed is reflected back by all that surrounds her and captures her fascination.

THE DAY AFTER THE QUESTERS TOLD THEIR STORIES, we all hiked back down the mountain. The final day of the quest we spent at the ranch, focusing on the "reincorporation" phase of the quest, practices and tools that would enable people to sustain their visions when they returned home. Then there was packing, cleaning up, and organizing of rides to the small local airport and other destinations. We had all loaded our gear into cars and were hugging and saying good-bye in the parking lot in front of the ranch house, where white gravel, reflecting late afternoon sun, made it hard to look too closely at teary faces. Then and there, Lucas astonished me.

"I am truly and completely in love with you," he said.

I'd heard similar declarations. Every teacher who facilitates the process by which someone taps into his own marvel receives a share of the exhilaration that results. Men had told me they were attracted to me, women had said they wanted to be like me. What I tried to offer in response was the same mirror I'd held up to them in the first place: a belief in their own capacity for wisdom, leadership, conviction, a big voice, love, courage, freedom from self-doubt, passion for work — whatever it was they believed had been bestowed on them by me, when it fact it was a quality burgeoning in them.

But something in Lucas's tone made this avowal different. It sounded as if he really meant it. I was startled, flattered. I couldn't think of anything to say, so I hugged him again, a quick guide's hug meant to give a young follower a dose of compassion and gratitude, braced with emotional distance. Then I climbed into the car with Bill for the ride out of the mountains.

But those words began to work on me. That night, as I was doing my laundry in a Durango hotel, walking into town for dinner, packing my bags with clean clothes, and waiting in the airport the following morning to board my plane for home, Lucas's words sang in my head. "I am truly and completely in love with you." On the plane, I looked out the window and saw, imprinted on clouds, a flattered middle-aged woman. "I am truly and completely in love with you."

My husband, Andy, picked me up at the airport in Newark, and for a while, during the three-hour drive north to our home in rural Pennsylvania, as we talked of the events of the past two weeks, the words temporarily rested. The next day they were back. "I am truly and completely in love with you." They rang in my mind, and when they fell silent, I deliberately rang them again. An exceptional man was in love with me. This knowledge made me — an aging woman who had been happily monogamous for twelve years — glow with desirability. It made me feel beautiful. It made me feel like the woman I might have been, if only I had been more fearless and magical and outrageous. No, it was more than that: those words, that declaration of love, made me feel as if I really were the woman of the high mountain cave who confidently sang her people up to their own heights.

I felt flattered for two whole days. Hot and sensual, my pleasure kept beauty and vitality stoked in me no matter what else I was doing. At the same time, there was a certain grandiosity to my attitude. It seemed Lucas's words reached up to me at that lofty place where I presided (or might have), the portal of the cave in the mountain. I received them with grace and dispassion.

Then the truth hit. Andy and I were in his old yellow van, driving along the interstate to a furniture warehouse to buy used file cabinets. I was leaning out the window in the passenger seat, feeling the hot, sunny air flap at my face and whip my long hair toward the green chenille hills we streamed past. Below me the tires sang to the high-way the words I could not get enough of. "I am truly and completely in love with you. I am truly and completely in love with you."

Suddenly I was struck by an epiphany. The reason those words kept singing to me was not because I was flattered, but because I was in love with Lucas, too.

CHAPTER TWO

Desire, or the Fall

THE DELICIOUS MADNESS OF TUMBLING INTO LOVE

What a shock. The man was not an apprentice at all, he was a paramour.

The sun and wind slapped my cheeks, awakening me to this new consciousness. Apparently Eros had been stalking me for days from some perch in the clouds. When at last he let his arrow fly, down to the shimmering parking lot at the ranch, my determination to maintain my distance as a guide had created a shield so impenetrable that the arrow was deflected back up to the sky, where it had hovered for the next two days. Now, two thousand miles to the east, shaken loose from the stratosphere by a hot, hard wind and a song of love hummed by tires to a faithful road, the arrow had come unstuck. It had found its way unerringly to my heart, and instantly I melted with desire.

It is possible to resist desire, but when the force hits, so strong is the magnetism that not even the gods *want* to resist it.

Shiva, deep in meditation, felt a sharp pang of desire, inflicted by Kama, who, like Eros, does his mischief with infallibly aimed arrows. Annoyed, the god pushed the distraction aside. His meditation continued. No doubt whole universes were created and destroyed in the path of his intense concentration.

Kama approached again. This time he pierced Shiva with fascination. The god succumbed.

Desire itself is desirable. Desire transforms whatever it touches into necessity. The urge to melt into the fascinating, all-too-remote other is the catalyst that drives seeds to moist soil, planets to wheel around the sun, and men and women to abandon duty and common sense for the sake of one, just one, kiss. A rush of longing for Lucas flooded me, and I tumbled into an incomparably sweet void. I was bathed in love. This was love received, like waters in a deep, sun-laced pond surrounding and caressing my whole being, and it was love given, gushing out of me with such force that it swept every other sensation, physical and cognitive, into the outpouring. It was love, it was lust, it was give, it was take. The seams of me burst wide open. Longing poured in. As the galvanized air of late summer strummed at my face and hair, I accepted my readiness to fall in love again, now, in late middle age.

"WOULDST THOU COUNSEL ME TO FALL IN LOVE?" Julia asks her waiting woman in *Two Gentlemen of Verona*. "Ay, madam," replies Lucetta, and then, considering the well-being of her young charge, adds, "so you stumble not unheedfully." But falling, falling, falling in love is one uncontrolled act we not only accede, but aspire, to. Falling in love feels, while we're in the midst of it, like destiny. Falling in love at first sight or, as I did now, without any prior inkling that emotional stumbling had lain ahead, seems especially portentous. A thing of such velocity and mass must be cosmic, urgent, necessary. Plunging past all things familiar, hardly pausing to consider what we might be leaving behind, and our only prospect of a landing the hope that it will be in the new beloved's arms — we abandon ourselves to the delicious danger.

Upended by love, we feel *euphoric*, which *Webster's* defines as "a sense of well-being and buoyancy." Psychologist Michael Liebowitz proposes that the euphoria love inflates us with may be associated with rising levels of certain bodily chemicals, such as phenylethylamine, a molecule that speeds up the flow of information between nerve cells and bathes the brain in sensations of excitement. This adrenaline-like substance may originally have benefited humans by masking pain but then took on an evolutionary role as it began to surge in moments of pleasurable physical closeness.[1] Imagine those moments between our protoancestors when the man, tired from the hunt, arrived back at camp and glimpsed his woman bent over the fire, and the woman, hearing a familiar footfall in the brush, looked round to see her man, and both their hearts leapt with joy. The reunion after each parting tickled them with another little plunge from mundane preoccupation into mood-changing pleasure. What an incentive that would have been for them to come together again and again, especially once they discovered that the feeling bubbled up in a new form when they held their child in their arms.

The act of falling into love takes over our senses and shuffles our old beliefs. Johnny Cash spotted June Carter, the soprano daughter of the musical Carter family, across a theater where both were performing and promptly informed her that they would marry one day. Carter, who was not only already married but deeply loyal to her life of singing, touring, and living as a principled Christian with her family, laughed him off. Not long after that night, however, she had fallen for Cash as well and penned the combustibly erotic song "Ring of Fire" for him. She was falling, falling right down into hell, she told her sister, who was the first to sing the song Cash himself later immortalized, "and the flames got higher." Cinderella feels, after whirling round the dance floor all night with Prince Charming, that love is the antidote to all the degradation she has suffered at the hands of her stepmother and stepsisters. We tell Cinderella's story over and over, because it holds out the promise of another kind of fall facilitated by love, the fall into salvation, which will sweep us away from all that has held us back and all who have misunderstood us. And when we land, the story further implies, our tired feet will be eased into magical glass slippers, so that we may walk the ground anew.

Falling in love is irresistible, even when there's no certainty that love is returned. Closely observing and trying to interpret all the looks, words, and actions of the object of desire is an obsessive skill every adolescent excels at without ever being taught. When I was in my early teens and besotted with my best friend's handsome older brother, I kept a diary in which I faithfully recorded and analyzed all the ways in which he did or did not turn his attention to me. Not-yet-requited love opens up for microscopic inspection all the beloved's small, formerly private gestures, such as a sigh or the way a hand touches an object on a table close to the adoring lover. The ways the characters in *Pride and Prejudice* pluck and tweak such "symptoms of love" move the plot as much as any of the things people actually say to one another. Two hundred years later, movies and romance novels continue to titillate audiences with tales in which the passionate union of hero and heroine is the payoff we love to hope for and never take for granted.

If one-sided falling smolders in private, mutual love burns. Its heat is coaxed by the ardor of both lover and beloved, who come forth to meet it in each other and stoke it further. Mutual love, even mutual attraction not yet quenched, is an exquisite ache, and now I let Eros's arrow wound me again and again. It seemed I was burning to be in love. At this stage in my life I was savage for passion. There was one person on earth I could not know enough about! There was someone who could not know enough about me! We were vast, oceanic mysteries to each other. The mystery of each of us pouring into the other's depths was not a conundrum I needed to solve, but an invitation I could not turn down. There was no bottom to such a mystery, no limit to such a quest. There was, however, an enormous gate to be passed through.

I pulled my head back into the van. The comparative stillness there sobered me, and after a moment I reached over and placed my hand on my husband's knee. Andy and I smiled at each other. I knew that, though I ached to be stabbed repeatedly by Eros's arrow, there was danger in becoming such a target.

I HAD FALLEN UNDER THE SPELL of the man who became my husband because I had recently broken up with a sad, sexually confused man and found in Andy both great physical passion and a tirelessly creative mind. I had a crush on him for several months before we became lovers. He was ten years older than I, a slender man with sandy hair, blue eyes, and wire-rimmed glasses who loved looking into the under-pinnings of his world and considering how everything worked, or might. The possibilities of things excited his curiosity, imagination, and wonder, and his extraordinary memory gave him a personal rela-tionship with each phenomenon that rose up before him. Oh, yes, he knew about the rotation of sunspots, and the ineffectiveness of air attacks during World War II, and an experimental treatment for cancer devised by a Canadian doctor in the 1940s. He knew why Pennsylva-nians didn't have to worry about the killer bee that was ravaging Texas, and what typefaces were most effective in conveying the messages of the text. When his daughter, Justine, and her boyfriend visited us shortly before I left for Shandoka that summer, they had complained about a tax they had to pay on the old brownstone they'd just bought in Brooklyn, and Andy had launched into an explanation of why the New York State tax laws had been amended in 1931. Justine and I exchanged a glance — knowing, tolerant, fond: wasn't this just like our Andy?

He loved pulling together disparate forces and turning them into something new, and he did it with objects as well as ideas. Around our home, cupboards, gates, lampshades, rugs, bowls, spoons, paintings, prints, and garden paths came into being because he could discern how one thing might be relocated and refitted to become something else. In the past four or five years, he had begun to devote more and more of his energy to making ceramics, a passion he had shelved as a young man, when he had been persuaded that the "high arts" of painting and printmaking were more intellectual, hence more respectable, than the functional crafts he truly loved. In fact, though, his crafts were art. A clay pot, for instance, he regarded as an entity that, when turned in a viewer's hands, revealed a small world of colors, textures, and lines leading into and away from one another like a narrative. At the time I left for Shandoka, he was experimenting with painting abstract calligraphic lines on each pot, as if, translated, these scrawls might tell a story or a poem and, if not, told one anyway through their travels around the pot.

My husband and I liked walking together and staring at things, then talking about what we encountered. We were both drawn to those wisps of strangeness that flitted among known things in the world. One fall afternoon, for example, picking our way through the woods behind our house, we noticed brown moths struggling to climb up maple trunks. Caught short, we stopped, our faces inches away from the bark, and silently watched. When the spell broke, Andy speculated that the insects, perhaps gypsy moths, were females, and that they were making their way up to the branches to lay their eggs. The eggs would hatch in the spring, when the leaves opened to feed the larvae. This made sense, but it was the doggedness of the moths that had impressed me. They dragged themselves over the ridges and grooves in the trunk as if they were blind or drunk, so servile to the imperative they moved to that they would not rest or pause to find a path of less resistance. They reminded me of pilgrims trudging over harsh lands to reach a holy shrine. Andy and I considered each other's points of view for a moment, then slipped back into our own more rewarding musing. He liked to solve the mysteries he encountered, and I liked to mystify facts.

We pursued our own interests enthusiastically and found, for the most part, that they did not conflict. After twelve years of marriage, whenever one of us returned home after having been away for a few hours, the other always hurried to the door with a welcoming hug and kiss. I fell in love with him several times a day.

On occasion, however, I also fell, if not exactly in love, then certainly in desire, with someone else. I indulged in these fascinations in a way that blended elation with utmost secrecy.

I HAD ALWAYS MAINTAINED a circumspect relationship with desire. My mother, a beautiful woman, a dancer full of litheness and hope before she married my alcoholic father and traded her optimistic ease in the world for a survival struggle, used to say that a well-brought-up young lady never showed her emotions in public. (A favorite story she proudly told was about how, one night at a restaurant, my father had thrown a drink across the table at her and she had not even flinched.) When I got older, she presented a coda to this rule: "A nice girl never lets a boy know how much she likes him." I was a child who took her responsibilities seriously, so I interpreted my mother's teachings to mean "Don't let anyone know you desire something. Ever." That included: a wax ballerina *en pointe* atop a friend's ninth-birthday cake, a cat, editorship of the high school paper, a boyfriend, admission to a certain college, a prize, a man, a job, praise, money, attention, sex, love.

Desire, I thought, weakened you. Admitting you desired something weakened you further and practically guaranteed that you wouldn't get it. Your failure to get it, then, assured that you would be ridiculed for your arrogant presumption to desire in the first place. No one wanted you to get what you wanted. Those who didn't have it would hate you, while the ones who already had it and deserved it more than you did anyway would make sure you lost it. So, to get along, indeed to survive, it was wise to hide your desires.

Many of us adhere to this philosophy. We move from one decision to the next, not because we're beckoned ahead into partnership with what attracts, but because we're nagged from behind by fear and a stubborn belief in our own limits. Fear, like a grim judge watching over our shoulder, holds us back, warning that it is dangerous to aim too high. It carps that our parents would be disappointed if we exceeded the short, polite reach we were born with, or the Church would disapprove, or the whole town would gossip, or our friends would abandon us. Limitation chides that we're foolish to hope for anything different, that we'll never be brave enough, creative enough, smart enough, pretty enough. Desire whispers, "Come, come. Here is something you may love. Give yourself over to it." Fear and limitation worriedly pluck at your shirt: "Stop. Something terrible may happen. The rut is safer than the pathless wilderness. Don't go there. Don't."

The myths confirm that dealing with the disciplinarian over our shoulder is part of the heroic journey. Consider Psyche. Night after night, she lay blissfully in the arms of her lover, even though, for a reason unknown to her, he had forbidden her to look on him by day. At first she didn't mind. The two of them were ecstatic together, and her eyes didn't need anything her fingertips weren't already full of. But her sisters, representing the judge over her shoulder, intervened. "He's probably a monster, Psyche. Why else won't he let you see him? Go on. Have a look. It's for your own good." Eventually she capitulated. *What if* overrode *What is*, and late one night she shone a lamp on her sleeping lover. There, lying before her, was a beautiful young man, and she was just drawing in a breath of joyful relief when a drop of oil from the lamp spilled on his shoulder. Eros, god of love, awakened and fled.

And consider Perceval, an earnest young knight in search of the Holy Grail. As a guest in the melancholy castle of the Fisher King, he sat in awe as the mysterious vessel he had sought so long and hard passed before him, illuminating the dark stone walls with its holy light. With all his heart he longed to ask about the strange sight he was witnessing and why his host and all the kingdom ailed. But he held back. "He recalled the admonishment given by the gentleman who had knighted him, who taught and instructed him not to talk too much; he was afraid that if he asked they would consider him uncouth, and therefore did not ask."[2] As self-doubt and longing battled within him, Percival sat mute. He could only console himself with a weak promise that he would ask someone for an explanation the following morning. By then, of course, it was too late; the Grail and all its attending company had vanished, and Percival had lost his chance to restore the kingdom to vitality.

Orpheus was another hero brought low by the tug of limitation. He had received permission, unprecedented in the Underworld, to lead his dead wife, Eurydice, out of the realm of the dead and back to life. The only stipulation made by Hades was that Orpheus make the entire journey without ever turning around to look behind him. He was doing fine, filled with anticipation of the bliss that every brokenhearted widower dreams of, when the judge at his shoulder started nagging: "What if you've been duped? What if you're all alone here?" He turned.

Yes! Eurydice was there! And then, quite suddenly, she wasn't. She was gone forever.

By choosing safe, predictable stasis and flinching from the call of seductive mystery, we dry out the rich and fertile potential that life requires to pollinate us. As for me, when I was a young woman wrestling with immense, secret hungers for love, fame, passion, scotch, metamorphosis, Zen peace, and Medea-like revenge, I contrived little ways to get what I wanted without letting anyone know what I was up to. Eventually, I got sober, I got married, I went on a vision quest, and I started venturing with growing temerity onto paths that attracted. Still, I kept my desires to myself. And when Kama occasionally zapped me with fascination for a man other than my husband, I would revive an old and reliable way of loving in spirit when physical love was impossible. I called it the Immaculate Love Affair.

The Immaculate Love Affair is a union characterized by intense metaphysical intimacy on the part of two people and perpetually unsated sexual desire on the part of at least one. The reason the pair abstains from lovemaking varies: commitment to another, religion, class, distance, the mores of business. In any case, the withheld sexuality in an Immaculate Love Affair is no obstacle, but the engine that keeps allure going. Imagining the ultimate physical union, aching for it, yet resigned to its impossibility, we never have to be disappointed by a partner who turns out to have smelly feet or who talks too much at romantic moments or who rolls away after lovemaking, abandoning us to our fading pleasure. We remain actively enchanted with each other, basking in the heat of being-in-love. We want to know everything about the other and to reveal things about ourselves that we seem only to uncover in their perceptive, adoring presence. Then, energized by the contact, we can go on to live our own life with something of the lover's ichor in our veins. We are what we were, but more so, for the Immaculate Lover does things the way we might do them, or sees in us what we cannot yet see in ourselves. The Immaculate Lover is Orpheus reformed, the gentle sweetheart who leads us into the light without ever turning around to grab us prematurely and hence keep us sentenced in the dark.

Immaculate Lovers are not mates or even prospective mates, and so, freed from expectations of how mates ought to behave with each other or preoccupation with how successfully each progressive phase of the partnership is unfolding, these lovers simply drift, godlike, in the endless, dreamy bliss of being-in-love. Immaculate Lovers are a long ride through wilderness on a luxury train, embers winking in the hearth, a puzzle, a big cuddly prize won at a county fair, reflections of sunny creek ripples brushing dreamily on boughs above the water, a cool dessert with mint, a lozenge to suck on at odd moments throughout the day. We indulge like epicures in the Immaculate Love Affair, relishing the fruits we share with the chosen one. Time and place, as we bend over these feasts of the psyche, vanish.

One of my Immaculate Lovers was a man I worked with when I had been married about three or four years. I was in New York, writing multimedia shows, and he was producing them. He had a master's degree in philosophy and loved abstract conundrums, yet when he jackknifed his tall frame into a leather chair around a polished conference table at a Fortune 500 corporation, his demeanor, posture, and cant bespoke such comfort with his surroundings that clients instinctively trusted him. I learned from him that one can be professional and eccentric at the same time, and authentically so. We would go to lunch together, allegedly to talk business, but actually to plunge into investigations of the meaning of beauty, the unconscious rituals of corporate America, and what kinds of things we would do if we could turn invisible. I'd look up from the conversation and note that the restaurant was full, duck back into the dense talk, and look up again to see with a start that the room had emptied. (The end of that friendship came abruptly and by tacit mutual consent. One day a waitress spilled a drink all over the back of his white shirt. An hour later, as he walked me to the subway, I tripped over some construction materials, fell into the street, and sprained my arm. Both of us must have gotten the message: our supposedly high-minded congress was heading into dangerously physical territory. We did not speak again until years later.)

Is an Immaculate Lover really a lover? Is it love if it's not declared? Yes, I say, if both people are magnified by the contact. I add, as another of my lovers (so out of my range and radar he did not even count as Immaculate), Albert Camus, wrote, "There are no limits to loving, and what does it matter to me if I hold things badly if I can embrace everything?"[3] A person who pursues another who wants only to be left alone is not an Immaculate Lover, but a pest, or even a threat. One who nurses secret — or not so secret — hopes that the beloved will make adjustments so the two can be together in body as well as mind robs the existing relationship of its best treasure, the freedom to indulge in the savory juice of the present moment. But it is human to want more from the one we love, and the impossibility of consummation can eventually cease to be alluring and can become instead simply frustrating. For this reason Immaculate Love Affairs usually just taper off after a while. They go with a whimper, not a bang. I used to think they slipped away without a trace except for a sweet, if insubstantial, memory. However, as I was to discover when my desire for my newest love interest, Lucas, gradually underwent a metamorphosis, an Immaculate Lover can sometimes evolve into an Escort to the divine Beloved of the soul.

ALTHOUGH I NEVER TOLD Andy about these brief, disincarnate flings with Immaculate Lovers, I had told him that I had a propensity for them. He'd told me he indulged in chaste little trysts as well. He tended to become fascinated with women briefly, intensely, and regularly. Any woman could engage his interest, he said; the line of a cheek, a laugh, a scent, the way a woman opened her purse to ferret out a piece of paper would seduce him, and he would richly consider the possibilities of making love with her. The moment would pass, the reverie scatter and fade. So we each had our little ways of indulging in polygamy of the imagination, and we each considered the diversions not just permissible, but healthy. How else could a marriage thrive? A person needed a little outside defibrillation now and then to get his or her own erotic pulse back in sync. We would dally in these daydreams, we agreed, but we would not act on them. And — at least as important, and maybe more so — we would never compare the object of our momentary fascination with the beloved partner we planned to spend a lifetime with.

So Lucas and I would not be lovers. I was married, and so was he. I was fifteen years older. He was the father of a ten-year-old girl and a six-year-old son. We lived three thousand miles apart. And there was yet another reason why I was not going to indulge in an extramarital affair with him. As a young woman in the grip of out-of-control drinking, I had been enslaved to secrecy. Sustaining alcoholism demanded the constant negotiation of deceit, half-truths, and exaggeration. How often I drank, how much, and what I did under the influence were matters of such toxic shame to me that the poison seeped into every other aspect of my life. No matter what I did, even if it was something estimable, it became tainted by its proximity to the ugly and inappropriate. Shame was an impetus to drink, to block out the shame, and the consequences of drinking caused more shame and more secrecy. When I stopped drinking at age thirty-two, I gladly gave up the keeping of secrets, and I would not, under any circumstances, reassume that burden.

Yet Lucas had said to me, "I am truly and completely in love with you." He was truly and completely in love with me.

There was another possibility. Organizing files in my new file cabinet on the night I was slapped into consciousness by the hot wind of desire, I wondered if Lucas would be amenable to engaging in an Immaculate Love Affair. This was a risky proposition, and I knew it. None of my previous Immaculate Love Affairs had been mutual, or at least they had remained chastely undeclared, which meant they smoldered in place and threw no sparks. I didn't want to lie to Andy or to deceive him, yet I wanted to be with Lucas, and as anyone who has ever really wanted something knows well, a palisade of excellent reasons to refrain can be easily bent by a one-track desire to go ahead. During the quest, Lucas and I had talked about our shared wish to learn advanced wilderness survival skills. He had friends and teachers among the Salish Indians who he thought might be willing to teach us in the Canadian forest that was their homeland. What would happen to that plan if we were Immaculate Lovers? The answer was easy: what had been immaculate would soon get sullied. Wrenched by desire, lust, love, curiosity, caution, and need, I felt I absolutely had to be with Lucas, and I absolutely had to stay away.

I NEEDED HELP. And so, leaving my files, I went to the computer and broached the subject with Bill.

With my partner I was mature and realistic. "Remember my telling you that Lucas said he was in love with me?" I emailed. "Well, I have realized it's mutual! Still, is it possible to fall in love with someone only after you've parted? And is he really in love with me? I'm his anima," I wrote reasonably, referring to the inner feminine figure that Carl Jung had theorized was the guide to a man's spirituality. "He dreamed me up to the cave of his potential."

Writing this email was not, for me, a logical response to a personal crisis. But although I had spent a lifetime trying to deny desire, the chasm that longing now cleft in me forced me to do something radical. And who else but my partner, after all, could hear what I had to say? He knew the man, the cave, the dream. He had been in the car waiting for me at the very moment I turned away from the magic words. I had even reported them to him. But even as I reasoned sanely to my friend, desire spun its own hidden intent: I wanted Bill not to counsel me but to argue, *Surely it's truly you he loves.*

I had an email from him the following morning. He did not oblige: "Lucas is a lover. He loves people. You took the role in his dream of the inner feminine who leads him to his soul. That wasn't you, it was him." He suggested I write Lucas and ask him to clarify his meaning.

Without giving myself time to consider whether it was a good idea, I took his advice. I emailed Lucas immediately and told him that his words of love would not let me go. I asked what he'd meant by them. I acknowledged the impossibility of our being lovers and declared myself available for an ongoing tryst of the mind, heart, and imagination. I confessed that I loved him, too. I thought it the bravest thing I had ever done.

CHAPTER THREE

The Love Wolf

UNREQUITED LOVE AND ITS TRAPS

I did not hear from him. A day passed, and then another, and the phone did not ring, and his name did not spool out in the SENDERS column of my email, which I checked many times a day. In the absence of an answer, my longing swelled. This is the nature of desire. It is shaped by what it does not have. When the outline of desire, drifting about like a silk pouch puffed up with wind, is filled in at last with the solid object it was made to hold, it ceases to be desire, or it shape-shifts and wants anew, rounding a gap of a different form. Almost as soon as I realized I loved Lucas, I ballooned with wanting. Loving was not enough now; reciprocity was demanded. Love wants to be loved back, not with sweet words heard days earlier, but with current words, current affirmations, current expressions of desire. That melodious refrain that Lucas had imparted to me in the parking lot faded in the clamor of my need for a new one.

Even as I planned my next vision quest, which was to begin in just over a week, organized files in my file cabinet, and took walks with Andy through woods and fields as overripe with late summer as a peach just past its prime, I thought of Lucas constantly. I pored over poems of erotic longing, seeking companions for my misery. "Aglow with desire," Izumi Shikibu, an attendant to the empress of the Heian court in feudal Japan, expressed her yearning to a lover who, by stroking her black hair, had burnished her to a beauty more splendid than that she had possessed before she knew his touch.[1] So, too, had Lucas begun to beautify me in some way I felt I would never fully realize unless he attended to it. I combed through memories of the vision quest, thinking of things about him that would have attracted me if only I'd known I was going to fall in love with him.

He followed a dream up a mountain. He ate meals in our mountain base camp from a bronze Tibetan singing bowl, out of sympathy for the monks who carried but one vessel for both physical and spiritual nourishment. He knew how to tie a wonderful knot that made it easy to adjust a tarp in a high wind. He offered wilderness rites of passage to teenagers. He was hoping to find a female mentor who could guide his daughter through puberty. He listened as if he were a bird, with two great wings folded around the speaker, housing her in feathery attention. I wanted all these aspects of him bundled together for my well-being, like the remedies assembled in my wilderness first-aid kit. I wanted him as a cure for an illness I had not known I suffered from. I wanted the solid reality of his love to fill out my voluminous silken emptiness.

I got silence.

We always told vision questers that, in the radical act of leaving behind their old ways and striking out into the wilderness for clarity and insight, they had to give up the need to understand. We told them that it was best simply to dissolve into the chaos as the caterpillar melts into its cocoon before the mess remakes itself as a butterfly. It occurred to me that I should now be following that advice myself, but I didn't want clarity and insight, I wanted Lucas.

> He is the love-wolf
> gobbling in my cave...
>
> eating of the bread
> offered to the gods.[2]

So pined an anonymous Egyptian poet more than ten thousand years ago. The love wolf is a ravenous beast. He had been gobbling people for millennia. Now he was eating me up, and I loved the cut of his sharp teeth.

IN THE ABSENCE OF LUCAS, I corresponded with Bill, sometimes two or three times a day. "Still no word," I wrote. "I'm feeling vulnerable and foolish and embarrassed, particularly since I confided all this to you."

He wrote back, commending me for opening up. "I'm your co-guide, for godsake; if you can't be vulnerable, foolish, & embarrassed with me, then with WHOM??" He thought it was great that I was dangling out there, needy and uncertain; he saw it as a vast improvement over the woman he'd come to know, who fought back her tears and never needed help.

I found that I looked forward to confiding in him. The articulation of desire was a practice entirely new to me, and having it witnessed and accepted was a thrill I wanted more of. I realized, I confessed to Bill, that I had always cultivated an attitude of toughness. "I've tried all my life to be tough," I emailed. "I've strived to be a warrior who never showed any weakness, never let on that she wanted anything. But after all these years of being a Touch Guy, I think I'm turning into a softie."

"Do you realize," he replied, "that when you write me about the Tough Guy, you (mis)spell it as 'Touch Guy'? Take a look at your keyboard. Notice that the 'c' is far enough away from the 'g' to make it definitely something other than a slipped digit. Perhaps the Tough Guy has secretly longed to be the Touched Guy."

Writing Bill, I tried to talk myself into a more rational approach to the gnawing of the love wolf. "I need to embody my adult feminine self in a way I never have before, following my heart, not secretly but openly. I need to learn something about love and desire that I've missed up till now."

"Right on!" Bill wrote. "I believe that the Tough Guy has been somewhat (not seriously) a barrier to the growth of your full guide power. Let me be the first to welcome the Touch Guy home as a heroine!"

Despite Bill's conviction (and my efforts toward conviction) that it was desire for some inner lovemaking that tore at me, deep down I believed, or wanted to believe, that it was Lucas himself who was the only answer to my hunger.

In the garden, the tomatoes ripened on the vine. The squash, yellow commas among prickly, fan-shaped leaves, fattened each day and featured in each evening's dinner. Grass and leaves were fading from summer emerald to the citrine hues of fall. The birds had begun to migrate south, and the absence of their song was filled with the hum of cicadas, sending their tireless tonal prayer to the sky. I picked dill, cilantro, thyme, and basil and took them up to the attic to dry on lines of string as heat poured off my skin. Andy and I sat by the pond and watched frogs as fat as Buddhas lazily catch insects with their quick tongues. Moving about in the heavy brocaded heat of late summer, my body melted, as if to the touch of the man I desired. And every time I checked the messages and saw nothing from him, I despaired more.

The giddy infatuation that buoyed me when Eros first slapped me into wakefulness was receding. In its place oozed the agony of absence and unrequited love. Unrequited love is not romantic. It is lonely and desperate. Roland Barthes compares the lover who yearns for the "migrant, fugitive" beloved to "a package in some forgotten corner of a railway station."[3] The beloved may spurn the adoring one gently or cruelly, deliberately or by casual neglect, because of personal taste or the inflexible facts of life. It scarcely matters. In the eyes of the rejected one, whatever life the beloved now goes on to construct becomes a fabrication purposefully designed, like the hexed gown that Medea, the vengeful, spurned sorceress of Greek myth, sent to her rival, to taunt with its beauty even as it burns its victim alive. If shared love makes us shine, unrequited love dims us. Then we may depend on the lover to light us as, in another Greek myth, mortal Clytie so obsessively follows the path Apollo blazes across the sky each day with the sun that she turns into a sunflower, a bright head bobbing faithfully in his direction. In a twentieth-century British version of the tale, Dora Carrington, a minor artist and fringe member of the Bloomsbury Group, devoted herself to making a home for the one man she adored, her "bugger-wug," the brilliant, and homosexual, author Lytton Strachey. Other unrequited lovers accept their fate without entirely giving up on the rewards of partnership. Calamity Jane, for example, sucked up the sorrow of Wild Bill Hickock's rejection by turning herself into a tough, sharp-shooting, hard-riding cowgirl, as if, by becoming a version of him, she could possess what she loved. Or the unrequited lover may resolve to remake herself in the image of the one the beloved prefers, or would seem to. In *All's Well That Ends Well* Helena disguises herself as the woman her uninterested Bertram is smitten with and slips into bed with him, while poor Aschenbach, in Thomas Mann's *Death in Venice*, gaudies himself up like a painted doll in order to attract the handsome Tadzio, only to be melted down by plague, heat, and the boy's obliviousness. Medea committed murder; sorrowing young Werther committed suicide. In a bizarre real-life crime story from 1957, Burt Pugach hired a hit man to throw acid in the face of the woman who had spurned his advances, Linda Riss. Fourteen years later, when Pugach got out of jail, he and Riss were married. And every now and then we sigh with relief to hear of a happy, or at least virtuous, outcome of unrequited love. One such lover, Florentino Ariza, in Gabriel García Márquez's *Love in the Time of Cholera*, waits fifty-three years to embrace his Fermina Daza and, in the process, bestows his ever-accumulating love skills on 622 other women. Perhaps the most exalted pair of unrequited lovers in history are Dante and Beatrice, he the great poet who chronicles the soul's journey from death to eternal life, she resurrected by his words to become the wise and loving guide who ushers him to Paradise.

I knew the stories. But as the days went by and Lucas did not respond, none of them mattered, because I, of all the unrequited lovers in the world, was hopeless, pathetic, and certainly unredeemed by noteworthy narrative.

AND THEN SOMETHING SHIFTED. I was walking in the woods one afternoon about a week after I returned home, sunk in obsessive longing, when suddenly, overcome by it all, I sank down on the ground beneath a big Scotch pine and lay my head on my knees. Grief washed over me. I was pining for a young man who had not responded to my heartfelt, heartsick plea, and I saw myself as an abject creature at the mercy of a gigantic, ravenous desire. I was dying of appetite. I was like those hungry ghosts of Chinese legend who roam and roam, crying piteously, for they crave sustenance and are perpetually denied it since their needle-thin throats can't swallow a morsel.

I began to sob. I sobbed for my helpless tumble into desire beyond my control and no-holds-barred vulnerability. I cried because I was drowning in a bottomless pool of unquenched love, and I didn't even know what kind of quenching would revive me. I cried because this was probably the last invitation from Eros that I was ever going to get, and there seemed no way it could be sated. I abandoned myself to my despair so utterly that, sooner than I would have believed possible, sooner than the circumstances surely deserved, sorrow floated away. The woods rushed forth to reassert their presence. From a high branch a crow called. That harsh call grabbed me and pulled me up, so I glimpsed myself as if I were the crow looking down and noting a woman huddled under a pine. What the bird-self saw, surprisingly, was an extreme reaction to a small stimulus, a case of emotional anaphylactic shock, the condition that erupts when the immune system reacts hysterically to a bee sting or some other allergen and, in a frantic effort to destroy the alien invader, musters all defenses to the task, willing to destroy even the very body it depends on for life.

I observed in that moment of dispassionate clarity that the intensity of my desire was out of proportion to the reality of gestures,

looks, and words that Lucas and I had traded in the eleven days we
had worked together. Desire was not in the picture there. It wasn't
even an undercurrent, suppressed during working hours, biding its
time for a more convenient opportunity to gush forth. I had not fallen
in love with Lucas until two days after I last saw him, after his incantatory words had caught up with me. This was no love at first sight, or
even at last sight! Could it be that a few simple words had been the
instrument that injected this love poison into my bloodstream?

A precedent occurred to me. A short story by Chekhov, "The Boa
Constrictor and the Rabbit," shows how easy — and seductive — it
is to fall in love with lovely, insubstantial words.4 Pyotr Semyonych,
a self-important man of no obvious charm, slyly sets out to seduce N.
N., the woman of his fancy, by making her believe he sees her as no
one else does. Repeatedly he drops hints to her husband about how
desirable and beautiful he finds her, how she is the ultimate Russian
beauty and ought to have her portrait painted by a master, how most
of the dull citizens of their acquaintance could not possibly understand
so exquisite a creature. The husband, on whom any kind of subtlety
seems to be lost, goes home and tells his wife all this in tones of baffled amusement. The woman, of course, hears the comments as she
was meant to hear them: as love messages mouthed for her. She becomes consumed with passion for the one man who can discern her
exceptional nature, her true beauty, and is increasingly persuaded that
only he can release her stifled love. His solicitations continue, her
longing grows, until, late one night, she turns away from her sleeping
husband, climbs out of bed, and goes to meet the destiny that has been
strategically plotted for her.

Not able to recognize that it is she herself, the reflected image,
whom she must come to cherish, N. N. falls instead for the bearer of
the mirror. It's the words that do the trick. The words ignite her longing, even though she believes, as her seducer intends her to, that without the wielder of the words, she will remain dull and nondescript.

Words are potent, no doubt about it. In the Beginning was the

Word. Words charm, they propitiate, they curse. "Abracadabra" and "Open sesame" fling open the doors to magical realms. "All words are spiritual!" proclaimed Walt Whitman.5 And in that moment, pining under the pine, I acknowledged to myself at last that words had set off in me a chemical reaction that was only just beginning to bubble and transform. I saw clearly that it wasn't Lucas I was in love with, but the dream his psyche had placed me in and that he had delivered to my keeping through his words.

CHAPTER FOUR

TRUTHS AND CONSEQUENCE

FINDING MEANING IN LOVE'S ABYSS

I sat for a while against the pine, getting accustomed to a truth I had not wished to perceive: I was not in love with Lucas, or at least not in the way I'd imagined.

Finally, I stood up. Through the woods, the meadow to the south looked like a brilliant golden tapestry hung behind the dark grille of the trees, and I headed in that direction. Five years earlier, on a rainy afternoon in October, I'd held a menopause ceremony in this meadow. Draped in golden scarves and jewelry, which women friends from different phases and places of my life had adorned me with, symbols of all the blessings and lessons my soul had received during my first forty-five years, I had danced in the center of the circle they formed around me. Then, spontaneously, I began to remove my finery and drape it over the branches of the apple trees on the verge of the meadow and over the necks of the women themselves, a token of my hope that I might spend the second half of my life giving away the bounty to others.

Now, the air was hot and still, except for the ceaseless prayers of the insects. Among the grasses, milkweed pods thickened their woody armor, and white yarrow flowered above feathery stalks. The goldenrod grew as high as my heart. As I trailed my fingers through their globular blooms, pollen sifted onto my fingers. I walked directly into the sun, my body sifted along by the tall plants. I was suffused in heat, in light, in the peace that follows an emotional release. In the woods to the east, beyond the brush fence that marked our property line, the cool fingers of fall had already begun to redden the maple trees, drawing the next season toward themselves. The present, I thought idly, hungers always for the taste of that which has not arrived.

I lay on the ground and peered up through the grasses into the blue sky. The still, late summer air, the bowing insects and honeyed sunlight pressed me down, heavy and compliant, into the earth. I was no less aswim in desire than I had been before. My outburst had washed away the specifics of need, as rain erases the details of a chalk drawing on a city sidewalk, leaving behind only a wash of colors. Desire tossed me still, but it had become unbounded and diffuse. I closed my eyes and gave myself up to the pleasing experiment of surfing desire without any object.

Before long, heat and light pushed me down into a dreamy state, where I bobbed between wakefulness and sleep. Perhaps I had lain there for hours, or perhaps I was only a remnant of consciousness, restful but restfully attentive, like a cat. The sun slid out from behind some trees to dazzle my closed lids, and with that movement, that passage of bright energy, I had a sense of a presence moving toward me. In my mind's eye a woman, dressed in a gown the color of yellow chrysanthemums, picked her way out of the woods. She was tall and slender, her face beautiful, not with youth, but with experience and, more than that, with pleasure in how experience was shaping her. Her hands gathered her long silk skirt. Her headdress was cone shaped, with a yellow veil wrapped around it, one end fluttering loose. She carried her head high, her body gracefully. Two whippets romped around her legs, trying to get her attention.

Alert yet entranced, I watched her come, a woman from the age of the troubadours. As she neared, aspects of her character clarified along with the details of her physical presence, as, during sleep, some omniscient librarian discreetly provides background on the plots of our dreams. The woman was in her late thirties or early forties. She was married and had lived a life of privilege since childhood. Grace, modesty, and gentility were skills she had learned early and wielded well. I remember being surprised at how easily she moved in the woods, an aristocrat who would have grown up expecting someone else to remove any obstacles in her way. As her legs swung against the flowing silk of the gown, she reveled both in her muscles' power to cover space and in the sensuality of cool fabric against her skin.

And I realized that she had done this before. Approaching someone from a distance, that both she and the other might be known more intimately by the time they finally stood face to face, was one art she had not been taught but had taken care to master. Her way of moving showed consciousness, but not self-consciousness, of her own beauty and desirability. Her expectation that whatever she passed on the way to the one who awaited her was also suffused with desirability, since all of it was a part of the narrowing distance between her and him. She walked in this way when she moved down a staircase into a crowded room, or across a jousting field, past a gathering of her peers, toward the young knight who was her beloved.

In this reverie or vision or half-dream, I saw nothing of the beloved himself. I only sensed him waiting, sensed his smiling and his expectation. What was important was not his identity, but the charged energy of the space between seeker and sought. Approaching what seduced was itself a quenching of desire and an activation of it. Drawing near to the one who held out his arms to her, this woman moved into the world as into the arms of a waiting lover.

I saw her step into the meadow, and then it was as if the sun itself gathered her into its brilliant embrace. She faded. I bobbed up to wakefulness again.

That this particular vision, with its attendant insight into the nature of desire, should arise before me on that afternoon of longing, anguish, and self-candor was amazing only in hindsight. I knew little about the world of courtly love. A few months later, as I studied the subject, I was amazed to learn that the force that drove religion, culture, literature, and ethics at that time was nothing less than longing for the unattainable beloved. Between the lady and her lover — often a man younger than she — distance, duty, and society imposed painful separations symbolic of the gulf between human and divine. To love, then, was to suffer as the unrequited one, but it was also to find meaning in the void by filling it with honorable deeds and lofty poems worthy of the absent beloved. The correspondences between my own circumstances and those of lovers who had lived seven hundred years before me would prove abundant and instructive.

At that moment, however, lulled to visionary drowsiness in my cradle of sun and grass, I was simply struck by the way the woman walked. That walk was an epiphany. As I witnessed it, my entire perception of what had happened with Lucas was transformed, as if it were a woodland herb that, crushed under this golden woman's foot, released its curative perfume. Granted a glimpse of the way a lover moves toward her beloved, I understood that how I went forth from here — not whom I went forth toward — would make all the difference in the world. I realized that, instead of pursuing Lucas, my task was to track desire itself.

I HAD SCARCELY BEGUN TO CONSIDER how that project might unfold when, the next day, Andy confronted me.

We were in the kitchen. He was making his lunch, and I was washing some dishes. He remarked, with what I recognized as forced casualness, that I had not been as forthcoming with stories about this past vision quest as I usually was, and he asked me if something was wrong. Brisk and efficient, washing silverware as if it were urgently needed by royalty, I denied that anything was amiss. My voice was hearty with confidence. And then, just as quickly, I saw that the whole unfolding mystery would be worth nothing if I were to go on keeping desire secret. I asked him to come up to my studio.

His feet were heavy on the stairs behind me, and I climbed slowly, casting in vain for enlightenment on how to do what I had to do. In my room, I gestured him toward the old velvet armchair by the window, while I sat beside him at my desk. Fear clouded his eyes.

Then I told Andy that a strong attraction had sprung up between me and a man on the vision quest. I assured my husband that he was the one I loved, that nothing was going to happen with this man, that he was married, younger, lived far away, on and on. I talked too much, too fast, too nervously, too brightly, desperately trying to locate an island of calm for us both and speeding ahead until, I hoped, I would crash into it.

"This was a thing that happened because of something I need to change in myself," I said. "I don't really understand it yet, but I know it's the truth."

Finally I fell silent. Andy didn't say anything. He sat in the little chair, looking down and considering. Nervously, I waited for the blow.

"Are you in contact with him?" he asked.

"No," I replied, and, really, it was true.

When he spoke again, he did not ask what the other man looked like or what he did for a living or how we had spent time together. He did not ask me if I had kissed or touched him. He did not walk out of the room. He did not get angry. The fear in his face was gone and had not been replaced by the hurt and feelings of betrayal I sat waiting for.

What he said was, "You know, I'm surprised this hasn't happened before."

I stared at him in disbelief.

"I mean, that's the point of what you're doing, isn't it?" he went on. "You take people away from their ordinary life and into the wilderness so they can find their true beauty. You spend all that time together, removed from the things you normally have to think about. There are no distractions coming from the outside world. You're focused only on this personal search. So you may be dirty and smelly on the outside, but inside you're seeing each other's beauty."

I was speechless. I would have reached out to him, except at that moment, he seemed too rare a thing to touch.

"You might as well get used to it," Andy said. "You're a beautiful woman to begin with. And the longer you keep doing this work that you love, the more beautiful you're going to become and the more men of all ages are going to fall in love with you."

I took his hand. I could only say, "How could I even imagine wanting anyone but you?"

We would not speak again for several weeks of what we later came to call, when we mentioned it at all, my "attraction." From that moment on, it seemed we carried on as if nothing at all had happened, although we both knew that something had. Perhaps I was a bit more playful with and attentive to him than I had been since I returned from the mountain; perhaps he was more relaxed with me. Surely, when we hugged each other, as we did frequently throughout any day, there was nothing coming between us now.

AFTER THAT CONVERSATION with Andy, the shift in my perception that had begun with the crow's-eye view of my predicament and clarified with the vision of the golden woman stepping lightly and confidently toward her lover, gained yet a wider scope. Andy was right about the power of the vision quest to coax forth a person's inner beauty. And, not infrequently, that personal beauty was revealed through an image of the mysterious, alluring soul-lover. I recalled the powerful lover figure who had appeared in the dream of one quester and how timely her arrival had been for him.

Lawrence, a wealthy, successful businessman, had come to Shandoka with Bill and me the year before I met Lucas there. His intention for the quest was, as he put it, to bring forth his feminine, intuitive side, which he had previously ignored in order to pursue his ambitions. A couple of nights before his solo, Lawrence dreamed that he was standing in the massive marble lobby of a bank building, waiting for the bank manager to come meet with him. The man arrived, but when they greeted each other with a handshake, the manager's hand sloughed off into Lawrence's. The manager went outside, and Lawrence followed. There, his attention was drawn to a red-haired woman who was naked from the waist up and who held a banner with some kind of message written on it. In the other hand she carried a violin. She tried to get the bank manager's attention, but he got into his car and drove away. Captivated, Lawrence approached her. He saw that she was very beautiful, and he felt a strong sexual attraction to her. Beside her a lake shimmered. Holding the violin high above her head like a sword, the woman walked to the lake and stepped in. Lawrence waded in after her. The woman walked deeper and deeper into the water until she was completely submerged, and Lawrence, never pausing, followed.

Lawrence's anima had taken the form of the sacred lover in this dream, and she was obviously in full accord with his hopes for the vision quest. His former world — rock solid and foursquare like the bank building and representing the money and prestige he'd strived for — had ceased to be well suited to him; he could not shake its hand, grasp its authority. But when, and only when, he risked stepping outside his old environs, he encountered the beautiful, alluring woman warrior-artist of himself. She had a message that the bank manager of his unconscious was unable to read or uninterested in reading. But the psyche of the dreamer was ready and aroused. He let his sensuous soul guide lead him into the creative, fluid depths of his unconscious.

Who was the soul-lover awaiting me? I wondered. Was he, even now, trudging up to the cave of my unconscious to meet me? Or was it I who was striding across the distance toward him, as the enraptured lover of the troubadour covered all the space between herself and her beloved, painting it as she went with her joy and desire and compassion?

THE DAY AFTER MY ENCOUNTER with Andy, emboldened by the success of confession, as well as by the realization that I would not be able to give myself over to the pursuit of desire as a force unto itself as long as I was in thrall to an uncommunicative, if decidedly still enticing, human object of desire, I called Lucas.

I hadn't had such an attack of nerves since I was fourteen and forced to invite a boy to the Christmas dance at my all-girls school. Leaving a message with Lucas's answering service, I imagined the woman chuckling and gossiping to her colleagues at the phones, "It's her; it's that older woman who's chasing him." But he called back ten minutes later, so I plunged in before I could change my mind.

Had he gotten the email I'd sent almost a week earlier?

He had gotten it, he said, and had written back immediately. What? I hadn't received anything? He would resend it right away. Did I have a fax machine? What was the number, he would fax me a copy, just in case the email went awry again.

I will be frank. After that, the conversation did not go the way I had hoped. To begin with, he couldn't even remember those potent words he had unleashed. "I know I said something like, 'I feel love for you,'" he began carefully.

I did not insist, "No! That's not it! You said, 'I am truly and completely in love with you!'" I was embarrassed to admit how well I knew those words, how much I had caressed them. So, even now, in the midst of her bold advance, my mother's daughter sat primly and refrained from showing her emotions.

Lucas went on, explaining sweetly. How could he help but love the guide who had inspired him to venture up to the cave that called to him? I was so dedicated to my work. I did it with such passion. He had learned so much. I had about me both a fierceness and a femininity that he found appealing. He cited moments in which something I had done or said had inspired him. "So of course I love you," he said.

I was listening closely. This was all well and good — and leading inexorably to the big "but."

"But," he went on, "I'm afraid that's all I meant."

It was a rejection, and it stung. I felt chagrined. But I wouldn't surrender, and I wouldn't let him go, not just yet. I had brought him this far, or he'd brought me, and I could not just accept and agree. I might keep his precious words a secret, even from him, but I wouldn't hide their medicine.

So I left my mother's daughter on her little chair, knees together, hands in her lap, and told the man how much I liked him. I told him that his words of love had swept me into their spell until I was thoroughly infatuated with him. I admitted my admiration for what I saw as his ability to express his love so openly, to let a dream propel him up a mountain, to step so easily between the spiritual and material worlds. I told him that I was both drawn toward and frightened away from exploring my intense feelings for him, which probably had something to do with opening up to some alluring, passionate, feminine aspect of myself that I had previously refused to curry.

And he said all the right things: we were connected in a cosmic way, we had known each other in other lifetimes, would have more to teach each other in this one. Could we always be friends, "soul friends," he asked?

Of course I said yes. We hung up as if we had given each other a big, friendly hug. I sat there at my desk, alone and considering. I felt emptied and a bit desolate. Betrayed, even. I sensed threads of embarrassment and foolishness unraveling from my aplomb and could have knotted them together into a sturdy fabric if I'd wanted. Instead I chose to focus on the exhilaration I felt for having declared my desire outright. I will admit that I was extremely proud of myself. And I felt relief. No longer was it possible to nurture the illusion that an outer lover stood before me with his arms outstretched. If I were to continue on — and I had every intention of doing so — I had to find the inner lover who had been calling me all along. There was more. I also had to find the inner woman who loved to step through dense woods, toward the sunlit meadow of her beloved's embrace.

CHAPTER FIVE

Soulful Yearning

THE DEEP DESIRE FOR A HIGHER LOVEMAKING

When I returned to Colorado, I came as a woman both weaker and stronger than I had been when I left two weeks earlier. In that short time I had been split apart and tied back together by passion. I felt whipped and glorious, like a flag flapping in the wind. I was ready for adventure. The newborn Touch Guy showed up right away, when guides and vision questers met one another for the first time. Feeling the customary stares of the six participants, their wariness as they assessed my worth as a guide, as well as their desire, like that of a potential lover, to be captivated, I did not resort to my usual bright chumminess in an effort to ease their anxiety. I did not pretend that a person could be deciphered at a glance. I allowed the looks to try to fathom me, and I looked back. Two days later, as we set off for the hike into the canyon, I let one of the young men help me with my backpack instead of trying to shrug into it manfully by myself, as I usually did, as proof of my competence to guide. The next morning, in our base camp at the mouth of a canyon beneath red, bulbous slick-rock slopes, Rose, my co-guide, and I talked to the questers about the eternal longing of seekers to discover their wild, bold, authentic self. Seized by inspiration, I found myself comparing that search to a long walk toward a distant lover. You know that the beloved one is there, I said, loving you completely, and the desire to feel that dearest of all embraces compels you to keep going, on and on and on, as though the world itself were your waiting lover. Going on a vision quest is announcing to yourself that you are ready to do whatever you need to do for that embrace.

No transition is seamless, of course. If acclimating to one's own betterment were so easy, we would not need psychiatrists or cookbooks or refresher courses in French, and we would always learn our lesson from just one mistake. Congratulating myself one morning on the changes I seemed to be manifesting so effortlessly, I caught myself thinking, "Now that Lucas and I are just friends and not partners in an Immaculate Love Affair, now that I've learned so much from my infatuation with him, we're free to *really* fall in love with each other." I had to smile. Really, it is hard to be moderate when madcap passion is the alternative.

On the second day of the questers' solo, I went for a hike, leaving base camp to Rose, who settled under a juniper tree to weave a basket. I headed out through the sandy, stone-filled wash so as to avoid the broad swath where new grass sprouted in patches of fragile cryptobiotic soil. Part lichen, part moss, part algae, part fungus, and part bacteria, cryptobiotic soil — the Greek roots mean secret (*crypto*) and life (*bio*) — lodged on top of the sand and, left undisturbed, formed crusts that became the desert's topsoil. "Crypto," as the locals called it, stabilized the soil by sending out slimy filaments that wound their way over and through the earth, stabilizing the shifting sand, sopping up rain water, and drawing down nitrogen from the air.[1] After several years, when the crypto was mature and ready to nurse seeds, it resembled elfin villages with warrens of earthen buildings. Avoiding it was a challenge, as well as an ecological necessity that could place limits on where a quester claimed a solo spot. Grass seeds at loose in the winds, I thought, must long for this soil that will hold them snug and nourish them.

Where the wash met the trail, I turned and walked west, paralleling the Dolores River, which sang invisibly behind a scrim of willows and reeds. To my left opened another side canyon, smaller than the one at whose mouth we had set up our base camp. Because the side canyons in this area faced east and west, they housed no ruins of the Anasazi, the ancient people who carved their high abodes into south-facing walls. But the sensuous red Entrada sandstone was a source of enchantment unto itself, with its gentle slopes, broad saddles, towers, sentinels, turnips, and slides. Even in bare feet you could climb on it, explore it, take off your clothes and lie naked on its slanting beds to catch the sun, and trek up to the phantasms at its summits.

Walking, I met longing everywhere. Under a deep, cool, north-facing alcove at the mouth of the small canyon, where peregrine falcons dived for prey — or maybe simply because peregrines are engineered for such aerobatics — spread a circular declivity of dried mud. Clearly, this sheltered area thrived each spring as a grotto, fed by showers of melting snow that cascaded down from the rock lip above. The muddy circle would flourish as a pool. Wild roses and ferns would bloom in the crevices of the rock wall, and swallows would dart through rainbows of spray to build their nests on tiny ledges. Now, crimped slabs, curling at the edges, heaved out of the earth. The plants in the wall were brown wisps, barely hanging on. The place was long-ing for water. Staring, I felt a stab of something like empathy. I, too, thirsted to be quenched down to my roots.

Wandering farther into the canyon, I came to a massive hole high in the rock wall. The wall begged for the hole-shaped boulder that had broken loose and rolled down to lie unbroken in the wash forty feet below. On a rock a lizard scuttled across shade to pump a spot of sun. The lizard longed for a bellyful of heat. A wild aster, rooted under a stone, craned its purple bloom up and out, longing for the sun. A fat, inquisitive bee longed for the aster's sweet pollen.

Longing abounded and grabbed for what would enliven it. We were all made up of the architecture of longing, like the cryptobiotic soil, reaching down and up and sideways, readying ourselves for the one wind-borne seed that would root in us and transform us into the luxuriant beings we were born to be. I often told vision questers, "You're drawn to where the lessons are." If you keep your senses open and your attention keen, the phenomena of the natural world that will attract you, as a sunny rock invites a lizard, are the very ones whose particular essence at that particular moment mirrors your soul. Longing itself was the lesson that drew me now. I needed allies in the quest for that vital, missing Something that beckoned just out of reach. I needed evidence that the elusive, alluring other was a universal force that, even if never found, never held, still needed urgently to be sought. I couldn't say exactly what it was I longed for, but I knew that, whatever it was, it felt like being in love.

"Life means Longing," wrote Sufi master A. H. Jaisinghani. "Progress is only possible through Longing. And as the Path of Progress is infinite, there should be infinite Longing. Thus Longing becomes itself a form of the Infinite, to be desired for its own sake. This is why the Mystics idealize Longing. The other name for Longing is Love."[2] Longing, he continues, springs from the memory of an encounter with the divine. Sorrow foams in the wake of memory, since separation from past wholeness plunges one into current exile. Exile makes reunion the heart's imperative. Longing is the victuals for the road.

It was longing that compelled the gods to create their people in the first place. They had gotten lonely enthroned in the center of their universe. The world they had made was splendid, but dull. With spittle, breath, mud, clots of blood, and other primal goo, they shaped the companions who, they expected, would honor and obey them. The Judeo-Christian God made it clear that it was love he demanded above and beyond all other forms of fidelity. "You must love the Lord thy God with all thy heart, and with all thy soul, and with all thy might," is the first commandment Jehovah gave Moses when he called him away from the grumbling Israelites and summoned him up to Mount Sinai.[3] Surely it was not too much to expect that creation would faithfully honor its creator. However, things did not always go as planned.

The origin stories of many lands relate that the reason humans have reached their current discontented state is because their ancestors did something unforgivable, cutting the people off from their close relationship with the holy ones. They committed some act of disrespect or failed to follow a sacred practice and, often after being given a second and even a third chance to mend their ways, were exiled from the holy favor they had taken for granted. Anthropologist and analyst of the sacred Mircea Eliade claims that the central theme in all religious traditions is the "nostalgia for paradise" and the purpose of the religious quest to recover what was lost. In the Judeo-Christian tradition, Eve is the culprit who disobeyed God's warning about which fruits in the garden were off-limits and hence got herself and Adam and all humankind estranged from paradise. Not just prayer and sacrament, but guilt, shame of the body, and distrust of the feminine have been practices that worshipers have used for four thousand years to win forgiveness for Eve's audacity. The Hopis, having failed to take care of three previous worlds that the creator had granted them, escaped a cataclysmic flood by climbing up to the present world through a hollow reed. Once they arrived, they had to prove their good intentions by setting out from their prospective new home in what is now the Four Corners area of the United States and making their way to the ends of the earth in all four directions. Then, most important of all, they had to find their way back to the starting place.

In the Japanese myth, Susanoo was an exile in heaven, pining for the earthly half of himself that he had never known yet missed desperately. Born of the water droplets that fell from the body of his father, the first male deity, as he purified himself in a stream, Susanoo was a god out of control, howling and shrieking and constantly causing disturbances in the heavens with his demands that he be allowed to go to the home of his mother. Finally, the other deities could stand no more and obligingly cast him to earth, where, after more misadventures and bad behavior, he finally found peace by marrying the daughter of the earth-spirit and founding a long line of royal descendants.

The vague yet relentless longing of Susanoo for the earth hounds seekers in a contemporary version of the myth of exile, which author and activist Chellis Glendenning, cultural historian Morris Berman, Al Gore, and others have explored. According to this theory, we humans have gradually, if unintentionally, cut ourselves off from our primal intimacy with nature, original provider of spiritual and aesthetic as well as physical sustenance, and have become addicted to a technological lifestyle increasingly devoid of meaning and touch. To make matters worse, unlike poor Susanoo, we can't even figure out what ails us. In our addictive need to gobble up new products and experiences, we are not only destroying our home planet, but we are also eroding our own awareness of the consequences of our compulsiveness. Like any substance addiction, the craving of materialism tightens its awful bonds, and we attempt to blot out our fear and isolation by consuming even more. "The froth and frenzy of industrial civilization," Gore writes, "mask our deep loneliness for that communion with the world that can lift our spirits and fill our senses with the richness and immediacy of life itself."[4]

Another modern interpretation of the pervasive yearning for completion centers less on society than on the crisis of the individual who has lost his soul, or sense of wholeness, and feels adrift in the world. Fractured by childhood trauma, self-doubt, and cultural imperatives to conform, this troubled self longs desperately to be healed. Mending the split is the aim of psychotherapy and also of the eclectic, but often influential, self-help and New Age movements. These practices and techniques aim to integrate the fragmented selves so that the suffering individual may find purpose and meaning in life. There is a presumption here that a preordained wholeness awaits one at the end of these efforts, that all the scattered pieces can be fit together to form a unique human landscape.

According to philosopher and psychologist Julian Jaynes, it is the structure of the human brain itself that accounts for humanity's persistent yearning for a lost, more perfect union. Until about 3000

B.C.E., Jaynes speculates, the brain was bicameral, or two-chambered, with "an executive part called a god, and a follower part called a man."[5] Neither part was conscious of its own existence or of that of the other. Human beings, therefore, acted without subjectivity, without recognizing themselves as responsible for their acts. Their volition, planning, and initiative seemed to them to be revealed not internally, but by hallucinatory outer commands: by the voices of the gods. Nostalgia for the unequivocal promptings of this ever-present authority has had lasting consequences, says Jaynes, from the insistence of poets that it is not their own talent but possession by the muse that harnesses inspiration, to Marx and Engels's conviction that dialectical materialism could restore society to an ideal classless state, to the search of modern physicists for a unified field theory that will explain, with one neat equation, the whole, vast cosmic arithmetic.[6]

Whether alienation from the source is a mere illusion caused by the physiognomy of *Homo sapiens* or memory of a primordial union with the creator, or whether our DNA simply contains some undiscovered gene of yearning that goads us to move onward into change, even as we grasp wistfully at our own dim, undifferentiated evolutionary past, almost all of us seek to be embraced by a sublime Other. P. L. Travers, author of the Mary Poppins books, cofounder of *Parabola*, the magazine of myth and tradition, and lifelong student of myth, called it the "Something Else": "'There must be Something Else,' I would say. Achingly, I would say it. But all, I knew, was Here and Now, and if all, then within the all that Something Else awaited me, infolded, implicate."[7] Freud hypothesized that an infant craves the "oceanic feeling" of the womb, reexperienced early in life as the sensation of being one with its beloved, its mother, and the intimate environment it floats in. Individually and culturally, we try to reclaim what we sense must have been our primal and rightful wholeness. How we long to be loved by a force greater than we, to have our soul's thirst quenched, to be guided flawlessly in the right direction at every baffling fork in the road! How we long to throw off the shackles of timidity and the tiresome need for approval and to dance ecstatically! How we long to love what we do and do what we love, and be loved by others in the process! Lizards and bees and wild asters and even boulder-shaped holes in canyon walls know exactly what they need to restore them to wholeness. We humans, on the other hand, are driven to search, on and relentlessly on, for the great Other we can scarcely fathom and feel sure we will recognize the instant we find it or it finds us and folds us in its warm embrace.

I LEFT THE CANYON and headed toward the river, parting the dense vegetation and sidling through. The Dolores, dark brown, stippled with silver ripples, hurtled past, rounding a bend on liquid sinews. The river longed for the sea. High on the rock cliff on the opposite bank, a canyon wren sang its inimitable song, a ribbon of sound unfurling and fluttering into the sky. The wren longed for its mate.

It occurred to me that I could immerse myself in the river and hence become part of something wild and unfettered. About twelve feet from the bank, the water splashed round the sides of a flat rock that looked a little longer than a human back. I took off my clothes, draped them on the reeds, and stepped cautiously into the cold, quick water. The current was strong, and I had to lean upstream to keep my balance. My feet moved tentatively over slippery stones, through satin mud. When I reached the rock, I tested it: it supported me from my shoulders to my knees. I adjusted myself, feet upstream, head down. Immediately, my long hair took off behind me. My hair longed to go with the flow.

Sun, water, and air moved over me and swept me up in their force. The sun massaged my skin. The river pumped at my feet and plowed my toes. The bubbling water sang just below my ears, and the more I listened, the more I discerned the many voices of its chorus: low gurgling, as deep waters made their way around stones; a sibilant whisper; a mercurial trickle; a rush; a roar; a sigh. A breeze stirred, and the rushes on the bank brushed against one another in a papery intimacy.

I thought of the story of Changing Woman, the holy being in the Navajo myth, who brought the people the most valued aspects of their culture: sheep and the knowledge to care for them, weaving, ceremony, respect for the four sacred mountains and the bejeweled properties they contain, the brakeless drive of things — children, sheep, words, a new morning — to be born. Earlier in the story, just after Changing Woman and her sister, White Shell Woman, have reached maturity, they are walking on the sacred mountain, Ch'óol'í'í, when each finds herself irresistibly attracted to an alluring presence: Changing Woman to the sun, White Shell Woman to the stream.[8]

Changing Woman, considering the sun, wonders aloud, "Could it not be, I wonder, a living creature like ourselves? A creature with a spirit like ours who is waiting just like we wait now?"

White Shell Woman reflects on the stream, "Perhaps it, too, longs for whatever it is we long for. Perhaps it is as lonely as we are."

They have to find out. Changing Woman makes her way to a flat rock and, lying down on it, spreads her legs. White Shell Woman finds a flat place in a shallow pool by a waterfall and lies on it, open and receptive. The Sun moves over and into Changing Woman. The Stream moves over and into White Shell Woman. Each woman feels pleasure burst within her. Each gives herself over to the presence that wants to fill her. Soon, they both know they are with child.

Of course a woman could make love with the earth. A human body was of the earth, after all. Before we were protohumans, hairy and apelike, taking our first tentative two-footed steps over the veldt, before we were chittering creatures swinging in trees, or blind cells swallowing and splitting, we were but chemicals swirling around in search of other chemicals to bond with. Our oldest living ancestors are hydrogen and copper, sulfur and zinc, chemicals that still constitute our twenty-first-century bodies. How can we help longing to merge more fully once again, in joy this time and in full consciousness, with mineral and water, with bear and oak, with salmon, and with red dust of desert whirlwind? We would forget for a while our human concerns and lie down with the great beings whom we vaguely recall as teachers and lovers.

I wriggled my body around until my feet were planted on the rock and my knees were spread, and then I asked the sun and the river to make love to me. There was a moment while I waited, while my body settled down from its efforts, then I felt the response. Sun lay on me forcefully, pressed insistently on my belly. The breeze found the hot spots on my body and blew them cool. Breeze riffled through sun, and then there were two of them on me, moving sun, warm breeze, interlaced. The river pulled my hair into its hands and combed it, strand by strand, like the lover Izumi Shikibu dreamed of. Ah! I was human caressed by wild and wet, and I was in rapture.

The canyon wren trilled again, and I fell in love with everything that flowed around and through me. I was in love with a life that could fissure me like dried mud and then liquefy me into delight. "There is some kiss that we want with our whole lives," wrote the Persian poet Jelaluddin Rumi in the thirteenth century.9 Kissed by the river, kissed by heart-breach, kissed by the love of longing itself, kissed by the potential I could hardly imagine, I would have kissed back if only I could.

Then the breeze blew chilly, and consciousness, chillier still, swooped over me. I sat up and thought about warm clothes and dinner. I wanted to tell Rose what had happened. The moments when longing is sated are few and brief, I thought. Rapture sustains us for a while, then longing, faithful to its nature, pulls ahead and teases us forth once more.

AND LONGING IS THE PREHENSILE PASSION that enables religious mystics to cleave to the great mystery, the creator and sustainer and occasional provider of rapture, even when that sublime force feels furthest away. Like Changing Woman and White Shell Woman, mystics insist on knowing their god directly. They want not just to learn the truth, but to be sizzled by it. They plead for — and frequently receive

— direct communication, personal messages, prophetic revelations. But it's not just words of wisdom they want. They long for nothing less than to make love with the divine.

"Why should I flail about with words, when love has made the space inside me full of light?" asks the fifteenth-century Indian poet Kabir, answering himself with the only answer there is:

> Listen, brother!
> The Guest, who makes my eyes so bright,
> has made love with me.[10]

For Kabir, both a Sufi and a follower of Hinduism's bhakti path of devoted action, the Guest was the indwelling presence of God: the truth teller, source of ecstasy, flutist who never ceased playing, quencher of soul-thirst, lover. That same divine guest, who comes and goes at will, tantalizes its welcoming hosts in every major religion and moves poets to use the language of Eros to express their yearning for more. "O infinite goodness of my God!" cried Saint Teresa of Avila in the sixteenth century. "O Joy of the angels, how I long to be wholly consumed in love for Thee!"[11] The eighth-century Sufi poet Rabia was in the habit of climbing onto the roof of her cottage at night and there, under the grandeur of the stars, singing to Allah:

> O my joy, my longing,
> O my sanctuary, my companion,
> O Provision of my way
> O my ultimate aim!
> You are my spirit;
> You are my hope;
> You are my friend
>
> . . . .
>
> O radiant eye of my yearning heart!
> You are my heart's captain!

As long as I live, never from You
Shall I be free.[12]

Would Rabia have wished to be released from God's captivity? Never!

John Donne, cleric of the Church of England and poet of desire, was another prisoner of divine longing. Held captive to God, he wished only to be bound tighter still:

O'erthrow me, and bend
Your force, to break, blow, burn, and make me new.

Take me to you, imprison me, for I
Except you enthrall me, shall never be free,
Nor ever chaste except you ravish me.[13]

The longing for ravishment, to be engulfed by the sublime, is also reflected in the song that Uvavnuk, an Iglulik Eskimo woman, sings to the sea:

The great sea
frees me, moves me,
as a strong river carries a weed.
Earth and her strong winds
move me, take me away,
and my soul is swept up in joy.[14]

Swept up in joy or bound down like a prisoner, filled with inner God-light or singing in starlight, the mystic yearns to be taken body and soul into the presence of the ultimate. Ecstasy is an end in itself.

THAT NIGHT ROSE AND I TALKED about the events of the day as we played a game with the moon. Sitting on the ground in the low camp chairs that sheathed and buckled around our folded sleeping pads, we watched radiant light surge over the top of the dark canyon wall and round into a globe a couple of days past full, fanning over the plain behind us. After a few minutes, we would move our chairs several feet closer to the wall so we could witness the whole spectacle all over again. "Junkies for beauty," Rose called us.

Not an inappropriate term, considering that we had been talking of longing and its poor cousin, craving. "Craving is painful," Rose said. "There's only one thing that can satisfy it. Craving traps you."

I told her a bit about my old love affair with alcohol. No matter how much I drank, I had needed more and ever more. As I've heard it said, "One is too many, and a thousand isn't enough." Even after I stopped drinking, my need to be filled with what I hoped — vaguely, irrationally — would transform me continued to nag. I sought alcohol's substitute first in cigarettes, then in food. Recovering from those addictions, I got into debt with credit cards. But even before outward addictions had been loosed upon me, I had hungered both for constant affirmation from the people around me and for escape from all of them. I still demanded approval from Andy, more than I liked to admit. It had always seemed that only some potent medicine from an outside source could fill the abyss of incompleteness I foundered in.

On a vision quest in the Utah canyons the previous April, I had sacrificed to the ceremonial fire an old watch of my mother's, gold and set with six diamonds. It was elegant, but it wasn't me, and besides, it hadn't worked in years. It no longer served, like my need for fame and validation from others, which the watch symbolized. For four months I'd bided my time, wondering if anything had shifted within and what would happen next. Across my path stepped Lucas, en route to his cave in the mountain. Lured by a flattering dream and words of love, I could not help but follow. I trudged after him, pining for him to turn around and take my hand, but on he went, alone. Then, in his wake sprang another kind of longing I was only beginning to grasp. It had to do with the pursuit of the woman of myself who sang from the mountaintop cave and the warrior who would find a way to join her there as if his life depended on it. Only in their meeting would my own exile end.

The moon draped its veil over us and the grassland, turning us all silver. "Shall we?" I asked. Rose nodded. We stood and moved our chairs another twenty feet closer to the wall. Now there was no trace of moon in the sky, just a swipe of sapphire light above the black rock.

"Spirituality can be a kind of craving, too, you know," Rose said. "A lot of people go from one workshop to another, or one spiritual practice to another, looking for the one that's going to tell them who they are. They never settle into anything, they just keep hopping around."

"Maybe that's not entirely a bad thing," I said, "as long as they know it's the seeking, not the finding, that's the point. I mean, if you're just running around, pounding on doors and hoping God or your guru or true love, or whatever, will answer, that's craving, and it will probably make you miserable. But if the search is filled with wonder because you know the secret could be anywhere, that's joyful."

"I'd rather be free of longing," Rose said. "I think it's better to be content with what you've got. I mean, I love guiding these quests, I love the whole process and what happens to people. But I always miss my family so much. I miss Ed and our children. I'm really happiest when I'm home with them, in my community. Then I don't long for anything else. If I could find some way to guide vision quests in my backyard, I would."

"You see!" I crowed. "You are longing for something. You're longing for uninterrupted oneness with your family."

"I *have* oneness with my family," she argued. "Maybe I'm a Buddhist at heart. I seek nonattachment, nondesiring. And don't tell me I 'long' for it. I just want the peace of mind that comes from being happy with what I've got."

"I think longing is part of everyone's search for truth," I said. "Do you know the Arabic story of Layla and Majnun?"

She didn't.

"It's about a man, Majnun, who is so in love with a woman he can't have that he devotes his whole life to searching and calling for her. He's miserable without Layla, but he's thoroughly, totally alive and receptive to life, and he's ecstatic, because his search is so all-encompassing. That's the longing for God."

Rose yawned and got to her feet. "Right now," she said, "my longing is to crawl into my warm, cozy sleeping bag."

I spread my own sleeping bag out in the meadow and lay there watching the moon. The moon longs for its fullness, I thought, unable to let the analogies go, and then, perhaps, it longs for emptiness.

I considered Rose's position, that nondesiring, rather than desiring, was the real point of spiritual practice. But even that path necessitated a search, an ideal. Why, then, should the search itself not be a desirable thing? I thought about the Hindu myth of Krishna and his many lovers, how longing for another encounter with the god so stimulated the women's hearts that, in a sense, he made love to them even in his absence. As for me, I had yearned to be an initiate of the cosmic unknown ever since I was a little girl trying to discern the secret language of trees, to spy out the magical world I was sure flourished beneath an icy pond in the Connecticut woods where I walked with my grandfather. I still wanted oneness with mystery, or Spirit, the great, ineffable, unknowable All that suffuses and enlivens the universe, and I wanted it personal and immediate, as I had experienced it that afternoon with the river. The god I wanted to make love with would seduce me daily into a revelry of things coming alive — people, ideas, acts, nature, potentiality. I wanted to be passion itself.

Like Majnun, I thought, returning to that haunting story. The son and daughter of chieftains, Majnun and Layla were children when they met at school, and the moment they gazed at each other, they recognized their soul's true beloved. Majnun's ardor for the young girl quickly took hold of him. He could not stop staring at her in the classroom and whispering her name day and night — "Layla!" Alarmed by such intensity, Layla's father warned the boy's father that Majnun must never come near his daughter again.

But Majnun had already abdicated all choice in the matter. Consumed by the fire of his passion, he began to wander the desert, shouting Layla's name as if it were the Logos of creation. The young man's loving father tried to help, tried to bring him back to the fold of community life and responsibility, and even rallied the family to carry him to Mecca on a litter, in hopes that prayers made in the holy city might cure him of his madness. Majnun would have none of it. Madness on behalf of Layla, he exclaimed, was preferable to sanity without her. Love itself kept her essence burning in his heart, even though he was prohibited from seeing her in person.

Gradually all human concerns slipped away from Majnun, and he became a star of white-hot longing for his beloved. His hair, which he pulled at in his delirium, grew dirty and unkempt. Blisters oozed on his feet, and his clothes were nothing but tatters. Wild animals began to accompany him, for he himself had become more wild than human, and his needs were as spare and sharp as theirs. He slept in caves. Children mocked him. Still, everywhere he went, he continued to call out the name of his beloved: "Layla! Layla!" Eventually, even as people gawked and laughed at him, they had to acknowledge that he was the epitome of devoted love.

Eric Clapton borrowed the gist of this story when he wrote "Layla," perhaps the most passionately asserted love song of the modern era, about his obsession with Pattie Boyd, the wife of former Beatle George Harrison. At the time, Clapton was also addicted to heroin and alcohol, and the craving for the woman and the substances so fused in his mind that, after playing the song for Boyd for the first time, Clapton threatened to overdose on heroin if she did not leave Harrison and come to him.[15] This was the kind of longing Rose distrusted, and rightly so.

But the story of Layla and Majnun, rather than being a tale of addictive love for another human being, is actually a parable about the ardor for God, ever unattainable and beguiling, whom the devotee would rather adore in wild despair than ignore for the sake of maintaining a shallow, socially acceptable contentment. As long as the "Beloved," the Sufi endearment for Allah, thrives in this breached, seeking heart, love burns.

IT WAS A BELOVED LIKE THIS, I realized, splendorous and vividly experienced, that I longed so desperately to know and feel and learn from. That was the seducer whose presence, subtle as a scent, I had detected in so many places on my walk that day.

Goethe calls such an ache the "soulful yearning," the deep desire to be penetrated by a great force that will shatter old preoccupations with distance, darkness, and difficulty and fill us with a sense of sacred purpose and meaning. "Distance matters nothing now," he writes of the determination to satisfy "a longing for a higher love-making [that] grabs you and sweeps you up."[16] Jungian psychologist James Hillman traces the roots of such exalted longing to the Greek word *pothos*.

> *Plato defines it...as a yearning desire for a distant object. Its associations in the classical corpus are with longings for* that which cannot be obtained: *yearning for a lost child or a beloved...longing for sleep and for death. As late as the Church Father, Gregory of Nazianzus,* pothos *was described as a striving power in plants. It is the "vegetable love,"* a via naturalis *of which Andrew Marvell has written, or "the force that through the green fuse drives the flower drives my [green age]" of Dylan Thomas.*[17]

POTHOS, UNLIKE FANTASY OR ADDICTIVE CRAVING, does not limit us; it transports us beyond ourselves. It pushes a wanderer on and on over mountains and deserts, in search of wonders that can never be possessed but must ever be sought, since the seeker needs to marvel at them in himself. It impels scientists to their quests under the microscope and beyond the telescope. It drives artists, writers, and musicians to wrestle with the inexpressible until they have expressed it in the only way possible, through their art. *Pothos* urges pilgrims to far-off shrines and lonely caves in search of intimate communion with God. It grabs hold of men and women and persuades them that spending time alone in the wilderness, without food, company, shelter, or diversion is the best, indeed the only, way to take their hard-earned vacation. "*Pothos*," writes Jean Houston in *The Search for the Beloved*, "is an impetus to all our evolutionary striving...it is the memory of a union that fails to go away, a union that could only be partially explained and mirrored through human loving or partnership."[18]

Once we make room in our life for the great, mysterious Other that beckons, we realize that longing itself is a potent force, for every breath we take louvers us wider to the light of that remembered or hoped-for presence. Soulful yearning is active. It expands its own boundaries in keening for what it loves and does not have. We are stretched wide open by a God-shaped hole and wish with all our hearts never to be closed up again. Exile, our ache and our bliss, keeps us moving toward the best of ourselves.

And the one who awaits us, arms outstretched, is the Beloved.

CHAPTER SIX

THE BELOVED

THE QUEST FOR THE SOUL PARTNER

I found it a beautiful word: *Beloved*. Pronounced in three syllables, it sounded classical enough to belong to the myths and traditions from which it did, in fact, come, yet there was also something hauntingly familiar about it. Like the figure it referred to, it rang of a poignantly sweet intimacy that had once been known and had never quite faded from memory.

The Beloved personifies the object of the soul's longing for union with its highest expression. Elusive and alluring, the Beloved seduces us into our own becoming, compelling us to keep moving through tangled paths, wild deserts, mockery, misunderstanding, and, more often than not, a Vulcan's forge of yearning love that we discover we cannot bear to live without. As long as the Beloved is within our sights, or even within the scope of our belief, we willingly make our way through obstacles and doubts in hopes of being clasped in his or her embrace — that moment of self-realization, rapture, or revelation with what is at once greater than us and intimately, exquisitely, our truest self. Even knowing that those moments of sublime connection are rare and all too brief, the lover of the Beloved remains faithful, for the longing itself constantly widens us to make more room for what we love. Part of the human heart, part of the immense mystery beyond our ken, whether you wish to call it God, the creative force, the soul, the unconscious, or the interplay of subatomic particles that gel the universe, the Beloved is the desired one, the lover desiring, and the abyss of desire itself. Standing just out of reach, in the green glade of our vision and our dreams, barely perceptible in dappled sunlight, the Beloved beckons to each of us alone: "Come. Come. Come to my arms and fall in love with yourself and all your world."

BEGINNING IN THE FALL OF THE YEAR I fell in love with Lucas and realized it wasn't him, after all, whom I loved, but some force that had grabbed my heart by posing as Lucas, I set out to learn about the Beloved. The vision quest with Rose was my last program for that year. Now, like a bear, I hunkered down in my home cave. I spent time with Andy, wrote a couple of articles, read, earned a living by abridging audiobooks, occasionally saw friends, and drew energy from the stark austerity of bare trees, animal tracks in snow, ice on ponds, and the sere sleep of the gardens. Occasionally I went into New York to spend hours at the public library on Forty-second Street, absorbing books on mythical lovers, divine messengers, and invisible friends. Throughout that fall, I continued to feel a little off balance. The attraction to Lucas lingered, despite my certainty that he had been but a substitute for that "higher lovemaking" Goethe refers to. I felt both deserted and expectant in some way I could not quite define. I told myself that the inner lover would move into the void, but, really, I often lacked faith that anything would come of this pursuit.

Once I set out to track passion, I looked for clues everywhere. A primary source was other people. Brazenly telling my story wherever I could, I discovered that some friends, including those I had always considered open-minded and interested in new approaches to personal transformation, were shocked. They felt I had come dangerously close to betraying Andy. One even advised me to give up this Beloved business altogether and be grateful for what I had. These were the exceptions, however. Most people identified in some way with the precipitating event, and several told me that they, too, had struggled to wrest meaning from an unrequitable love. One friend described a difficult, volatile lover who, on the very day she had put her foot down and told him he would have to move out of her apartment, suggested she accompany him to the *zendo*, where he practiced Zen meditation. The moment she walked into that clean, tranquil place, her eyes filled with tears, for she felt that she had come home at last. "I couldn't live with him," she told me, "but he introduced me to the spiritual path I've now been following for thirty years."

"I can't relate to what you're calling the Beloved," said one new acquaintance, a dedicated and compassionate eco-psychologist. "It makes me think of how religious people talk about Christ." Contrarily, a neighbor laughed uncomfortably when I told her what I was working on. "I don't know," she said. "That sounds kind of paganistic to me."

But, in truth, religious mystics the world over have spoken of God as the Beloved. "When I close my eyes in solitude," wrote Hazrat Inayat Khan, who early in the twentieth century introduced Sufism, the mystical branch of Islam, to the Western world, "I see Thy glorious vision in my heart, and, opening my eyes amidst the crowd, I see Thee acting on the stage of the earth. Always I am in Thy dazzling presence, my Beloved."[1] *Ani L'Dodi v'Dodi Li*, proclaims the Jewish prayer: "I am my beloved's and my beloved is mine," or "I am the beloved of God and God is my beloved." Equating divine love and painful longing, St. Thomas Aquinas wrote, "The beloved penetrates the lover, coming to his interior; and because of this it is said that love wounds and transfixes the lover."[2] And it's not just the mystics, those oddball members of the flock who seek to know God up close and personal, who use the imagery of Eros to evoke the holy. Since its beginnings religion has not only made room for, but has actually depended on, the elements of sexual love, desire, and wedded union to depict primal cosmic oneness, the lust to create, and the blissful, juicy conjoining of heaven and earth.

ALL ORGANIZED RELIGION has its roots in ancient rites enacted to acknowledge the human longing to be embraced by the holy and mysterious, and we all have ancestors who were zealous participants in these rites. Sacred marriage ceremonies, in which a human, temporarily suffused with the presence of the goddess or god, made love with a mortal or with another inspirited agent of the gods, were necessary to assure the well-being of the people and the fruitfulness of the crops and flocks. To reach orgasmic unity in the name of all that was holy was to participate body and soul in the reproductive powers of the cosmos, to actually re-create creation. Sexuality was a communal affair at these occasions, enacted in mass orgies, ritual prostitution, and joyful licentiousness. A man and woman who, the day before, might have passed each other on the lane with only a polite nod of recognition, and who would do so again the day after, could, on the night the bonfires danced into the sky, tumble into a freshly plowed furrow and partake of the sacred coupling themselves.

Hinduism, the world's oldest formal religion, which began to emerge separate and distinct from its rough tribal predecessors in the second millennium B.C.E., depicts the fundamental principle of existence as erotic union. The voluptuous energy generated by the original cosmic pair, Shiva and Shakti, was monumentalized in a pair of images that anyone, high priest, princess, warrior, or beggar, could relate to: the *lingam*, or erect phallus, and the *yoni*, receptive vaginal vessel. Like the coupling impulse of these two physical members, states the Upanishads, all complementary forms and concepts were originally clasped together like a man and woman: "Just as a man closely entwined with the woman he desires no longer distinguishes the outside from the inside, so the man who embraces the divine no longer distinguishes between outside and inside. In it he finds his real form, the one that satisfies his desire, the supreme being who is all that is desirable."3

Sexual bliss as a symbol of ecstatic plenitude found expression in the sensuous erotic sculptures in the temples at Khajuraho, in the graphic instructions for lovemaking in the *Kama Sutra*, and in the oral tales of Krishna and his adventures. So explicit is the eroticism in all these mediums that it could never have been intended to serve simply as a workable simile for talking about the concreteness of religious devotion. Titillation itself attracts. Sex is interesting. And stories and pictures about sex make people want to pay attention. When one hears the story about the abashed young women who emerged from their bath in the river only to find that saucy Krishna had stolen all their saris and climbed up into a tree with them, one takes on the undercurrent of desire, takes it on not just with the imagination's eye and, perhaps, with the soul's understanding, but with the libido as well. The story is meant to teach that we must go naked to the god; since erotic interest holds us in the grip of the teaching longer than a lecture might, we're more likely to get the message.

Christianity, at least as it has come down to us, has taken just the opposite approach: sensuality and sexuality are considered the bait the devil uses to lure weak-willed humans into his perilous waters, far away from God's safe haven. So despised, in fact, are the body and its urges that in Church doctrine first set forth by Matthew in his Gospel and codified almost two thousand years later in a papal bull issued in 1854, the central figure, half-divine, half-mortal, had to be delivered into this world of a woman so stripped of sexuality that she not only got pregnant without having engaged in intercourse but was herself conceived in a similarly vague, decidedly uncarnal way. Even though Christianity has long insisted on a uterus-free Virgin and a male father-God, a different view emerges in texts written at the same time as the other New Testament gospels, then hidden in the sands of the Egyptian desert for safekeeping and only discovered in 1945. In one of these Gnostic Gospels, the creator is an androgynous being, both Mother and Father, who lustily copulates with itself "and with those who love me." Another text, whose title, *Thunder, Perfect Mind*, conveys its forceful, uncompromising language, is delivered in the voice of a divine female in whom all opposites are united: "I am the first and the last. I am the honored one and the scorned one. I am the whore, and the holy one. I am the wife and the virgin. I am the she whose wedding is great, and I have not taken a husband. I am knowledge and ignorance.... I am godless, and I am one whose God is great."4

It is not surprising that this fierce Christianity was pushed, literally, underground by the Church hierarchy, which must have viewed it not as the word of a God even more omnipotent than they had dared to imagine but as that of the devil. Sexlessness and patriarchy prevailed. Jesus is presumed to have been celibate, and the suggestion made by films like *The Last Temptation of Christ* or by the scholarship of feminist Christianity, which posit that Mary Magdalene might have been his lover or even his wife, rouses righteous indignation. Jesus did embody love, as no other religious figure before or after him has done, but his brand of love was compassion — for the sick, for women, for the poor, for the humble, for the doubters, even for those who persecuted him. It is hard to imagine him shifting tactics and turning his back on sexual love, if not for himself, then at least for his beloved followers.

Judaism identifies the passionate longing that drives the soul as the search for the Shechinah, God's female half, said to have been present at the time of creation. After the Word had set the world in motion, the two split off from each other, and the Shechinah descended to earth, where she continues to wander in exile. Facilitating the reunion of the divine pair, the kabbalists teach, is the essential task of the Hebrew people. They compare the Torah to the Shechinah's "outer garment" and claim that a scholar becomes a Bridegroom of the Torah by courting its mysteries as he would woo the woman he loves until, little by little, the covering falls away like the gown of the modest bride, and he will understand the most arcane of passages. Feminist author Barbara Walker puts it well: "She opens the door of her hidden chamber ever so little, and for a moment reveals her face to her lover, but hides it again forthwith. He alone sees it and is drawn to her with his heart and soul and his whole being."5

Unlike Hinduism or Judaism, Buddhism honors neither a mythology nor a deity. Its iconography centers on the enlightened one himself, the Buddha, in various phases of his spiritual journey through his earthly lifetime. This imagery, very different from that of its direct religious ancestor, Hinduism, is solitary rather than conjoint. It focuses on a single meditator, a lone seeker, and it is undramatic, just the opposite of passionate, its aim to evoke inner peace, divine bliss, transcendence over personal suffering, and compassion for the suffering of others. The Buddha, seeking to live as simple a life as possible, chose the path of celibacy, and he urged adepts to follow that path as well, encouraging them to channel their desire for a home, intimacy, and family into the sangha, or spiritual community. Understanding that ordinary men and women could not live by such strict precepts, he taught his followers that sexuality was natural but that it needed to be kept in mindful balance. One branch of the Eightfold Path toward liberation from suffering is right action, and that includes appropriate sexuality, not acts or fantasies that would harm others.

A more exuberant view emerges in tantric Buddhism. A blend of Buddhism from India and the animistic native religion of Tibet, Tantrism teaches that spiritual ecstasy is the germ of creation and that, with discipline and training, it can be unleashed in every experience and emotion. Tantric practitioners attain ecstasy through meditation, mental control of the uncoiling snake of kundalini energy rising through the body, dance, art, and intense engagement in even the most mundane of daily tasks. Since they also seek ecstatic states through sexual union and the relishing of sensual pleasure, they have been misunderstood by many, both critics who condemn them as licentious and would-be followers eager to indulge in merry orgies. In fact, tantric practice seeks the awakening of the mind to all life, the ecstasy of which is but a part of the agony, and its rigorous practices include meditations on what is dying and putrid as a way of controlling the senses and burning up the dross of dualistic mind-sets and negative emotions.

Like Buddhism, Islam has no mythology; unlike Buddhism, it permits no imagery. Even its history is as tough and spare as the desert in which it unfolded: a man of Mecca, called Muhammad, received prolific teachings from an angelic messenger of Allah, or perhaps from Allah himself, and these communications became the Koran. All Islamic ritual revolves around the assimilation of the Koran, the word (in fact, *Koran* means "reading"), and everything a person needs to know can be found in that complex and musical scripture. The Koran teaches that Allah created man and woman from a single soul so that they might live together in serenity, and it sets forth many guidelines for doing so. For the Sufis, the enigmatic revelation that is the Koran is not a fixed text that must be interpreted by priests, but a constantly flowing cascade of divine power that can flood the one who devotes himself to it, just as Allah's word engulfed Muhammad. Sufis drink this sublime truth like wine, sipping not only from the dense passages of the Koran but also from the events of ordinary life and by entering mystical states they have learned to attain. They celebrate their ecstatic love of God and his creation through poetry, whirling dances, and misleadingly simple parables, all of which must be intuited, not interpreted, in the center of wisdom, the heart.

THERE ARE THINGS THAT CAN'T BE UNDERSTOOD except by pecking through them, as the chick in its egg ekes out the light of life. I pecked. I sought the Beloved all over the place and found it where I did not seek. Passing late one afternoon by Saint Lucy's Roman Catholic Church in a mixed ethnic neighborhood of New York City, I entered, remembering the winter celebration of St. Lucia that my Swedish grandmother used to tell me about, when she, as the youngest daughter of the family, would wear a white dress and a wreath of candles round her head and awaken her family with a tray of coffee and cakes. But Roman Catholic Lucy had a darker mission than her Lutheran twin. In the sanctuary of the church was a picture of her with her face upturned to the Lord, blank eyes blinded by torture or by her own hand. She appeared unconcerned about her fate, content to sacrifice her old way of seeing for inner vision, and confident that God would have a use for her in any state. Sacrifice was often the price of enlightenment, as vision questers regularly and willingly learned. As for me, the ways of seeing the world that I'd recently given up included feeling the shame of desire and acting the tough guy who never needed help. I'd give up more, I thought, to know the personal Beloved, whose heritage I now seemed to grasp more closely than the holy soul guide himself. When I left the church, sunset had layered the sky with the colors of passion: lavender, mauve, fuchsia, tangerine, hot pink, bittersweet red. Tears came to my blessedly sighted eyes. Every now and then the Beloved found me after all.

TRADITIONALLY, THE BOON OF RECEIVING direct personal knowledge of the divine has been bestowed only upon the lucky few. When it has extended to ordinary folks, it happens only on special occasions. For generations, a succession of female oracles at Delphi in southern Greece shaped the policies of the city-states, decreeing which nations were enemies or likely to be, warning of plagues and treachery, stating what kinds of offerings would please the gods and which men they favored, and people traveled long distances to ask their most burning questions of the mortal woman who was "filled with the god." In the long age of the prophets, from Abraham, Isaiah, and Malachi to Muhammad a thousand years later, humans took on the role of God's mouthpiece, declaring the end of the world, praising God's miracles, and preaching correct behavior, often in stirring, beautiful language that few doubted could come from any other source than the tongue of the divine. Muhammad accepted the treasure of Allah's teachings for twenty-three years, a gift and burden he never refused, although it is said that, at the very last revelation, his camel sank wearily onto its knees.

For millennia, the tribal people of Africa, Asia, and the Americas have drummed and danced and abandoned their human personalities in order to take on the spirits of their elders, the animals. Shamans in the dense rain forests of South America ingest sacred mushrooms and herbs to receive visions about the intricate, conscious functioning of nature, and Christians in Paris, Dubuque, and Dubai take holy communion so that they might incorporate into themselves the holy body and blood of Christ. In services of the Pentecostal Church, the Holy Spirit zaps ordinarily sober men and women like a blast of electricity, then speaks through them in tongues. In these fevered services, commented an early observer, people are sometimes healed from persistent afflictions, sometimes they run around the church as if they've gone mad, and sometimes women kiss men who aren't their husbands.[6]

There are Sufi adepts who can depart the mundane world regularly to meet with Muhammad, Jesus, and such a host of saints and teachers that, as one master declared, his head felt like the dome inside a mosque.[7] Native American lore is filled with stories of people who are visited by the Great Spirit in the form of a bird or animal, occasionally a plant, that seeks them out and makes a sacred compact with them. If the human being will vow to protect the animal and all its kind, so the offer usually goes, then the animal will bestow on him or her a special knowledge or skill. These are not little favors that quickly lose meaning, but compacts that often thrive way beyond the lifetime of the recipient, since, in fact, they are almost always intended to benefit not just her, but all the people. A Blackfoot story, for example, tells of a young woman who is so loved by a buffalo that she and her people are granted permission to kill the animals for their meat, hides, bones, and sinews if the people, in return, will perform a dance to bring the animals back to life, that they may give themselves again. And so on in perpetuity.[8]

THE GODS PENETRATE THEIR FAVORITES in many ways. And astonishingly enough — or maybe not, given the intense personal charisma of the man — it is Jesus Christ, the presumably celibate man of a sexless mother, who has ravished the souls of the female devout in ways that got women who weren't under the protection of a convent burned at the stake. Mechtilde of Magdeburg, for example, a thirteenth-century member of the Beguines community near Berlin, wrote a narrative poem, "Flowing Light of the Godhead," about her intense spiritual romance with the young eighteen-year-old Christ. In the poem, Christ comes to her and admits that he has been wooing her. He asks her for an assignation in the woods. They dance together, and he begs her for another meeting. The ensuing inner debate does not go quite the way one would expect: it is the senses, typically portrayed as the rash perpetrators of sin, that urge caution on Mechtilde. She informs them that she intends to drink the "unmingled wine of divine love" and leaves them behind to return to her Bridegroom, implying, as psychiatrist John P. Dourley points out, that "all souls are made for such love because they are of the same nature as their divine lover."[9] Mechtilde continues:

> Then the beloved goes into the lover,
> into the secret hiding place of the sinless
> Godhead. . . . And there, the soul being
> fashioned in the very nature of God, no
> hindrance can come between it and God.[10]

Another thirteenth-century nun, Gertrude of Helfta, was so modest that, by her own account, she had to skip over sections of scripture with references to carnality. All that changed when Jesus sought her out as his bride. The Lord loves her unconditionally, she writes, and tells her he finds no pleasure in anyone else. "Burning and panting" with desire, she goes to him, and the couple engages in physical acts torqued from a concept of sex that could only belong to someone with no personal knowledge of it. In one meeting, Gertrude has a vision of Jesus placing her soul on his breast, where it melts like wax in a fluid she insists is *not* his perspiration. In another she feels her "devastating coal," her "fiery furnace of ever-increasing heat" suck the marrow from her bones as her flesh dissolves. Often Jesus bends down to implant on her soul "the sweetest kiss." When Gertrude is ill and worried that, by her absence from chapel, she is displeasing her lover, he chides her gently: "Do you think that the spouse takes less pleasure in his bride when he is alone with her in the privacy of the nuptial chamber, and they can delight one another with the charm of intimate converse and tender embraces, than when he leads her forth in all her beauty to be seen by the crowds?"[11] Such detailed notes from the bedchamber, sanctified though the place may be, are reminiscent of romance novels in which the heroine must be reassured over and over that she is the only one loved by her beloved. Other nuns, like Teresa of Avila in Spain and Sor Juana Inés de la Cruz of Mexico, were also ecstatic recipients of Jesus' passion. They spoke to him with a lover's wooings, and he responded in kind. They were always available to him, and they ached when he was absent. Like the moth in the flame, they gave themselves up to be consumed in rapture. *Agape*, compassionate, charitable love of God, had fermented into *Eros*.

All these spirit-driven utterances, divine favors, prophetic teachings, and visionary gifts were unpredictable, uncontrollable, and as volcanic as "waves of liquid love," in the words of an early Pentecostal in Connecticut.[12] Most of us have had no dependable, sober way of persuading the god or goddess, passionate and fickle no matter what tradition they come from, to be our lifetime companion. The Greeks, however, by nature architects of the balanced life, had a more reliable means of staying in touch with the gods. They posited the existence of a personal, constant soul guide. It was loyal. It was wise and helpful. One did not have to relinquish sense and sanity to get the benefit of divine guidance. Best of all, it was a companion for life, not a ravenous *geist* that wrung you out like a mop until it was through with you.

From the time a person first takes seed in the womb, Socrates taught, he is accompanied by a semidivine guardian called a daimon. The daimon remembers exactly why the person was born and nudges him into making the appropriate choices so that he can fulfill his destiny. It conveys his prayers up to the gods and relays their counsel back down. Upon the person's death, the daimon accompanies the soul to the Underworld for judgment and assignment to another body, at which point the daimon itself moves on to become helpmate to another soul. Socrates never calls the daimon the "Beloved," but he does state that the force binding each human to his lifelong soul companion and to the gods is Eros. In the *Symposium*, Socrates tells his students about a conversation he had with the Mantinean priestess Diotima, in which she identified Eros as the active agent linking people and gods. Eros, she said, is a great spirit (daimon) whose task "is to interpret and ferry across to the gods things given by men, and to men things from the gods... and being in the middle it completes them and binds all together into a whole. For God mingles not with man, but through this comes all the communion and conversation of gods with men and men with gods. These spirits are many and of all sorts and kinds, and one of them is Love [Eros]."[13] This Eros was no aloof deity lolling on a couch on Mount Olympus, but a dynamic force on earth, kinetic in every person. Eros was the current that streaked from the desirer to the object of desire and charged with sparks all the space between.

Apuleius, the second-century Roman author who elaborated on Socrates' discussions of this personal "god," as he referred to the daimon, distinguishing it from the mighty Olympic gods, spoke authoritatively about its physiognomy, duties, and inclinations. Daimons had bodies "less dense and more attenuated than clouds." They "consist of that most pure, liquid, and serene element of air, and on this account are not easily visible to the human eye, unless they exhibit an image of themselves by divine command" — in other words, unless they want to be seen.[14] The Olympic gods did not have passions, since that would make them less than perfect, but daimons did, for they were "likewise in the nature of their mind having immortality in common with the Gods, and passion in common with the beings subordinate to themselves. For they are capable, in the same manner we are, of suffering all the mitigations or incitements of souls; so as to be stimulated by anger, made to incline by pity, allured by gifts, appeased by prayers, exasperated by contumely, soothed by honors, and changed by all other things, in the same way that we are."[15]

The name the Romans themselves gave to this immortal companion was *genius*, and they insisted that humans take some responsibility for keeping the relationship satisfactory and productive. Apuleius reminded that the genius could not be expected to do all the work of soul-crafting himself. If one "watches [the genius] in the right way, seeks ardently to know him, honors him religiously," then he will gladly assume a variety of roles on the human's behalf, becoming, in the words of Jungian psychologist Marie-Louise von Franz,

> the one who can see to the bottom of uncertain situations and can give warning in desperate situations, can protect us in dangerous situations, and can come to our rescue when we are in need. [He can intervene] now through a dream and now through a sign [synchronistic event], or he can even step in by appearing personally in order to fend off evil, to reinforce the good, to lift up the soul in defeat, to steady our inconstancy, to lighten our darkness, to direct what is favorable toward us and to compensate what is evil.[16]

What a mutually fulfilling relationship this must have been: the daimon given to steer a soul to its highest fulfillment, the human guided in decisions small and large and hence kept on the path he was born to follow. The holy ones themselves would have been happy, knowing that they were not forgotten and that a portion of divinity pulsed in the heart of every mortal. But as the tenets of Christianity tentacled over the polytheistic world, the Church hierarchy quashed the belief that an ordinary human might attain such immediate and fruitful access to God. The only reliable mediator was an officially sanctioned priest. The Church not only denigrated the benevolent, personal guide, but it also made sure that the significance of the daimon was perverted into the very opposite of itself. *Daimon* devolved into the homonymous *demon*, a supernatural agent bent on luring one not toward but away from the holy.

How sad, I thought, that modern people don't have a daimon, or don't know they do. I wondered if the invisible best friends that children so adore, and whose reality they tearfully defend to their uncompromisingly reasonable parents, might not be their daimon, still tenaciously doing its job on earth until disbelief and neglect simply shrivel it up. In Philip Pullman's brilliant children's series–cum–scientific-theological parable *His Dark Materials*, everyone has an animal daimon who is their very soul. Villains in the story commit the unspeakable crime of cutting people off from their daimon.

THE DAIMON HAS MANAGED TO SURVIVE, although in limited guises and with its access restricted to but a few. It has been most widely tolerated as the muse, personification of divine inspiration and companion of creative artists. Originally there were nine Muses, daughters born to Mnemosyne, Greek goddess of memory, and Zeus. Each had her own domain — history, astronomy, music, tragedy, comedy, lyric poetry, love poetry, epic poetry, and dance — and upon the purveyors of her field bestowed insight and superior creativity. From the start it was the poets who took their muse most seriously. Homer invokes her guidance in the very first line of *The Odyssey*: "Sing in me, Muse, and through me tell the story." From that time forth, the muse, solitary, sisterless, and capricious, became the resident spirit in the poet's dark atelier, she who transforms her human's inchoate grapplings over paper to pure, exalted verse. The poet relies completely on his muse; he cannot begin to create without her. In the opening lines of *Paradise Lost*, Milton warns his muse that he has extremely high aspirations for their collaboration:

Sing, heav'nly Muse
I thence

Invoke thy air to my advent'rous song
That with no middle flight intends to soar
Above th'Aonian mount, while it pursues
Things unattempted yet in prose or rhime.

As a daughter of the goddess of memory, the muse does more than inspire the poet; she escorts him back to a great bygone truth awaiting only the proper words to be born anew. She knows what really happened at Eden, what words of wisdom Athena whispered in Achilles' ear. Mircea Eliade writes: "By virtue of the primordial memory that he is able to recover, the poet inspired by the Muses has access to the original realities."[17]

Male poets throughout the centuries have often portrayed the muse as an enchantress whose loyalty no amount of flattery or cajoling can assure. An interesting exception is Steven King's concept of the force that inspires his work. The bestselling author of horror novels has described his muse as a team of burly construction workers who live in the basement of his unconscious and tell him what to write in plain, no-nonsense language.[18] Women artists have claimed muses of both, or neither, gender. To the Russian poet Anna Akhmatova, the muse was female, but she was no personal guiding force, no daimon with whom the poet enjoyed an exclusive relationship, but *the* Muse, the one and only, the same commanding spirit who had once "dictated to Dante / the pages of *The Inferno*."[19] The nineteenth-century feminist author and Transcendentalist Margaret Fuller imagined her muse as neither male nor female, but as an impersonal dynamic, "that unimpeded clearness of the intuitive powers, which a perfectly truthful adherence to every admonition of the higher instincts would bring to a finely organized human being.[20] Poet and naturalist Diane Ackerman describes the muse as a "he / she / it gender-blur / who's mainly a him (because he fills / my hollows and limbs)."[21]

The twentieth-century poet and mythographer Robert Graves did not believe a woman could even have a muse; she could only serve as one to a man, and, furthermore, a wife could not be a muse, since domestic drudgery would pervert the sacred relationship that had to be focused solely on the creation of poetry. Graves's own muse, to which he devoted an entire difficult book, was the all-powerful White Goddess, a multidimensional being who could assume many forms, animal and human, benign and diabolic, when she appeared to him in the throes of his poetic rapture: "The poet is in love with the White Goddess, with Truth: his heart breaks with longing and love for her," he wrote.[22] Graves's longing for his muse dictated his life. The older he got, the more he pursued her, not just in the abstract, as he bent over his desk, but in human form, in a succession of beautiful, increasingly young women who became his lovers. The muse, at least when she is not forced to take on human form, is as driven as her poet. She cares for nothing but his art. Family, sanity, fiscal responsibility, sobriety — what do they matter as long as the poem is unfolding as it's meant to?

Another messenger between mortal and divine, the guardian angel, like the daimon, is more dedicated to guiding the whole soul toward its fullest realization. In the Zoroastrian tradition, immediately upon the death of the body the soul had to cross the great Chinvat Bridge to the high peak of judgment. On the other side, those who had lived an unrighteous life were gobbled up by a hideous monster, while the righteous were greeted by the angel who represented their true, complete, and perfect identity. Angels are typically portrayed as ethereal, luminous beings, belonging far more to the celestial realm than to the earth, although the plethora of modern films and television shows about them sometimes feature a comic, scruffy, eccentric representative of the heavenly host. First-person narratives about the miracles angels work abound and range from the sublime that one would expect to the very mundane. Many people have reported the sudden presence of a celestial being, surrounded by light and kindness, bearing news that a loved one is close to death, offering comfort during war, or bringing together two people who are the only ones in the world who can meet each other's exceptional needs. In recent years, there has been a resurgence of interest in angels — or, according to Sylvia Browne, who has written widely on the subject, a resurgence of angels themselves, come down to earth in response to a time of global and personal crisis and "in rebuttal to the hellfire and demons" whose presence is evoked by the very fundamentalist preachers who fulminate against such evils.[23]

Muses and angels are two recognizable entities who have survived the death of the daimon and been allowed to bridge the gap between God and human with their attention and favors. But, even unnamed, some waiting presence continues to haunt us. We know it's out there, wishing, as we do, that we might be united with it. This presence, this mystery of love, wafts about on the far side of a river sparkling in the sun. It comes to us in dreams and folds us in an embrace we wish never to awaken from. It hopes we will burst into the brilliant flame of our own radiant self, and it breaches our heart every time we fall in love. The old Prince, in Giuseppe Tomasi di Lampedusa's novel *The Leopard*, meets the beguiling soul guide as he lies on his deathbed with the urge to live still crashing over him like a tempestuous sea. Then he sees her, the one he used to perceive sometimes as he gazed at the nighttime sky. Gently she sidles past the gathered mourners to close the distance between them: "It was she, the creature forever yearned for, coming to fetch him; the time for the train's departure must be very close. When she was face to face with him she raised her veil, and there, modest, but ready to be possessed, she looked lovelier than she ever had when glimpsed in stellar space. The crashing of the sea subsided altogether."[24]

The banishment of the personal soul guide by the forces of both religion and rationalism has robbed most of us humans — by nature inquisitive beings, always pondering the mysteries we cannot solve but wish ever to be part of — of the chance even to conceive of an intimate, faithful companion who could elevate our aspirations and transform us through love. It has been the task of psychology to resuscitate the attentive, wise, immortal advisor and bring it back to its rightful place in the psyche, or whole self. Carl Jung was convinced that certain archetypes, or prototypical images common to peoples throughout the world, were stomping around and carrying on just underneath the thin, polite crust of the conscious mind and that they were powerful allies on the road to psychological health. Jung's preferred term for the invisible and alien behind the material and obvious was the "unconscious," although he acknowledged the value of descriptive synonyms like daimon, mana, and God, because they enabled people to grasp hold more easily of a slippery concept.[25]

Jung encouraged his patients to enter into dialogue with the archetypal figures who appeared in their dreams and whose presence continued to nudge their unconscious even as the dream dissolved. Either alone and engaged in the process of "active imagination," a kind of automatic writing, in which they wrote down both their own questions and statements and those of the dream figure, or in the company of the analyst and speaking both parts aloud, patients could gain profound insights, not only about the importance of the dream to their own psychic history but also about how they might transcend the familiar, limited self and begin being true to the soulful, integrated Self in as many ways as possible. You could say that, in these numinous conversations, they were like poets in the grip of the muse. Among the most common archetypes, which first showed up in the world's folk- and fairy tales and returned again and again to play roles in the dreams of individuals, were the wise old man and wise old woman, the parent, the monster, the tyrant, and the child. Another was the lover. Jung called the lover the "contrasexual other" and considered its incorporation into the psyche a sign that a person had reached a high level of psychological development.

Jung enjoyed a dynamic relationship with his own inner feminine, to whom he felt he was writing letters as he worked out his theories about her and her ilk, and with a personal "vision figure," a "pagan" he called Philemon, who served a role like that of the Greek daimon.[26] Jung frequently took walks with Philemon, asked him questions, heeded his wisdom, and treated him as "what the Indians would call a guru." He describes the relationship touchingly: "Philemon represented a force which was not myself. In my fantasies I held conversations with him, and he said things which I had not consciously thought. For I observed clearly that it was he who spoke, not I. It was he who taught me psychic objectivity, the reality of the psyche."[27]

Through regular sessions of active imagination with archetypes like these, Jung resolved inner disputes, gained insights about the struggles of his patients, and pieced together his theories of the unconscious and its perpetual search for its own spiritual realization. Not through intellect alone, but through partnership with numinous guides who could not be seen or heard by anyone else did this giant in the new field of psychology solidify his ideas.

Several of Jung's followers have expanded and elaborated on his ideas of the inner lover who leads the individual closer to his or her own divinity, including Jean Houston, whose experiential process of "sacred psychology" culminates in the encounter with the Beloved, "one's double in the extended realm of the soul; the exotype of the archetype, the one for whom one yearns, after whom one wanders, in search of potential union";[28] Caitlín Matthews, who focuses on the daimon of women as their "true, universal experience of the masculine, which becomes clear when women begin to live from the ground of their authentic selves";[29] and John P. Dourley, who explores the psyche's journey to its own divine center, "at once the source of all consciousness and so of whatever meaning exists in the universe."[30] I read their books hungrily, looking for clues to the identity of the personal soul guide. One Jungian in particular, Nancy Qualls-Corbett, entered my life in a way that not only provided intellectual inspiration but also facilitated a strange and wonderful net of synchronicity, Jung's term for those seeming coincidences in which the inner and outer worlds meet, inform, and ennoble each other.

DURING THAT WEEK IN LATE SUMMER, when longing for Lucas had soaked up all my concentration, I had confided in my good friend

Barbara Vernovage. Barbara, who lived with her husband on a large farm not far from me, was a passionate student of Jungian thought, had gone through Jungian analysis, and had belonged to a Jungian study group, and she was fascinated with the archetype as personal teacher and companion. We sat one morning on her sunporch, blinking into the bright sun that rose over rolling green hills as we drank coffee and spoke of lovers real and imaginal. So excited had we both become by the cataract of ideas the subject generated that we decided to get together once a week for breakfast to keep the discussion going. In our area of rural northeastern Pennsylvania, there are not a lot of dining choices, but we covered them all over the next weeks and months and years, for it was the mental fare that nourished us, not the scrambled eggs, watery orange juice, and margarined toast. At one breakfast, Barbara had loaned me Nancy Qualls-Corbett's book *The Sacred Prostitute*.

In it Qualls-Corbett explores the figure of the sensuous priestess who gives imaginatively and generously of her femininity and who, resident in the psyches of both men and women, can stoke the fires of spiritual, sexual, and creative passion. For centuries throughout the Middle East, the sacred prostitute served the goddess of love by initiating the stranger in the temple into the mysteries of divine union. Whispering, touching, lovemaking, and attending to this seeker, she taught him through example what it was to give, receive, and contain love. For the contemporary man, Qualls-Corbett writes, developing fidelity to the sacred prostitute of himself means tapping into his emotions and opening more comfortably to his experiences of beauty, joy, spontaneity, and laughter. The woman who cherishes the sacred prostitute of herself comes to trust her own autonomy and to cast off "the yoke of servitude to many masters." She "serves the goddess of love by attending the holy fire of her inner feeling."[31] Qualls-Corbett believes that by exploring the potent figure of the sacred prostitute and consciously welcoming her into our psyche, as she welcomed the stranger into the sacred nuptial chamber in the temple, we can restore to society a positive, life-affirming image of the feminine as manifested by both sexes.

I was still enthusiastically immersed in *The Sacred Prostitute* when Barbara told me that she was expecting a weekend houseguest.

The previous spring, around the time I was burning my mother's gold watch in a desert wash, Barbara had joined a tour of Pompeii, Amalfi, and other sites in southern Italy led by her former analyst, Eugene Monick, and Nancy Qualls-Corbett. The purpose of the trip was to study the rites of Dionysus, the semidivine embodiment of passion and ecstasy, as they were revealed in temple frescoes and sculpture that abounded in that region. One afternoon, standing by a stone wall that overlooked the glittering aquamarine Bay of Naples, Barbara had fallen into conversation with another participant, Melissa Werner, a child development expert from Birmingham. Melissa told Barbara that she was studying the ways Native Americans raised their children, which she believed could provide a valuable model for majority-culture parents. When she mentioned that she had recently done research on the Navajo and Hopi reservations, Barbara, knowing that I had written extensively about the Navajo and Hopi during the late 1980s and early '90s, asked if she had ever heard of me. "After I finished scraping her off the floor," Barbara crowed in a message scrawled later that day on a postcard showing the Ariadne fresco at Pompeii, "she told me she knew you at college."

It was true. In 1969–70, when I was a senior at Stephens College, I worked a few afternoons a week at the receptionist desk in one of the freshman dorms. Seniors, of course, rarely deign to associate with lowly freshmen, but there was one young woman — Melissa Werner — with whom I developed an unusual and mutual empathy. Although we never socialized beyond the confines of my desk, Melissa would frequently pause there as she went in and out of the dorm, and we would talk as peers of many things. I had not seen or heard of her in twenty-eight years. And now she was coming for a visit.

Melissa arrived on a cold night in January, and, after the two of us had gazed at each other for a moment in tearful disbelief, trying to bring into focus the middle-aged woman before us and the young student we remembered, the three of us women drove to a country inn for dinner.

We were seekers, students of dreams, unravelers of myth, and delvers into tradition. Quickly our conversation turned to the subject of the Beloved. I told Melissa about Lucas. All my friends knew the story by now, for I had not gotten over my enthusiasm for admitting to desire. Leaning forward, elbows braced on the white tablecloth, as wind shook the holly bushes outside the low windows of the green clapboard inn and riffled the pines lining the lake, I described what I was learning about the universal figure of the Beloved. In particular I raved about the book I was reading.

"Qualls-Corbett talks about the erotic feminine principle as it relates to both men and women. She says that if you can solicit — that's the word she uses at one point, *solicit* — the sacred prostitute of yourself, you break out of the bounds of convention and doing things simply because they make sense or somebody else says they're correct, and you take on divine madness. That doesn't mean you go crazy, it just means your personality is enlarged, it's liberated. She's brilliant. Even her writing is sensuous. And the way she works with dreams is so perceptive," I exclaimed. "I've never really had any interest in going into analysis, but if I ever did, it would be with Nancy Qualls-Corbett."

"She's my analyst," Melissa announced matter-of-factly.

Then she went on to describe the work that she and Nancy were doing with a positive male figure who had first come to Melissa in a dream, the inner lover. She called him Casizza. Sometimes Casizza appeared to her as a Middle Eastern man; more often he made his presence known not visually but viscerally, as a spiral of energy that she could feel coiling up her spine. Tuning into his presence, she felt an erotic charge permeate whatever she was doing at the moment. At first her dialogues with Casizza had occurred only while she lay on the analyst's couch, but recently, encouraged by Nancy, she had begun calling him up whenever she set out for her daily morning walk in a local park. This was her rendezvous time with Casizza, she said, and the regularity of the practice had substantially contributed to its fruitfulness. Casizza was helping her to advance the work she was doing in analysis, since he accepted and unqualifiedly loved what she had identified as her two dominant female subpersonalities, the erotic self and the mothering self. These two aspects of her psyche had always warred with each other, and she had regarded them as incompatible, but her inner lover did not see it that way at all. "Casizza loves all parts of me that come from my deep self," she told Barbara and me. "He wants them to be united, and I can only unite them if I'm true to myself." Developing a relationship with the inner lover took patience, Melissa added. "Part of the attraction is the wooing. Casizza is a kind and gentle presence. I have been used to more aggressive men." By wooing, she meant not expecting too much of her Beloved, allowing him to reveal himself slowly. She meant playing with the growing intimacy between them, as if the two of them were engaged in the mesmerizing explorations that kindle lovemaking.

FOR YEARS I HAD BEEN AN AFICIONADO of deep imagery, the practice of entering into dialogue with dream figures, archetypes, and other aspects of the unconscious, yet it had never occurred to me to use it to ask the Beloved to show himself to me. The method I worked with, the Personal Totem Pole Process, was developed by Eligio Stephen Gallegos in 1982 as a way of taking advantage of the deep wisdom of the unconscious to bring about individual healing and wholeness. Inspired in part by Jung's experiments in active imagination, Gallegos's work differed in several respects. First, it did not wait for dream figures to appear as guides but plumbed the reservoir of imagery in the unconscious as needed. Moreover, Gallegos did not limit imaginal encounters to a few known archetypes but insisted that people could call on an infinite number of inner guides cohering around every conceivable human concern — fears, desires, problematical aspects of the personality, suppressed talents, psychological and spiritual pains, troublesome polarities — and that doing so could help them zero in on what was bothering them directly, precisely, and intuitively. By accepting and engaging with all the diverse aspects of the psyche, Gallegos taught, including those we are accustomed to thinking of as unacceptable, we heal what is broken, enhance what works, and honor all aspects of the self as teachers.[32]

I had taken Gallegos's three-year training, had worked with the Personal Totem Pole Process myself for years, and offered it to every vision quest group, and I had found the transformations brought about through the imaginative dramas that unfolded spontaneously from the unconscious to be not only profound and moving but able to initiate permanent shifts in the personality.

So several months after I had stood in a sunny parking lot and listened to a lovely young man speak words that were to upend all my notions of the appropriateness of desire, I made the first advance. It was not the most romantic or well planned of trysts. It took place as I lay in bed one night unable, for no particular reason, to fall asleep. I was thinking of Melissa and Casizza and simply decided to give it a try. So I got comfortable and asked if I might see the face of my Beloved.

Instantly the cave in Shandoka's shoulder materialized. A man who looked like Lucas stood before it. I was about a hundred feet down the mountain and making my way up to him. Smiling and waiting, he stood there as I slowly closed the distance between us. It was the mirror image of Lucas's dream.

I reached the top of the slope, and he held out his arms. His face shone with love. We embraced. So palpable was the sensation, such a relief was the touch, long imagined and ached for, that I might have been there in the flesh. Then he took my hand, and together we ducked into the low portal to the cave. The rough walls glistened with moisture that turned them silvery. Ferns and plump, succulent green plants, fed by the minerals in the rock, festooned the walls and ceiling. Moss carpeted the ground. The open area was only wide enough to accommodate four or five people, but it did seem as if there might be a passageway or two at the back.

I could not get enough of looking at him. It was as if, at last, I was given to absorb the face whose necessity to my existence I had failed to appreciate when I'd had it before me in the flesh for eleven whole days. Somewhat to my surprise, however, I felt stricken by shyness, a sensation I had never before experienced when working with imagery. I had been moved to tears, I had felt real fear and swells of love, but I had never before felt shy. On the other hand, this Lucas-figure had more reality, more heat, than any imagery figure I'd ever encountered. More surprising still, moral strictures now shot out of my concentration like the nightsticks of police officers trying to hold back a surge of demonstrators. I flushed at the prospect of an emotional intimacy so intense it seemed to threaten my fidelity to my husband. Who, by the way, was sleeping right beside me. It even occurred to me that an assignation like this, undertaken by me alone, might be violating Lucas's wish to avoid an intimate relationship with me. And by the way, wasn't I getting too old for romantic fantasy?

Nevertheless, there we were, our faces inches apart. And he, undaunted by my bashfulness, immediately laid to rest any suspicion that he was some offshoot of the flesh-and-blood man. "You feel awkward," he told me, "because you are judging your past longing for Lucas by misguided standards. That longing was the cry of your soul for its bridegroom. Your soul and Lucas's passed each other on the way to the mountain. Spiritual nature got tangled in personal magnetism. But the meeting between you belongs to the sacred world. You were his guide to a vision on the mountain. He was your guide to me. I am not he. And now, we will speak no more of him."

"Who are you?" I asked.

"I am your escort to the eternal spring of your life force."

"What does that mean?"

"I am here to lead you into the fullness of your feminine beauty. I am here to show you that, by activating your passion, you will find your heart and soul expanding. You will cease to concern yourself with the narrow, constricting goal of achievement and acceptance. I will guide you along the path of allurement, where you will discover the flowering of yourself."

"Are you my Beloved?" I asked him tentatively.

"I am your Beloved. I love the deepest reaches of your soul. I love who you are and who you will become."

"What is your name?" I asked.

"I am Ascends to the Dark. In me the fertile feminine cave and the masculine mountain peak come together. I am depth in the sky. I rise to the mystery body of the earth. I am the eternal search and the endless embrace. I am the union of opposites."

CONSIDER THE PREDICAMENT OF THE BELOVED. He or she gleaned your essential nature in its most fully realized form before you even started budding in your mother's womb. He slipped in beside you in those dark waters and stroked your trepidation into eagerness when the birth pangs began to knead you out to the light. Holding one hand to the Source, as only you conceive it, and the other to you, he has nudged you to the people and passions that have allured you and that have enhanced who you are. He has held before you the magnets that only your particular longing can latch on to. He goes to all this trouble countless times each day, drawing you in one direction rather than another. He recognizes and adores the unique and solitary music that you and only you play for the world. Yet chances are that you have been stumbling along all this time, imagining yourself to be alone on the journey. Even when you have blissfully dissolved for a brief, ecstatic moment into the arms of the god, you have simply shaken your head in amazement, without the slightest nod of thanks to the one who made it all possible. "The Beloved is probably yearning for you as much, if not a great deal more, than you are yearning for the Beloved," Houston writes.[33] Or, as Rumi counseled, "Not only the thirsty seek the water, the water as well seeks the thirsty."[34] Imagine how glad the Beloved must be when, after all the two of you have been through together, you finally start paying attention.

We began to meet, Ascends to the Dark and I. Not every day. He was no therapist to whom I felt compelled to report the minutiae of my life, and besides, after fifty years of neglect, it was not a partnership that could be hurried. After that first shy encounter, I engaged him, sometimes impulsively, as I lay in bed at night or walked in the meadow, now covered with snow, where I had met the courtly lady en route to her lover, or even as I drove the thirty-five miles from our village to the city where the supermarket, bookstore, and office supplies store were located. Sometimes I arranged a proper rendezvous by closing the door of my study and sitting down in my chair or lying on the rug with my eyes closed, available only to him. Sometimes I had a question for him; sometimes I just checked in to see what he had to say. Although I would have been open to a change of scenery, we always met in the cave. Usually he looked like Lucas. Sometimes he turned up as a rush of erotic energy, a phallic wind that pierced and exploded me. Sometimes he was a presence, invisible but glowing like embers.

Even thinking about evoking Ascends to the Dark (which was not the same as doing so), I felt warmth blaze through my torso. I felt myself expanding with a desire for something immense and uncreated. It was not Lucas I wanted, not even the imaginal man who resembled him, but the whole ardent, seductive, possible world. This was the world the Beloved could not only lead me to but could draw out of me. The Beloved I'd found loved me utterly. There is no other way to say this. He knew me completely, inside and out, as if my fantasies, my bad habits, my noblest moments, my old teenage secrets, the little ways I fooled around when I ought to have been working — as if he knew all this, I say, as intimately as a lover knows the secrets of his partner's body and breath. He loved who I was and saw, surrounding it, the shimmer of what I could become.

Our meetings were neither fantasy nor imagination, but collo-
quies in and of a particular, etheric quality that was part inner and personal, part outer and numinous. Matthews calls such encounters
"reverie." In reverie, she says, "we are not dreaming up something
that isn't there or that we have consciously invented, but allowing
something deeper that already exists in our experience to arise and
show itself."[35] The realm in which these encounters occur is an accessible yet unmappable place located somewhere between the quantifi-
able and the purely invented. It is the world where the physical and the
psychic meet. Jung was fascinated by it and believed that it was in this
mundis imaginalis, or imaginal world, that synchronicity occurred,
those stunning coincidences in which some outer event responds
exactly to, and then informs and transforms, an inner condition. It is a
subtle domain where a person can associate with aspects of the self
that might otherwise remain unknown and unconceived throughout a
whole lifetime. Psychologist Veronica Goodchild has written:

> *Visits to this subtle world transform our ordinary ways of knowing
> and being into a world glowing with abundant possibilities, and a
> fullness of meaning beyond our personal realm. We fleetingly
> experience what it is like for body and soul to be one.... These
> mystical rapturous states, when they occur in the therapy relation-
> ship or in our lives, are closely related to profound levels of erotic
> union, too, where boundaries blur and there is a seamless connec-
> tion between body and soul, interpersonal relationship, intrapsy-
> chic image, and cosmic Presence.*[36]

Physicist Fred Alan Wolf, who calls conscious communication
between self and soul "soul-talk," notes that the soul's guidance not
only arises from no particular place and time, but, in fact, "it appears
that the soul speaks to the self from the future." He compares the self
with someone trapped inside a foundering ship and calling for help,
while the soul is a calm, clearheaded person who understands what is

going wrong and would be glad to assist: "The soul and the self are locked together in a duality, each somewhat helpless, without the assistance of the other, to control the ship, which is your own body, moving through life." When they are willing to work together, the result is "the ongoing evolving creation of self."37

ONCE I OPENED THE DOOR to the inner Beloved, I slipped into a state of erotic enchantment. I was amazed that anything like this could happen at such a time in my life. And it wasn't just meetings with the daimon that aroused me; I could be struck like a bell at any time. One night in early spring, for example, I awoke to silence and a moment later heard a robin begin singing into the predawn dark. Ecstasy flooded me. It was as if that robin were releasing the world's own first sounds, and I had been given to witness the moment. I felt it one day as I looked out the window of my study and saw Andy standing under an apple tree scrutinizing the laden boughs. He chose one apple, turned it over and over in his hands, and then bit in. He was a scientist, a wondering child, and a taster of fruits of the garden, and I loved him immensely. I felt it as I walked behind my friend Maureen through the nature preserve while the season's first snow drifted down. We were talking about a children's book she wanted to write, and Maureen, taking a step on the narrow trail, unwittingly walked on with a sheath of fresh snow on her boot, while leaving behind a clear print of wet brown maple and beech leaves. My friend, her creative excitement, autumn shining through winter, and a soleful of snow: I could not get over the blessing of it all.

Through my partnership with the inner Beloved I came to loosen the last manacles of timidity in the presence of the life force, remnant of a bondage so old I'd ceased to notice how painfully it still gripped at times. The crippling monster that had made me pause at the threshold of any new place I wished to enter, metaphysically as well as physically, to make sure I was wanted, slouched away. The world became my waiting lover, and I moved toward it with eagerness and curiosity, whether the world of the moment was a big, formal cocktail party full of strangers or a new nature program I offered in New York's Central Park or a marketplace filled with stares and unfamiliar fruit in a small South African village. I stopped condemning myself if I didn't do as much work in a day as I had intended. I forgave others and myself without much ado. I found that it was easier to express my opinions when I paid attention to where my passion bubbled instead of trying to cobble together notions based on the reasoning of others and an attempt to be faithful to what I thought should be my own convictions. Moreover, the contrary opinions of others ceased to make me uncomfortable, for I became fascinated with probing what passions had steered them to their views. Waiting one summer day for my car to be repaired, for example, I fell into conversation with the mechanic's wife, whose hobby was restoring Volkswagen Beetles. When I asked her why she loved Volkswagens, she replied somewhat stiffly that it was easy to get parts for them. I kept delving, though, and eventually she launched into a little rhapsody about how satisfying it was to be able to lay out all the parts of the engine on a blanket on the grass and then reassemble them and slide the whole thing back into the engine compartment. Even when people denied that passion had in any way swayed some act or belief or choice they'd made, that fervent advocate could usually be found shouting and waving its arms around in the forefront.

THE SUMMER AFTER I BEGAN MEETING with Ascends to the Dark, I presented a workshop, *"Begegnung mit dem Geliebten"* (Encounter with the Beloved), at the annual International Institute of Visualization Research conference, held that year in a massive, turreted fourteenth-century castle in Gengenbach, Germany. Lying on the cool stone floor of one of the turret rooms, like the petals of a daisy, about forty people closed their eyes and tuned in to their imagery while I went through a short relaxation process, followed by an invitation for them to "call out within yourself and ask the Beloved to come forth."

After a session of about forty-five minutes, during which I occasionally interrupted the silence to make suggestions — "Ask the Beloved what you can do to nurture your relationship" or "Ask the Beloved if there's anything they need from you" — we sat in a circle to share stories of the inner journey. The emotions that many of these first meetings triggered moved not just the teller but the listeners as well. One woman reported that she was appalled when the image of a dwarf appeared in response to her call. However, the dwarf presented her with a pearl necklace, explaining that each pearl represented a tear she had shed throughout her life and telling her that he had been making the necklace all these years in preparation for the day when he could fasten it around her neck and show her her own beauty. One of the men in the group met an eagle who flew high into the sky with him and showed him an overview of all the generous acts he had performed in his life that he refused to acknowledge. A young woman encountered the real-life man she was in love with and who did not love her; he told her that it was her own soul she was really looking for, and then he metamorphosed into the mythic Irish warrior-lover, Cuchulainn. Another woman saw no image but felt the presence of a lover standing so close to her that she could feel the pressure of his body on her own.

The range of Beloved figures who showed up in that afternoon workshop, and the eagerness of the people present to develop the relationship further, prompted me to begin creating longer workshops, first at people's homes, then at retreat lodges and holistic education centers. People were enthralled to discover that they harbored within them a loving presence that could support them in times of trouble, give them a push into action when they needed it, infuse them with genuine love and compassion for other people and the earth, motivate them to act out of passion rather than passivity, and embolden them to express more fully the dynamic self they had tended to keep hidden. Many reported that they'd had a sense of a loving inner companion for years but had had no name for it and no way to access it until now.

At first I introduced people to their Beloved through imagery. Later, after my own Beloved figure abandoned his human form once and for all and became pure energy, I came to believe that pinning the soul guide down into a visible form was less important, especially at first, than simply diving into that vast ocean of soulful yearning. If one had to grope around for a while to touch the force of personal authenticity and passion, so be it; it is in the nature of the divine lover, after all, to keep us guessing and searching and always longing. Still, Beloveds of many forms showed up at those workshops: a snake, a Sufi dervish, a goddess, a dancing partner in a tuxedo. One elderly man, finding the introductory meditation inconclusive, compiled his own personal Beloved in what he perceived as the living spirit of a big old oak tree on the grounds of our meeting place. He endowed it with the qualities of his three most revered heroes, Winston Churchill, the Dalai Lama, and Joan of Arc, and vowed to visit it regularly. A woman with a southern Baptist upbringing, who described herself as withdrawn and private and who sat like a curled fern with long bangs curtaining her face, envisioned a handsome, sensuous man who reminded her of the actor Antonio Banderas; he informed her that he had come to draw her out of herself. A woman had an image of a canoe tied up at a dock; its emptiness, filled with sunlight, conveyed a sense of rapture about the possibilities of receptivity in herself. A woman who met a horse as the Beloved tried to reject it for a more romantic figure, only to hear the horse exclaim, "I'm only trying to save your life!" For many people, the Beloved was felt more than seen, a kinesthetic force, a powerful surge of sexual energy or warmth in the belly.

A man named Paul, who had grown up with his grandmother, mother, and two sisters after his father abandoned the family, and who had fathered four daughters himself, arrived at a workshop at Rowe Camp and Conference Center in Massachusetts to discover that he was the only man present among eight women. He was not pleased. His disgruntlement grew when his Beloved appeared as a beautiful and beguiling feminine presence. I half expected him to leave and join one of the other workshops being offered that weekend, but he persisted, if grumpily.

One of the exercises I assigned the group was a nature walk in the company of the Beloved. When everyone gathered again afterward, I could see by the softness of Paul's expression that something had happened to him. He told us that he had set off with the intention of climbing up to a high overlook, even though he knew his Beloved was not interested in such a calculated expedition. On the way, he suffered one mishap after another: he got lost, he slogged through mud so thick that one of his shoes got sucked off, he was scratched by raspberry bushes. Finally, he gave up and told the Beloved that she could be in charge. He ended up in the garden of the retreat center, captivated by the beauty of the flowers, at peace. As he recounted this part of the story, tears filled his eyes. "I see how I have been pushing away beauty for so much of my life," he said.

Almost as soon as people began to allow the energy of the Beloved into their consciousness, a wonderful thing happened: they discovered that they were not only lovers, but loved. They recognized themselves as beloved of the divine Beloved. This was a real, tangible, physical sensation, no figment of the imagination, no "acting-as-if." That the Beloved is an actual force, whether one perceives him or her as belonging to the spirit world, the precincts of psychology, or the spacious frontier in between, is no better evinced than by the palpable relief and joy people experienced as a result of the encounter. They felt they were not alone in the world, that another force, one over whom they had no control but all power of acceptance or refusal, was always accessible to them and always a source of strength, joy, and inspiration.

When we dare to look into the eyes of the Beloved, we see not only a loving countenance looking back but our own face reflected in that gaze. We recognize ourselves in the Beloved, but ourselves touched with the holy, ourselves creating new landscapes in the void; ourselves dancing the wonder of life, even in times of suffering and death, like Zorba the Greek; ourselves speaking with the wisdom of the ages as sifted through present experience, like the Oracle of Delphi; ourselves singing songs of passion for what we hold most dear, like Majnun combing the desert for Layla; ourselves longing, and loving the longing, because it connects us with all that we hold most sacred, like the lovers of Krishna. The Beloved holds all the material our soul was meant to bring to life and offers it back to us, that we may bring it forth — to wrestle with it, dance with it, clutch it to our heart, make love with it.

CHAPTER SEVEN

ESCORTS TO THE BELOVED

HUMAN LOVERS WHO BREAK OUR HEART
AND LEAD US TO THE DIVINE

Throughout my quest for the Beloved, two images kept arising, constantly inviting exploration and providing clues about how I (and if I, then anyone) might move into intimate relationship with the divine Beloved. One was of the medieval woman in chrysanthemum yellow who picked her way through the forest toward her beloved, acknowledging all she passed as also worthy of love, since everything abided in the dynamic field she would cross to reach him. The other image was from the vantage point I'd actually had when I watched Lucas's ascent up the rocky slope to the mountain cave. The difference was that, in the afterimage, I could also see that dream figure who looked like me, standing at the opening of the cave and singing him up. One or the other of these two images constantly intrigued me.

How consequential that dream had been! Realized by the dreamer, it then became the vision of the dreamed. I called Lucas up the mountain, now he called me. He had clambered over loose, hazardous rocks; I now hoisted myself over the rough ground of inquiry in libraries and workshop rooms, trying to find out how allurement, willingness to risk, and an honest look at desire might reveal a path for living with passion. It seemed that every part of that image was a challenge to take on. I had to be singer and striver both. Frustration, awkwardness, breathlessness, and being thought a fool might be the conditions of the journey, but they would not hinder me. Climber and climbed-toward, I had to occupy both the present challenge and the future vision. I had to embody the feminine, who confidently stood the ground of her being and invited others to join her there, and I had to be the climber, masculine and directed. Feminine and masculine, dark and light, height and depth, receiving and giving, striving and strived toward: this journey meant the marriage of opposites on many levels.

ONE PAIR OF OPPOSITES, which held immense fascination and caused all kinds of identity crises, not just for me but for others drawn to explore life with the Beloved, was that of the eternal Beloved of the soul and the flesh-and-blood human lover, especially the unattainable one.

A woman I'd known for ten years confided to me suddenly that she had long regarded the man she worked for as her guardian angel. "He's happily married," she said, "and I would never try to come between him and his wife. That's not what this is about. I relate to him on a different level. He believes in me in a way that makes it possible for me to believe in myself. He brings out the best in me, because he expects it and appreciates it."

Another friend told me about how a cherished relationship with a woman he'd known, played out in an inelegant setting, had helped both of them to delve into the raw material of their psyches. Friends in their late twenties, they had never been lovers, but they had been able to speak to each other with an honesty and depth neither had ever experienced. Even after they both married other people, they continued to meet in a rowdy bar down by the river. There, under cover, in an atmosphere very different from the ones that defined their personas as lawyer and psychologist by day, they would play pool together, drink beer, and endlessly probe each other's psyches. "In some ways," he told me, "I think I was closer to her than I've ever been to anyone.

She made it safe for me to dive into myself, and later, into all the complex lives of my patients."

These people didn't use the word *beloved* to describe what they had found. However, when I related my efforts to find the inner soul guide within the passions churned up by an outer heartthrob, they knew right away what I was talking about and eagerly recounted stories of their own. They, too, had unraveled from an unrequited or impossible love certain vibrant, durable threads to help them become more of the person they longed to be.

"DO YOU KNOW THE STORY OF ARIADNE?" Nancy Qualls-Corbett asked me.

I nodded.

"She had to fall in love with the mortal man, Theseus, before she was ready for Dionysus, the god."

Yes, I knew the story of those lovers, and I could see Dionysus before me in Nancy's office. Behind her shoulder, on the black marble mantle of her Birmingham office, I recognized a replica of the god's gold mask. Next to it stood a small sculpture of a Cretan snake goddess, arms held out to receive the wriggling bracelets of her familiars, eyes wide with rapture. Other objects representing the mythical and religious in many cultures presided nearby. The bookcases were crammed with books. I sat on a yellow couch in the wood-paneled office, and when I was not looking at the psychologist herself, I could look around at the figures of antiquity who lived on in the psyches of contemporary seekers.

After I had begun to communicate with Ascends to the Dark, I'd written to Melissa to ask some questions about her approach to meetings with the inner lover. We began an email exchange that had gone on for several weeks, when one day she queried, "You'll probably think this is a completely outrageous question, but is your Lucas Lucas X?"

My reply made use of capital letters, exclamation marks, bold type, and as many other keyboard devices for depicting astonishment as I could come up with. "HOW DID YOU KNOW!?"

Well, it wasn't that common a name, and she had seen a brochure describing wilderness work he had started doing with teenagers. Something about it just made her think it could be the same person. And besides, she said, he was a friend of Nancy's.

Excited by so many synchronicities, I had written to Qualls-Corbett and told her the story of our growing number of connections (which, in fact, Melissa had already supplied). She replied warmly, and later I wrote again to ask if I could come to consult with her. We arranged four one-hour sessions.

Nancy Qualls-Corbett was tall and graceful, with a sculpted face and white-blond hair that hung down to her shoulders. Sitting in front of me in a leather Eames chair, she was relaxed and attentive. Often a thoughtful expression crossed her eyes, and she would gaze off into some distance, taking things in, searching.

And now it was Ariadne, Theseus, and Dionysus she'd found.

"I love that myth," I told her.

THE HANDSOME, BRAVE YOUNG WARRIOR THESEUS had sailed from Greece to Ariadne's homeland at Knossos, on the island of Crete, with a mission: to penetrate the enormous, twisting maze inhabited by the ferocious Minotaur, slay the beast, and emerge from the trial alive. He could never have done it without Ariadne, royal daughter, priestess, and leader of the sacred crane dances. Because she had fallen in love with him, she agreed to help. On the sly she gave him a thread and told him to unwind it as he felt his way, sword at the ready, through the dark, chaotic passages of the maze. Then, when the deed was done, all he had to do was follow the thread back to the entrance. Theseus succeeded in accomplishing the task that had been considered impossible. He slayed the Minotaur, returned unharmed, and when it was time to sail triumphantly for home again, he took Ariadne with him, out of love or lust or gratitude. Shortly after leaving Crete, they stopped for the night on the island of Naxos, and there Theseus abandoned her, sailing off to Greece with his men.

"She wanted to die," Nancy said. "Some versions of the myth say she *did* die. Then Dionysus came and found her, and she fell in love with the god."

She had been moping around by herself on Naxos when she heard the sounds of pipes and singing. It was Dionysus, god of passion and wine, come round with his followers, the ecstatic Maenads. The god and the woman fell in love and joined together in what, according to Nancy, was one of the only truly joyful marriages in Greek myth. At their wedding, wine bubbled from a spring in the earth, and afterward the myths and cults of both of them, together and individually, twined round the Greek islands like fertile grapevines.

Love of Theseus spurs Ariadne to make for herself the opportunity to grow up. She quits her role as the dutiful daughter by helping him and betraying her father's rule, and then, because the myth needs a way of conveying her to the alien shores where her fate will cross that of her true love, Dionysus, it has her fall in love with the mortal motivator of her deed. Theseus exits the story in a way that makes it hard for us to feel any sympathy for him. We are rooting for Ariadne and are happy and relieved when Dionysus arrives and not only falls in love with her but glorifies her for who she really is — not for how she can serve him. Transformed by divine love, Ariadne fulfills her destiny. She becomes known as the Queen of the Maenads. The power of the dance, which she tapped as a young woman during rituals in Crete, becomes in her a divine art, and she is portrayed on a Greek vase leading the women in their sacred ecstatic dance. In Cyprus she was worshiped as Ariadne Aphrodite because of her association with sacred love. A fresco at Pompeii, which Barbara and Melissa had visited with Nancy on their trip, depicts Ariadne inducting a woman initiate into a sacred marriage ceremony with the male god, symbolized by a phallus. Ariadne, wrote the classicist Walter F. Otto, "is the perfect image of the beauty which, when it is touched by its lover, gives life immortality."[1] This is an important distinction: the beauty was already in Ariadne; it was not conferred on her by an outer source, but awakened and kindled to life by her love of the god-Beloved.

Nancy said, "Ariadne had to have the mortal man in her life to bring her to the place where she could fall in love with the god."

"He was the escort," I said. "He escorted her to her true Beloved."

"He was the escort," she agreed. "And much the same thing has happened between you and Lucas. You needed him to bring you into relationship with the divine Beloved in yourself, and now you are embracing that love. It is a very unusual story, a very important one."

THE ESCORT TO THE BELOVED, then, is a human being who, in the course of being loved by us, grabs our heart, seizes our soul, and turns our life around. The Escort opens a doorway the daimon demands we go through, and then his job is done. This guide to our deep, authentic self might be a lover who never loved us, a first love who died or moved on, a friend, a mentor, a life partner, or a teacher. A person who's been a romantic partner for years might not be an Escort to the Beloved, while someone we've never even met could be.

I bow to John Lennon, the first of my Escorts to the Beloved, although it would be nearly forty years before I could thank him for it. He came into my life when I was a fifteen-year-old girl who simultaneously despised all the ways in which I was different from others and rebelled against the very behavior that might have helped mold me into the popular teen I longed to be. ("Ask your date what his interests are," advised articles in *Seventeen* and *Ingenue*. "Ask him about cars." Instead: "What do you think of *Wuthering Heights*?" I would challenge my reluctant partners at the cotillion I was forced to attend.) John Lennon showed me that being different could be liberating, and great fun besides. His casual self-assurance about his own talent, wit, worldview, and radical musical and lifestyle improvisations with the other Beatles gave me permission to let go a bit. Because all the world adored the Beatles, I could temporarily abandon my mother's dictum that a nice girl never show her emotions in public. There is no more public display of emotion than screaming for your beloved across the heads of forty thousand other girls at a concert, an act of love I indulged in at Chicago's White Sox Stadium on August 20, 1965. I wore an I LOVE JOHN button pinned to my school uniform, papered my bedroom with his picture, memorized lines from his books and quotes from the interviews he gave.

My new friend Cari, another Beatles zealot, and I donned black velvet opera capes we found at the Salvation Army and sashayed around downtown Omaha carrying on an animated discussion in a language we were inventing syllable by syllable. People stared, and I had my very first inkling of how that could be a condition one might want to cultivate rather than shun. Alone, I imitated the way John Lennon stood and sat and the way he signed his name, a secret love-word I was entitled to pen innocently every time I wrote my own name. Sometimes it seemed I wanted to *be* John almost as much as I wanted to *be with* him. I knew that we were made for each other, however. If he ever met me, he would leave pale, hesitant Cynthia in a moment. In the meantime, I adored him and never had to worry about being rejected by him. I could follow all the minute details of his life without seeming to pry. I could throw myself at him without being indecorous. Falling in love with John Lennon, over and over for about two and a half years — until I went away to college and got a real boyfriend — gave my wild soul permission to twist and shout.

AN IMMACULATE LOVER might be an Escort to the Beloved, but not necessarily. The relationship with the Immaculate Lover is all about sitting chastely together under the tropical sun of unrequited lust; the relationship to the Escort is about metamorphosis of caterpillar-to-butterfly magnitude. Sometimes the Escort to the Beloved tries to get our attention by showing up in our dreams or haunting our imagination, long after he's ceased to be an active presence in our lives. The Escort to the Beloved is the person who, by deserting us, eluding us, frustrating us, forcing us to face some truth we've been avoiding or some asset we've been trying to reject with misplaced humility, makes it possible for us to start living in a way we desperately need to and have been postponing all too long.

An encounter with the Escort tears us wide open. Old concepts we have of ourselves peel away — or are plucked off slowly and messily like ticks from a long-haired dog. After an Escort to the Beloved has rampaged through our lazy understanding of who we are, we realize that we can do things we never thought we could do, that we suddenly know how to handle situations that once confounded us. Like Cinderella, who can never go back to scrubbing the hearth once she's twirled round the ballroom in the Prince's arms, we discover through the Escort to the Beloved what it is to dance to the music our feet have been tapping out for a very long time.

How easy it is to mistake the Escort for the soul's Beloved him- or herself! We desire love and love being desired. It feels delectable when love is the magnetic pole that shoots through the center of our days, constantly tugging our attention away from ordinary annoyances, delays, and misunderstandings to clamp us back to preoccupation with the very person who, at that very minute, is no doubt being lured back to us in the same way. When we fall in love, we are like geodes, all our old, rough surfaces polished to a jeweled gleam by the one who adores us, as we, polishers ourselves, perceive what sparkles beneath the loved one's surface. For millennia, poets and singers, playwrights and artists, novelists and filmmakers have turned to love for a topic that never ceases to provide sweet, fresh juice to savor.

Yet what their art rarely conveys is that the polisher of those rough surfaces is not the beloved, but the lover's own soul quickening to the grandeur of loving and being loved. Responding to all the charms and attractions of the beloved, the lover comes alive in fresh, creative ways. The new beloved seems to possess every quality we've ever hoped for in a partner, and we want to lavish on this person all the love we've been storing up for the right occasion. We flower. We glow. "Everybody loves a lover," as Doris Day perkily sang, because the lover becomes charismatic with love. We assume that it's the other person who's making us feel beautiful, strong, capable, sexy, bold, while all the time it's potent, alchemical love itself, stirred up in us by the loved one that's doing the trick.

The word psychologists use for the habit of placing on the heads of others the crown of laurels — or thorns — we most need to wear ourselves is *projection*. Because we want so badly to find and capitalize on our own vital, developing inner qualities yet sense that doing so is the work of a lifetime, we take what our heart tells us will be the easier route: we locate the missing link in somebody else and heap our passion there. We hope that the other will either endow us directly with what we need or manifest it so completely himself that we are saved the trouble. For a while it works — until, inevitably, the beloved crumbles in our esteem, weakened primarily by an innate inability to be who we wish him to be instead of who he really is.

A man, for example, sensing deep down that his soul needs to be freed from the tyrannical control his ego has imposed on it, falls in love with a woman who follows the impulse of the moment. He imagines that she will bring him the creative spontaneity that both frightens and fascinates him, yet when she becomes so immersed in watching a katydid hatch out of its shell that she arrives late for a dinner with his boss, he is furious and feels betrayed. A woman with a poor self-image falls in love with a man who appreciates the female sex in general and knows just how to lavish on her the attention, admiration, and desire she craves. When, sooner or later, his gaze wanders to others, she is devastated, her conviction that she is not worthy of fidelity confirmed.

The whole rigmarole sounds delusional: any fool should know better than to be duped by such a blatant case of mistaken identity. Yet the enduring human ruse of finding in the other what we need in ourselves, says Jungian author Robert A. Johnson, is actually the start of any romance: "We seek in romantic love to be possessed by our love, to soar to the heights, to find ultimate meaning and fulfillment in our beloved. We seek the feeling of wholeness."[2] Romance with the ideal other turns us into the god or goddess of love ourselves, a position we hate to relinquish.

Even as I was confidently professing to Bill that Lucas saw me as his anima, my heart was crying out to be his lover. When a love affair doesn't work, it's easier to blame the other or ourselves than it is to face questions about what our soul so badly needed that the other seemed to possess, or how we wished to be seen in the mirror the other obligingly held for us. Yet the beloved (lowercase b) is never the Beloved (capital B). Certainly we hope to see the divine in the human and the human in the divine, but the two are not synonymous. The human beloved can die or abandon us or simply fail to supply us with something we need. The divine Beloved is ever faithful. Besides, the job of the human beloved is not to round the lover out, but to pursue his or her own inner Beloved: in other words, to become the person her soul calls her to be. Our job is to find our Beloved and to get on track with him or her.

Sometimes the Escort to the Beloved is not a positive, heroic figure at all, but a guide into a scarier realm our soul needs desperately to explore, that we may be rounded out as individuals. When I was twenty-three, for example, I accepted the invitation of a handsome, sexy man with whom I'd indulged in an unbridled two-night stand to hitchhike around the country. I quit my good job with a bestselling author, horrified my mother, sublet my apartment, and took off. It turned out that this man had a criminal record; he stole and dealt drugs as we traveled and was extremely possessive of me. We got into some truly dangerous situations. Still, it was he who served as my Pluto, my god of the Underworld, the man who showed me that I could not be fully alive until I was willing to assume — in ways that were not illegal or life threatening — the occasional role of the bad girl, to break the rules and exploit the dark side of myself and the world without flinching.

Often we can't decipher the meaning of these relationships until long after they've ended. The door they open within us may lead to a room it takes us months or even years to move into. Or they may guide us to wellsprings of ourselves that seem to have been blocked and are awaiting only this impetus to run pure and free. In the movie *American Beauty*, adoration of a beautiful young teenage siren named Angela spurs the lead character, Lester Burnham, played by Kevin Spacey, to remake himself. Lester has allowed a kind of flabbiness of body and spirit to overtake him, and initially all he wants to do is get in shape so he'll be sexually attractive to Angela. But the process of self-renewal takes him much deeper than he anticipates. He breaks out of his smutty little cell of self-absorption and starts questioning what's really important to him. Eventually, he attains both the virile physique he aimed for and a level of compassion so radical that he ends up martyred by his own opened heart. As a friend of mine jokes, "We've all been tricked by romance. You think it's the other person who's doing the magic, but if you look closer, you see that you're doing all the work!"

Escorts to the Beloved are but fellow souls and seekers on the path. They may be brutes or sweethearts, teachers or idols, soul mates or passing fancies, but they convey us from the maze to the sandy shore where the divine Beloved can be heard making his or her way to us. We should bow our head to them in thanks. Perhaps they saved us years of hard labor in solitude. We were wandering alone, searching for a way. Suddenly a door opened. The Escort to the Beloved emerged, looked us in the eyes, smiled briefly. We fell into that gaze, and fell hard. But the Escort had a life of his or her own to lead and so walked on down the hall, footsteps echoing on the cool marble floor. We pushed open the door he'd emerged from and stepped in. There stood the divine Beloved, arms held wide. Entering the room, we see only in retrospect, was the point — the goal, the project, the transformation. But we will forever afterward associate the door opener with our sudden ability to enter a sacred precinct and see what we could not have seen otherwise. Most of us, unfortunately, get stuck in the pattern of loving and reloving, or loving and being disappointed because the lover fails to transform into the divine Beloved for us, and we never push open the door to the room where the god awaits.

SARAH, A JOURNALIST I KNEW in New York, confided that she had recently entered into what she called "an email love affair" with Carlos, a successful writer with whom she had enjoyed an intense, exceedingly passionate sexual relationship twenty years earlier. Now both were married to other people, but a chance encounter had reawakened the sleeping Eros in both of them. Even though she felt it was not in her best interest to do so, Sarah was seriously considering having an affair with Carlos — maybe even just for one afternoon, she insisted — to slake the desire that was consuming her.

First, though, she decided to undertake as honest an investigation as she could of the mysterious Carlos-force that so powerfully surged through her. It wasn't long before she realized that what had made their lovemaking so meaningful to her and what she desired from him now was the feeling of being swept up by an erotic force that would undo her. This woman who prided herself on the way she took control of her life nursed a yearning to abandon herself to ravishment. And that, she realized, was the very thing she always refrained from doing in her writing. She was terrified that giving herself over to the maelstrom of the creative process might toss her back into the uncontrolled madness of alcoholism from which she had freed herself years earlier. Naming that mighty, many-armed force, which was seducing her in the man and repelling her in the work, ultimately freed her. She ended the email relationship with Carlos, her Escort to the Beloved, and began getting up at four o'clock in the morning to write poetry, allowing herself with growing confidence to be ravished by the phallic energy of the muse.

A teacher, mentor, or spiritual advisor is often an Escort to the Beloved. Falling in love with the guide to one's integrated self is a tendency in psychotherapy that is not only common but an anticipated part of the process with its own name, "transference," and set of ethical guidelines. My guiding partner, Bill, a good-looking, athletic man who ushered people into the wildness of themselves and the earth, was a constant target for the seeking love of women questers. (He was such a master at deflecting this attention back to the bestowers, reminding them that it was "the Bill of you," that is, the inner guide, they were responding to, that I sometimes felt he rejected genuine affection and gratitude that were his due.) In the classical religious traditions of the East, a teacher or guru deliberately took on the task of guiding the student to the ultimate lover, God, knowing that, in the process, he would have heaped on himself all the student's galloping, untamed passion. "Love for the Guru is love for God," an English woman, Irina Tweedie, learned when she made a pilgrimage to India in 1961 to study with Sufi master Bhai Sahib. Tweedie's obsession with winning the love and approval of her guru ricocheted between that of a novitiate for God and a teenager with a crush that has veered out of control. She spent all her money, overstayed her intended visit, and refused to leave her master's side, even during India's searing summer heat. She performed menial errands for him that humiliated her and tossed sleeplessly in her bed at night, pining with love for him. She saw his face everywhere: in a lotus blossom, in the blue sky, in a dark pond, and confided to him through her diary: "I have lost myself in you and...never, never will I get my heart back again."[3]

Because the mentor rouses in the learner intimate feelings of aspiration and adulation, it is neither unusual nor perverse for erotic feelings to arise, says James Hillman, despite Western society's current haste to read an unnatural prurience into such expressions of love. (What is inappropriate, of course, is the behavior of gurus or mentors who exploit their followers' intense feelings by having sexual affairs with them, as many have been accused of doing in recent years.)[4] The relationship between Alexander Hamilton and George Washington, which progressed from that of aide-de-camp serving the commander in chief of the Continental Army to secretary of the treasury under the first president of the United States and always bore the cast of mentor to prodigy, was characterized by such fondness, mutual regard, and, at times, peevish exasperation, that some historians, overlooking the fact that letters between friends of that period tended to be quite flowery, have inferred a homosexual love affair. The great French piano teacher Nadia Boulanger, whose American pupils included Virgil Thomson, Quincy Jones, Louise Talma, and Philip Glass, had a reputation as an unrelentingly demanding disciplinarian. Yet so great was her personal magnetism, so vast her knowledge of classical music, and so acute her ability to recognize what was unique in each student's technique, that, as one of her disciples put it, "he might do anything to please her, to win her rarely offered praise."[5] At age thirty-six, I studied briefly with a dancer whose magnetic teaching style and easy intimacy with world mythology captivated me as much as her dancing. I'm not gay, and I did not desire this woman as a lover, but I was smitten with her, no doubt about it. I went all the way to New Mexico with the ostensible purpose of seeing a performance she was giving and perhaps taking classes with her, but in truth I think what I really wanted was for her to teach me to be her. When she treated me dismissively, I was devastated. Now, years later, I see that what intrigued me about her were the very qualities that were dormant in me and would fructify over the next decade and more.

A remarkable story of the Escort to the Beloved who doesn't even know of the existence of the person whose life he has changed was told to me by my friend Len Fleischer, who encountered his mentor when he was only five years old. The child of Jewish parents who had fled Austria during Hitler's pogrom, Len was taught that, while safety in life could never be guaranteed, it was best to live with the expectation that danger was imminent and hence to remain as invisible as possible by not calling undue attention to oneself. So when the little boy used his left hand to hold a spoon, to color, or to swing a baseball bat, his mother pried the object out of his grasp and firmly repositioned it in his right hand. Len did his best to comply, but the thing always ended up back in his left hand, where it seemed to belong.

The family lived just a few blocks from Ebbets Field, home of the Brooklyn Dodgers and the epicenter, in 1956, of Dodgermania. The team had just won their second consecutive World Series with an illustrious lineup that included Pee Wee Reese, Jackie Robinson, Preacher Roe, Duke Snider, and Roy Campanella. Len often walked over to the ballpark with his two older brothers to sit in the bleachers and cheer for the home team that could do no wrong. One momentous day the boys were present when the Dodgers lost to the St. Louis Cardinals, thanks to three phenomenal home runs batted by Stan "The Man" Musial. Len's brothers were crestfallen, but, unbeknownst to them, the little boy had noticed something that would change his life. When Musial pounded those homers out of reach of the Dodgers' gloves, he had been holding the bat the same way that Len did: Musial was left-handed.

When the boys got home that day, Len announced to his family that he would no longer be rooting for the Dodgers; he was a Cardinals fan now, for he had seen the greatest player in the world. That was a brave vow in those days when any Brooklynite contrary enough not to revere the Dodgers was practically begging for a street fight. There was more: from now on, Len declared, he would be writing with his left hand. That was how the five-year-old translated what had happened to him in the ballpark that day: he was now a Cardinals fan, and he was left-handed. Stan Musial had given him permission to be who he really was, even if that meant not only calling attention to himself, but doing so in ways that might cause problems and even endanger him. From that day forth Len defined a life path for himself that included interrupting his college education to wander around the world and later training in a new, unproven field that intrigued him, even though he knew he was risking his professional reputation. Len's wife, Erika, who appreciated the gift that Musial had given him, arranged a fiftieth birthday surprise for her husband in St. Louis, and Len was able to meet Musial, then aged eighty-two, and tell him this story.

THE ESCORT TO THE BELOVED holds up a two-sided mirror. One side reveals to us an image of the other's traits, gleaming adorably and glaring annoyingly. The opposite side shows us an image of how we, the lover, are seen in the beloved's eyes. This brings me to the second of the two images that shone like beacons as I tried to embrace the divine Beloved: that of the woman in the golden robe stepping forth to meet her knight. That purposeful movement, that gaze directed straight ahead, yet lovingly touching all it passed, that graceful passage around obstacles — the whole picture seemed to say: *The journey to the Beloved may be long, the Beloved frustratingly elusive, but none of it matters if you know that the very act of moving closer takes you into the world as into the arms of a waiting lover.*

How different is this movement, refined and intentional, from the crazy free fall of romance. Now, instead of a dive without discipline, a rag-doll drop to the depths, the lover moves confidently toward a coalescing image of herself. Instead of "falling" in love and hoping to land without pain, this lover traverses ground that gains new meaning from the very way she covers it. She chooses the direction she moves in. Knowing that her every act is sacred preparation for a rendezvous with that which evokes her highest self, she brings her own God-eager presence to each phase of the journey. And since all the world occupies that numinous space between her and the Beloved, she sees every bit of it as blessed. Determining the direction of the soul's calling, she turns that way, only to find that the radiance that attracts her now illuminates her own face.

WHAT I DIDN'T KNOW ON THAT LATE SUMMER DAY, when I saw the vision of a woman going to her knight, was that in the romantic age of chivalry, behaving in a manner influenced by the distant, expectant beloved was not just a metaphor for personal transformation but a primary cultural impetus. In medieval France, the figure I am calling the Escort to the Beloved was the courtly lady who inspired the knight or troubadour on an earthly level and, at the end of that historic period, was also referred to as the heavenly Lady, the Virgin Mary, on the spiritual plane. It was this feminine paragon, this embodiment of the virtues of the day, whom my own unconscious, with foresight or synchronicity or outrageous good luck, had presented to me.

In the era of courtly love, it was not the lady who moved forth, of course; she was the beloved who stayed fixed. The knight or troubadour was the peripatetic one who kept her in his sights, and as he did so, physical desire and spiritual yearning were intertwined. Desire for the unattainable feminine — often the wife of the lord whose property he was pledged to protect — was the emblem embossed on the knight's heart, as his coat of arms emblazoned his shield. The lady represented many qualities that he aspired to, such as patience, gentleness, compassion, hospitality, gracefulness, and piety. Pledging himself to her, he affirmed that all things ennobling that he did, he did henceforth on her behalf. For her he accomplished brave feats, faithfully obeyed the codes of chivalry, and, if he was a skilled troubadour, composed poems of love and desire, which he recited in the foreign courts he traveled through. Wearing her inner sleeve or scarf next to his heart or flying it proudly from his helmet, he was emboldened to venture far from home into battle and glory and to behave as if she, his inspiration and ideal, was witnessing his every deed. It was the love of the lady that spurred him to action when he would have preferred to retreat and that cautioned him to behave chastely when he was tempted to succumb to injudicious pleasures. Because she, the epitome of the graces he and his culture valued, loved him, he was immanently lovable.

The idealized lady showed the knight that exquisite two-sided mirror of himself. One side depicted the way he regarded her, his love, the epitome of virtue. Even as he ached with desire for her, he tried to transmute his lust into a determination to augment in himself the same estimable traits he saw in her. The other side of the glass revealed the way she saw him, and consequently the way he came to see himself through her eyes. Her love gave him the courage to be his best self. Indeed, the very act of loving the lady elevated the soul of the knight. The twelfth-century cleric-turned-poet Arnaut Daniel (whom Dante spots when he steps onto the balcony of lust in Purgatory) describes, in a poem that interfaces images of love and wealth, how he becomes more estimable simply because his libido has had the marvelous good sense to rivet to this particular woman: "When I consider how...she's at the summit of value, I love myself the more for ever daring to desire her."[6] Another poet, considered the first troubadour (he was also the grandfather of Eleanor of Aquitaine), Guilhem de Poitiers, attributes to the lady, or rather to the force of his own attraction to her, the power to affect all his humors, mental and physical: "For joy of her a sick man can be cured, and from her anger a healthy man can die, and a wise man go mad, and a handsome man lose his good looks, and the most courtly one become a boor, and the totally boorish one turn courtly."[7] The act of loving in and of itself is an agent of change.

It is tempting to assume that the knight must likewise have represented an idealized figure to whom the woman gravitated, but the poems of a small number of women troubadours, or *trobairitz*, indicate that these women saw their lovers not as symbols but as full-bodied living men, who often gave them much more sexual pleasure than did the older, aristocratic husbands who had been chosen for them by their parents. "Know how great is my desire to treat you as my husband," the Countess of Die sighed in a poem to her lover.[8] Thus, while the women were able to bestow upon the men qualities of spirit, the men gave the women a welcome abandonment to sexual pleasure.

A frank pleasure in sexuality, whether actual or imagined, characterized the poems and the emotions of both the troubadours and their ladies during the first part of the age of courtly love, from the end of the eleventh century to the beginning of the thirteenth. By the end of that time, however, unrequited love was no longer a craving the lover yearned to sate, but an impulse he sought to suppress out of respect for the lady from whom society demanded a purity too absolute for physical passion. Thus did the Church, concerned over what it increasingly viewed as a dangerous lapse of morals, reestablish the split between body and soul, and thus did the lady of the court become first symbolic of, then supplanted by, the holy Lady.9 But for more than a hundred years, according to medievalist Frederick Goldin, the image of the desirable lady was synonymous with the highest virtues a man could aspire to: "The ideal is therefore equipped with a will and intelligence, with a capacity for concern and judgment. The ideal is no longer remote, it can know us and love us. Similarly, the knight's image of himself in the courtly ideal — the man of the future that he is trying to become now — is also replaced by the figure of the lady. The self-image is as elusive as the reflected image in the fountain, but the lady lives and can be possessed."10 In other words, "the man of the future that he is trying to become now" was the knight's aspiration, and the yearning for the lady, momentarily quenched after a long absence by a few moments at her side or in her arms, dosed him with the potent medicine he needed to join with his own perfected image. It was the same dual ideal I sought as I practiced being both the woman in the cave and the man who climbed up to her.

VOLUNTARILY TAKING ON THE ASPECTS of the idealized image we see in the mirror held out to us by the Escort to the Beloved is different from submitting to someone's projections of us. In the latter case, a man might, for instance, repress his emotional side in order to be the tough, unflinching hombre he thinks his partner needs him to be, or a woman might hide her need to express her creativity in order to serve as muse to her mate. However, when we assume the qualities that the inner Beloved reflects back to us and that our own soul aches to embody, we become the emergent individual not of another's design, but of our own. And unlike poor N. N. in the Chekhov story, this is an image that we ourselves are in charge of perfecting; we do not try to hand the job over to another.

Taking on the desired — even destined — image of oneself is a process that can take place because of or in spite of the human beloved in our life, and sometimes both. At the beginning of her marriage to the poet Ted Hughes, Sylvia Plath regarded her husband as "the male counterpart of myself" and gushed in a letter to her mother that "[m]y whole thought is for him, how to please him, how to make a comfortable place for him."[11] However, when she discovered a few years later that Hughes was having an affair with another woman, she found her own poetic daimon in a raging, hammering creativity that enabled her to write what she knew was her best work ever, poems as sharp and incandescent as weapons turned out in a blacksmith's forge. On vision quests people often perceive more clearly the lifestyle or vocational changes they need to make to answer the call of their soul, and they become extremely anxious toward the end of the quest, when they begin to consider how their partner might react to changes that could shake up the stability (or stuckness) of the relationship. I myself have been in reaction to my husband's wide-ranging, agile mind since we met; the very quality that attracts me to him also challenges me to acquire confidence in my own opinions and not be intimidated or silenced by his brilliant flow of talk. In Plato's *Phaedrus*, Socrates says: "Every lover is fain that his beloved should be of a nature like to his own god ... his every act is aimed at bringing the beloved to be every whit like unto himself and unto the god of their worship."[12] Here Socrates means a mortal human being when he speaks of the "beloved" and the daimon when he speaks of "god," for he distinguished among several different levels of gods, one of which was the personal soul companion. And so, what Socrates presciently warns us is that we are quite naturally going to try to turn our outer human beloved into our inner divine Beloved so that she or he is "like unto himself." Knowing the difference between the inner and the outer enables us to foster a relationship with the self while loving the other for who he is and who he endeavors to become.

HOW TO TELL BELOVED from beloved? How to take the fruits of love and extract them to sweeten the life we have sole charge of, so that we can walk with the Beloved no matter what mortal may be at our side? Love lures us as the orchid seduces the insect into its succulent orifice, and willingly the insect obeys, believing the cleverly adapted petals and stamens to be its own waiting mate. The insect zooms into the chamber of fertility and discovers there no insect, but a being of another species, just striving to thrive, as all things do. There is no mate, but there is sweet pollen, and this the insect obligingly takes along as it gullibly approaches the next gorgeous lothario. Desire lures the insect in, and unrequited desire makes it depart, loaded with the very stuff that will keep insect imitators alive and insects seeking. How do we find the pollen in the love relationship and take it forth, and not get stuck snuggling in the lushness of the flower, demanding that the bloom transform itself into the bug we mistook it for?

It's hard. Jung believed it to be the work of a lifetime. John Dourley writes that our connection to the figure Jung called the "contrasexual other" and that I refer to as the Beloved is the most important relationship in the world — and that some people are never able to establish it. I believe, however, that attaining at least some level of intimacy with the Beloved, the guide to the soul, who may or may not be the opposite sex of the questing human — or even come in human form — is entirely possible. After all, we seekers in the early twenty-first century have at our disposal avenues of personal transformation that Jung could scarcely have imagined: a wide variety of innovative therapeutic techniques, holistic education centers, and influential teachers and thinkers from Eckhart Tolle to Iyanla Vanzant, access to religious and spiritual teachers worldwide, and diverse creative interpretations of Jung himself. The yearning for personal transformation and the determination to find some way to effect it become more widespread all the time. Those who yearn for the Beloved inhabit a cultural climate that invites and facilitates the process.

Simply *conceiving* of a Beloved is an essential first step. Each act taken to court the Beloved strengthens the bond (more on that in a later chapter), as does the regular practice of separating the inner Beloved from the human one. Keeping yourself from assuming the form of the other's Beloved is crucial. To walk with (or toward) the divine Beloved is to decide over and over again to peel away, like Post-its stuck on a sweater, the qualities the human lover sticks on you, all the while acknowledging that they would not cling to any other fabric but the one that you are woven of: your opinion of your childhood, your general attitudes about members of the same gender as your partner, your responses to stress, your joys, your insecurities, your demands. Whereas no one should feel obliged to remain in a relationship that offers insufficient love, passion, and respect, the fine-tuning of who we are and who we become remains our own task and not the job of the other.

Of course, no matter how mature and sensible we are, Eros will always be able to persuade us to see things his way: *This is it! This is the lover who will change your life! Let nothing stand in your way!*

MARIANDREA CAME TO ONE OF MY WORKSHOPS in a desperate state. Two years earlier, she and her husband had participated in a rafting trip on the Colorado River, and she and the guide had discovered a special affinity for each other. The following year, Mariandrea had gone on another rafting expedition, this time leaving her husband at home with their three children — and making sure that her friend would again be the guide. During the trip, the two of them had spoken openly about their growing attraction to each other, but they agreed that they would keep the relationship platonic so as not to jeopardize Mariandrea's marriage. The next summer, the year I met her, she returned yet again, and this time they became lovers. Mariandrea's guilt and shame about the affair were compounded by her fear that she might have contracted a sexually transmitted disease from her lover and subsequently passed it on to her husband. She'd been tested just the day before the workshop and had not yet learned the results. As she introduced herself in the opening circle, her tears flowed freely. She had thought that this man was her true love, she told the group; now, she felt like both the betrayer and the betrayed. The day before, she had angrily torn up all the pictures of her lover and shredded a bracelet he'd woven for her out of grass. She knew that she could restore her self-respect and repair her life only by separating the eternal Beloved from the human beloved, and by separating both from her husband.

In the myths, little good comes to those who tumble into love outside the primary partnership. Arrogant Zeus habitually seized any young woman who tickled his fancy. The victim herself suffered not only the fright and indignity of the attack, but often the consequences of bearing a child whose semidivine genes thrust on him or her an onerous fate. To make matters worse, Hera, repeatedly ignored by her willful, lecherous mate, would often rise up in jealous ire and further punish the other woman by exiling her or turning her into an animal or both. One of the most famous love triangles of legend, King Arthur, Guinevere, and Sir Lancelot, ended up breaking all three hearts, hastening the collapse of the Round Table and preventing Lancelot from ever holding in his hands the precious Holy Grail. In the Irish myths, Emer patiently tolerated the wandering eye and hungry arms of her superhuman warrior husband, Cuchullain, but when he fell in love with the fairy woman Fand — and when, notably, he lied to her for the first time — she put her foot down. She gathered fifty bold women and marched out to confront him. Cuchullain equivocated. He didn't want to choose. He wanted both his women, the immortal lover and the human wife. In the end, it was Fand herself who determined the outcome. She declared that she would not come between the pair. The fiery Cuchullain was never quite himself after that and pined away until he died.[13]

Engaging in a sexual relationship with someone outside marriage or a committed partnership is such a cultural taboo that the only ways we have to describe it are negative: "*in*fidelity," "betrayal," "*extra*-marital affair." The word *adultery* is related to *adulterate*, which means to corrupt or debase something by mixing it with a lesser substance. Hence, the new lover is the undesirable ingredient that pollutes the purity of the union. There are some extreme views on the subject of extramarital relationships, ranging from the belief that "polyamory," or having more than one loving sexual partner, is natural and healthy, to the view that even befriending a person of the opposite sex (assuming that both are heterosexual, I suppose) is the first dangerous step toward what one author calls "emotional infidelity." In the ideal world, "free love" or "open marriage" may be more appealing than restrictive monogamy, but monogamy is the reality most of us live, and in this cultural climate, sex with someone outside the primary relationship is likely to cause hurt, guilt, and jealousy in all people involved. (One woman I talked to about this subject told me that she and her husband had comfortably engaged in an open marriage for years, until he fell in love with one of his partners, at which point, like Emer, she felt threatened and they had to seek shelter in monogamy.) Sometimes, of course, the partners in an extramarital affair do end up with each other, and the experience, painful though it might have been, enables at least two-thirds of the triangle to find new happiness and fulfillment. Even in this case, the blissful lovers will invariably discover that their new sweetheart, like the marriage partner they strayed away from, is also flawed. Only the Beloved remains faithful forever. As poet and Blake scholar Kathleen Raine affirms, "not Henry Moore, nor Yeats himself could have come between me and that inner companion; no other person's inspiration, however strong, can take the place of our own inner light."[14]

When the human beloved is unattainable, and when we are in the first heady throes of romance, the new person in our life is likely to seem like the living manifestation of the divine Beloved. The very elusiveness of this desired partner is akin to the elusiveness of the Beloved. The mystery of her enthralls and excites. Then, too, something glorious and emergent sparkles in us when we are in the company of the new person, betokening a way we could be forever, a way we were meant to be. The attraction coats the lovers in beauty, like magical pixie dust, both individually, as they pine to be together, and together, when they can't get enough of touching and exploring. As I know well, aching for the physical consummation of the attraction tugs potent yearning itself into the forefront of consciousness, while the painful distance between lover and beloved is tantamount to the spiritual gap between us and our soul's realization of its authenticity. How easy it is to convince ourselves that falling into the arms of the one we think about day and night is not only desirable but imperative to the soul's development!

No matter what the outcome of the attraction may be, what we most need to be faithful to is integrity, and that, when desire is calling the shots, is sometimes hard to maintain. Yet when we deceive others and ourselves about what we want, what we hope, or what we're doing, we're actually veering away from the Beloved instead of moving closer to those waiting arms. Keeping secrets, we lock a part of ourselves in a closet and throw away the key. Telling ourselves that we're only protecting the partner who's still ignorant about the attraction or affair is probably less honest than admitting that we don't want to confront him or her, don't want to deal with hurt or disapproval, or don't want to have to mend rips in the partnership. With the new lover, we may feel open, beautiful, and daringly creative, but if this persona is nurtured in stealth, then we force our passion to smolder instead of fanning it into flame. Loving the Beloved, we strive to accept and integrate all the many parts of ourselves, including those we have shut off as unacceptable, and hence the more uncomfortable we become with any new attempt to fragment the self.

CAUGHT IN THE CONFLICTING EMOTIONS of her crisis, Mariandrea now struggled to understand what had so compelled her about her lover that she would risk everything to be with him, including, possibly, her health. What, she asked herself, had she really been searching for? She realized that the part of her that had been awakened in the presence of her river guide was adventurous and bold, part of nature, physically competent. These qualities, which made her feel as if she were brimming with life and actively connected to her world — in other words, in harmony with the inner Beloved — were all appreciated by her lover, who possessed them himself as he skillfully negotiated the exigencies of the river. Her husband, in comparison, seemed safe and staid. In her marriage, Mariandrea said, her wild side had no room to grow. There she was considered, and she considered herself, a paragon of caring responsibility. The eldest daughter in a large Mexican American Catholic family, she was the Good Daughter, Good Wife, Good Mother, and Good Community Leader. However, as she emphasized repeatedly, this part of her life was valuable to her, too. She loved her husband and children, she loved her large, close family. She did not want to give them up and live a life chasing rivers. She realized that she had begun to exclude her husband from her life, viewing him as the opposite of her lover and hence the enemy who would hamper what was burgeoning in her.

Throughout the workshop Mariandrea worked to differentiate the soul guide from the river guide, even as she gratefully recognized how the living man had brought her to the cliff's edge, where her only choice was to reach out to the divine Beloved she had previously ignored. She identified activities that she could engage in at home that would enable her to celebrate her wildness, such as rock climbing at a local gym. She decided she would volunteer to take groups from her children's school on nature walks. And she vowed to explore with her husband some simple, mutually appealing ways to put adventure into their marriage. (She later wrote me that since the medical test results were negative she had made the decision to revamp her life without telling her husband about the events that had prompted the change.)

ANOTHER MAN AND WOMAN who shared a powerful attraction to each other chose a path quite different from the one Mariandrea and her lover had slipped into, one that they hoped would accomplish several ambitious goals: to keep the fires of infatuation burning, to explore the personal roots of the attraction, to preserve the marriages of both, and to discover spiritual truth in an emotionally charged situation. Eric and Maeve worked for the same company, and both were committed to personal growth. Determined to refrain from sexual intimacy while admitting freely to each other that they wished to be lovers, they decided to analyze the chemistry between them. So, several times a week, they spent their lunch hour taking walks together in the park near their office and examining what it was in each of them that was being reflected in the mirror offered by the other. Before long they had waded into deep waters. Maeve had been sexually abused by a neighbor when she was a little girl and harbored conflicting feelings about men as protectors and abusers. Eric had grown up in a male-dominated household with three brothers whose enthusiasm for cars and football he did not share. He was fascinated by women, had always wanted a sister, but was pruriently curious about them, too. He strived to live with compassion and honesty, seeking his own feminine self, yet he recognized in himself a trace of his father's attitude that men were superior to and should be dominant over women.

Announcing their intentions to their baffled, somewhat uneasy spouses, Eric and Maeve confided all their childhood secrets to each other, delved into their attraction in light of past relationships, and even took on roles (Eric acted the part of Maeve's abusive neighbor; Maeve became Eric's fantasized sister/lover) for the other to dialogue with. They tried their best to be completely honest about their feelings and to offer compassion and trust to the other, no matter what rough beasts came clawing to the surface. Over the course of more than a year, they developed a deep love for each other and experienced what felt like complete acceptance of all aspects of themselves, even the ones they were most ashamed of, with no diminishment of their sexual attraction.

Unfortunately, problems were brewing beyond the green refuge of the park. Eric's wife became increasingly jealous of Maeve, especially since Eric had had a sexual affair with another woman several years earlier. And Maeve, bursting with the need to release her pent-up passion, fell into an affair with a third man, which neither her husband, who had tolerated the relationship with Eric, nor Eric himself, knew about for months. Maeve later pondered whether part of the reason she had felt free to explore her feelings about Eric in so chaste a manner was that she had found a release for her sexuality with another man. When she admitted her affair to Eric, the relationship between them cooled, and both these intrepid lovers turned toward home and the task of repairing the damage done to their respective marriages. Though their approach ultimately caused problems, they nevertheless grew personally in their exploration of the potential for love and healing and learned a great deal about honesty and trust. Their experiment struck me as a courageous, if risky, approach to the tension and temptation stirred up when an Escort to the Beloved asserts a claim. Freud established the pioneering tenets of psychotherapy because he had noted how frequently and tumultuously the conscious and unconscious desires of a person could cause conflicts. A hundred and more years later, we still suffer the conflict and still experiment with ways to resolve it.

If, rather than an unattainable partner, the Escort to the Beloved becomes a core part of our life, a person with whom we create a strong, loving relationship even as we are simultaneously cultivating a relationship with the divine Beloved, then both loves can flourish. And as Socrates recognized, it is important for the human partner to share at least some of the most significant characteristics of the daimon. In other words, if a man's deepest personal need is for a mate who is intelligent, appreciative of his enthusiasm for bird-watching, able to give comfort in times of sorrow, and in possession of a hearty sense of humor, and if this man falls in love with someone whose nature it is to be this way, then the fact that the partner has an attitude toward money that is different from his or doesn't like socializing with his friends need not be cause for much concern. These gaps may annoy him, but they are exactly the ones the Beloved can fill. The Beloved, for instance, might encourage the man's fiscal responsibility and assure that he takes time regularly to be with his friends, rather than either giving up what is important to him or trying to insist that his partner meet all his needs. With the daimon, or Beloved, ever pulling us toward our authenticity, we can foster talents and tap reserves in ourselves that we once wanted others to supply. A husband, wife, or mate may not understand our relationship with the inner Beloved, and it may be easier to keep the details private. However, if the mate is contemptuous of the Beloved, or jealous, if the bond with the daimon is belittled, then it may be time to look for a human partner who will respect our need to woo the lover of the soul — perhaps a new Escort to the Beloved.

I myself could not have pursued my journey to the Beloved if it had not been for my husband, who gave me, first, compassion and empathy in the throes of a mighty infatuation and, later, enthusiastic support for the work that love had spawned. Andy and I had long conversations about the themes I was exploring in my writing and workshops and, after he met his own divine inner woman in a powerful dream and then began to think about his work with pottery as the path to her, we had a personal point of reference as well. I often expressed my gratitude for his compassion for my endeavor, characterized by his understanding reaction when I first told him I was attracted to another man. He told me once, however, that if I had pursued a relationship with "that man" (we never spoke his name), he would not have been so understanding. He recognized that the inner Beloved had no connection with "that man" — not even, as time went on, in the imaginal world — and he was truly happy for my own growing joy in exploring the Beloved and my uninhibited pursuit of what I felt called to do.

When each person in a partnership can strengthen the bond with the inner Beloved, all the while recognizing that the partner pursues a similar quest of his or her own, then each respects and honors the highest calling of the other — a spiritual impulse that Socrates referred to as a "thrusting upward." This is nothing less than the drive to persist joyfully in our own being, to transcend ourselves by loving ourselves utterly. Loving another person who consciously cultivates the inner Beloved while acknowledging the inner Beloved of their human love is a rare and mutually rewarding experience. The great Indian poet Rabindranath Tagore describes what happens:

> One day in spring, a woman came
> In my lonely woods,
> In the lovely form of the Beloved.
> Came, to give to my songs, melodies,
> To give to my dreams, sweetness.
> ...She stood beneath the tree, turned,
> Glanced at my face, made sad with pain,
> And with quick steps, came and sat by me.
> Taking my hands in hers she said:
> "You do not know me, nor I you —
> I wonder how this could be?"
> I said:
> "We shall build two beings, each to the other unknown,
> This eager wonder is at the heart of things."[15]

When each person is devoted to courting a sacred being who will, to some extent, always remain unknown even to that dearest of all humans, then "eager wonder" remains alive in all three partnerships.

ONE MORNING IN LATE SPRING, not quite three years after I'd met Lucas, I was sitting alone in a Canyonlands base camp, watching the sun stroke its way down blood-red canyon walls. All around me, six women fasted in the canyons and among the tall reeds fringing the Dolores River. I had been thinking about how each woman had chosen her place in an intuitive way that was nonetheless constructed out of the instincts, habits, needs, loves, and fears that currently drove her life. I thought about the people and events that show up now and then to haul us out of the emotional quicksand we get stuck in and set us on firmer ground. Then the idea came to me to thank the people who had been Escorts to my Beloved.

I considered the project for a while, as the sun caressed boulders and crevices into shades of ocher, blood red, tawny gold, and doughy white. Then I tore several pages out of my notebook, ripped them into smaller pieces, and wrote down a name on each. It was the unequivocal presence of each of these figures in my mind that dictated whether they would be counted, rather than any criteria I had set up in advance. And it was interesting who appeared, demanding to be included. Some, but not all, of my Immaculate Lovers showed up. John Lennon appeared immediately, and right after him came Albert Camus, followed by Emily Brontë, W. B. Yeats, Dante Alighieri, and Virginia Woolf, all members of the literary pack I'd adored for many years. My high school English teacher, Miss Lonnie Hansen, arrived then, and a well-known poet I'd had an affair with when I was in my twenties. Lucas was there, of course, and some of the men who had been my lovers before I married, though, surprisingly, fewer than I would have expected. Zuleikha, the dancer I'd followed to New Mexico, I included reluctantly, for she reminded me of the need to wrestle with vulnerability in the pursuit of the Beloved. I took my time over this name writing, for I wanted to include only those people who had set me on a new track in life and whose chemistry had mixed with my own to fuel me in a significant way. Not all were benevolent figures. One who came swooping into my consciousness was the man I'd hitchhiked around the country with. I wrote down Andy's name, though classifying him in any category seemed off the mark. I included my grandfather, Frederick Trebbe, who had loved me dearly and taught me how to draw, do crossword puzzles, and look at trees and stars as intimates, and who, just a month before he died, had sent me a rhinestone ring and a Valentine signed "Paul McCartney." When I was finished I had twenty-five names.

I wrapped the papers in a silk scarf and carried them up to a high, broad saddle of rock that spanned two turreted canyon walls. From all around that stony eminence I selected twenty-five small stones and an assortment of other wild beauties, including sand, burrs, a feather, juniper berries, wildflowers, pinecones, and twigs. I unwrapped the names, smoothed them flat, and placed them in a circle, with a stone over each. I arranged the names chronologically, in order of our first encounters, then festooned each stone and paper with the flowers and other embellishments. Finally I sat in the center of the circle and addressed each person in turn, telling them what they had given me and thanking them.

"Emily, when I read *Wuthering Heights*, I was fifteen years old and feeling different and lonely and unliked. You taught me that a woman can love the land passionately, that human emotions can be as wild and grand as storms and English moors. You taught me that strangeness and longing and sorrow are the very blood of writing and that they can save a woman's life.

"Danny, you were my first true love. You introduced me to French symbolist poetry, jazz, motorcycles, and the epic of Gilgamesh. You showed me that it was not as important to be a famous poet as to be a fiercely dedicated one. You opened me to sexual passion. Since you died, I have never stopped missing you.

"Zuleikha, you showed me that a woman teacher can be beautiful, seductive, alluring, and wise. You showed me how to radiate before a roomful of people just by doing what I love.

"Andy, you are the beloved who loves all of me every day. In you I sink into love. Your brilliance and confidence in what you know have forced me to parade my own ideas, even when I have felt them inferior to yours and even as I raged at you for not being more fascinated with mine. You help me to gain confidence in my own voice. You inspire me with your constant creativity and your attention to details.

You love me completely. I could write a love letter to you every day for the rest of my life and never say enough.

"David, you showed me that a person who is comfortable in his own spiritual wisdom can walk and talk with authority and generosity anywhere, from a powwow to a board room.

"Lucas, you gave me an image of myself that I needed to strive toward, and you told me you loved me in that guise. You changed my life totally. You escorted me to the Beloved. I thank you with all my heart."

When I had finished speaking to each person, I sat quietly in the center of the circle for a while and reflected on how formerly inert aspects of myself had been quickened by these people, men and women, living and dead, lovers and teachers, whom life had miraculously put in my path. Or whom, as I now would say, the Beloved had led me toward. I wondered how many of them I might inadvertently have delivered closer to their own Beloved, how many I had not included in my own circle of Escorts who had realized themselves through knowing me. I bowed to them, each and every one. Finally, I removed the flowers and other decorations and carried the stones over to a narrow ledge that overhung the canyon floor. I tossed the stones into the canyon like confetti and left the flowers, berries, and sticks in a shallow circle for the wind to take away. Then I dug a little hole in the sand and made a tiny pyre of twenty-four names, for, although I would always be grateful to these ushers along the path, I could now separate them from the qualities they'd passed along as gifts to me. With the smoke that rose from the fire I released them with gratitude. The one paper I did not burn was the one bearing Andy's name. That I tucked into the case of the pocket mirror I carried into the backcountry, for Andy was the beloved who continually mirrored my life.

CHAPTER EIGHT

Seized by the Rapture Bird

ALLUREMENT — HOW THE BELOVED BEGUILES US

The lover walks to the Beloved, who beckons from dappled sunlight.
What keeps the lover going?
Allurement, Eros's own pheromone.
Does the lover ever arrive in the Beloved's arms?
More often than you think.
And then?
Rapture!

It's no secret that a god sometimes develops a passion for a mortal, who, of course, has little choice about whether she, and occasionally he, will consent to the union. (Krishna, the great seducer of the willing and eager, was the exception.) Zeus was notorious for the creative shape-shifting he put himself through (bull, swan, shaft of light) to claim the women he desired. The Virgin Mary, though given considerate prior notice of God's intended conjugal visit by the angel Gabriel, was hardly in a position to refuse the request. When Fand made up her mind that Cuchullain was the man to serve her as lover and vanquisher of her enemies, she overcame his initial indifference by informing him that illness would eat him alive until he saw things her way. It's hard to refuse a god who has his sights set on you.

But make no mistake about it, the longing for union between divine and human is not the fancy of deities alone. The women who made love with Krishna yearned for him forever after, and the yearning itself became a ripe, expansive thing, imbuing their every gesture with meaning, since all was preparation for the next embrace. Parvati brought both body and spirit to the task of winning Shiva's love. Placing offerings before him, she let him glimpse her lovely breasts, then she took herself off to the forest to meditate in ascetic isolation. (Shiva was smitten, and their first embrace lasted twenty-five years.) The handsome shepherd Endymion fell in love with the moon goddess Selene and lay in eternal sleep in a glade in Latmos, dreaming only of her. Nightly Selene came to caress him gently, and though some say it was she who longed for a more robust passion than his somnolent limbs would allow, and some say it was he who yearned for more than her silken touch, it is longing between human and divine that drives the tale.[1]

The desire to be swept up by the mystery that they hold most sacred drives the faithful to dance, drum, pray, swallow hallucinogenic plants, fast, wear hair shirts, flagellate themselves, crawl into dark pits on sacred mountains, meditate, run marathons, and shut themselves behind closed doors to pursue an art or science. Such determination to experience oneness with the great, eternal Other has stimulated the spiritual imagination for a very long time. Clayton Eshelman, who has fused academic, poetic, and personal perspectives to probe the secrets of Paleolithic caves, suggests that those earliest of artists who crawled deep into the earth to render their vivid, animated figures of beasts were attempting not to mimic a successful hunt, but to enact a ritual rebirth from the "transpersonal or cosmogonic Mother."[2]

Of course, even the most dedicated adherence to these devotions provides no guarantee that the divine one will always reward the practitioner with a personal visitation. The muse is fickle. The gods have a lot on their minds. Often a mystical experience descends on one who is not even looking for it. Once it happens, though, life is never the same for that lucky initiate. The event itself is brief — indeed, it may last only seconds — but as William James points out in his seminal book *The Varieties of Religious Experience*, first published in 1902, one of the most significant aspects of the mystical experience is its "noetic quality": "Mystical states seem to those who experience them to be also states of knowledge. They are states of insight into depths of truth unplumbed by the discursive intellect. They are illuminations, revelations, full of significance and importance, all inarticulate though they remain; and as a rule they carry with them a curious sense of authority for after-time."[3]

And it's not just ecstatic medieval Christian nuns, Peruvian shamans, and Sufi adepts who are granted these "states of knowledge." Anyone can have what Abraham Maslow called a "peak experience" that makes them lose all sense of time and place; floods them with feelings of bliss, wonder, and awe; and returns them to ordinary reality "deeply inspired and touched."[4] My freshman roommate at college knew that she was going to be a priest in the Episcopal Church years before a woman was ever ordained in that denomination, for she had had a vision of Jesus, surrounded by light and looking right at her, when she was in high school. Moreover, although the experience is transcendental, it is not necessarily religious. Jean-Jacques Rousseau was thirty-seven years old and making his living as a secretary, teacher, and aspiring musician when he set out one day from Paris to visit his friend, the philosopher Denis Diderot. Casually scanning a newspaper as he walked, he came upon a notice that changed his life: a call for submissions to an essay contest sponsored by the Academy of Dijon. Rousseau recalled: "The moment I read these words I saw another universe and I became another man."[5] He entered the contest, won the prize, and was on his way to becoming the acclaimed, often notorious, always brilliant novelist, philosopher, and autobiographer who showed for the first time how an individual's private insights and difficulties influenced his public and social acts.

On vision quests, it's not at all uncommon for someone to be grabbed and shaken by a great awakening, and this doesn't just happen, as questers tend to hope it will, in the form of a miraculous vision — Crazy Horse himself come bearing tidings. Sometimes revelation waits in the small and humble, as a woman learned when she came to quest in the Utah canyon country. Marilyn, a respected psychologist, had been raised in a poor, working-class family with several brothers and sisters, an abusive father, and a cold, unemotional mother. She had risen to the top by competing and striving relentlessly, and she believed that anything worth attaining had to be won the hard way. When the group went out to find their solo spots, Marilyn, in character, clawed her way up to the summit of a high mesa, where, she had announced, she intended to sit for three days surveying the desert panorama far below. The climb was strenuous, and when she reached the top, she sank to her knees to catch her breath. There, right before her grew a clump of wooly locoweed, a tiny pincushion-sized plant of purple flowers set amid fuzzy green leaves. Seeing it, Marilyn burst into tears. Some dovetailing of the climb that betokened her whole approach to life and the welcome offered by that small, soft, thriving plant opened her heart, and she knew at once that she had to give up the fight and learn another way. Instead of exploring the mesa, she made her way back down to the canyon floor, where she chose a place under an enormous sheltering cottonwood tree beside a stream. There, during the solo, she allowed the earth to take care of her and teach her about softness, acceptance, and flowing around obstacles.

All these people were embraced by God — or spirit, or mystery, or, if you will, by some blocked dam in their psyche that required a certain dynamite, as big as Jesus or as small as a clump of locoweed, to be blown to smithereens, releasing the pent-up current of the particular human.

I, TOO, LIKE RAVISHMENT. In fact, I seek it out. I wouldn't guide vision quests or lie naked in rivers (and I probably wouldn't have spent years hinged to, unhinged by, alcohol) if I didn't love being lifted out of the everyday and given to glimpse the extraordinary. I'm a satori seeker, as I learned one night when Andy and I sat reading in bed and he read me a passage in one of Jack Kornfield's books, about two kinds of people: those who seek satori, the burst of enlightenment, and those who seek immanence, the path of steady practice.

I laughed. "I think all vision quest guides are satori seekers."

But we all need immanence to sustain us, as Kornfield makes clear: when you come back to earth after being transported by ecstasy, you still have to do the laundry. Fortunately, the Beloved offers both immanence and satori. The Beloved is different from those omnipotent gods who ravish when they will. The Beloved walks the earth with us, knows why we're here, and attracts us, through the power of allurement, to what we love and what needs to be shaped by us. Soulful yearning for a touch, a sight, a taste of knowledge of the Beloved keeps us on the path. And the constancy we develop, we find to our delight, opens us to the infinite ways the Beloved has of embracing us.

A SWEDISH TALE CAPTURES the magic of allurement. It seems a woodcutter was working alone one day in the deep woods, with only the chop, chop, chop of his ax, the occasional call of the raven, and the wind in the boughs to keep him company. Suddenly, through the trees stepped the most beautiful woman he had ever seen. She seemed both to have come from far away and to belong nowhere but there, in the forest with him. This was Huldra, one of the immortal ones, and when she smiled at the woodcutter, he forgot everything that had kept him tied to his routine, his work, his family, and the path toward home. He simply gaped, entranced. Then he dropped his ax and moved toward her. Giving him one last glance over her shoulder, Huldra turned her back and began to walk away through the forest. Now the man had no desire but to follow. Ever farther Huldra led him, and so he went, on and on, longing for the moment when she would turn and smile at him again.

The gift Huldra offers the woodcutter — and that he obligingly takes — is recognition of his own allurement. Allurement impels us to put down the tools of our old familiar trades and step into the unknown for the sake of something that, though it makes no promises for the future, fascinates utterly in the present. Allurement is the mesmeric, insubstantial Something that sparkles on a certain face across a crowded room while all other faces merge into the mass. Allurement forces us to stop, stock-still in our tracks, and get off the trail because some potentially wonderful thing in the brush needs looking at. "Either things signify or we do not notice them," says the Italian thinker Elemire Zolla.[6] Waving the fragrant spice of allurement under our nose, the Beloved grabs our attention and forces us to peer into some new mystery. Allurement keeps us engaged with our world.

We humans inherited this useful genetic trait from our elders, the animals. A cat creeps with fierce stealth to nail some invisible prey in the middle of the carpet. A dog greets the fun of the twentieth tossed stick with as much enthusiasm as he pounced on the first. Birds spontaneously engage in repetitive behaviors that seem to have absolutely no survival value. Ornithologist Alexander Skutch recounts many anecdotes of birds succumbing to allurement, such as one about the blackbird seen tossing an old walnut shell around, jumping on it, then tossing it again, or the flock of barn swallows playing catch. Swooping over a hill where ducks and geese had molted their white feathers, the swallows took turns diving down and seizing a feather, which they flew with and then let go. Another bird would catch the feather, fly with it, and drop it for yet another to grasp.[7]

I myself was once the object of fascination for a troupe of baboons. Sitting on a rock in the Drakensberg Mountains of South Africa, I saw them before they spotted me and watched as they picked their casual way through the brush in the midst of some routine foray. Suddenly a young baboon spied me and began to make a ruckus, screeching and staring and swinging from branch to branch in a small tree. This particular animal was no longer so small that it had to ride on its mother's back, but it was obviously too young to have earned much credibility, for none of the others paid any attention whatsoever. A few moments later, one of the watcher baboons, who travel on the outer rim of the troupe, noticed the anomaly, as was his job. The moment he called the alarm, they all stopped what they were doing and turned my way. For several minutes, they simply stared at me, a pale curiosity in an unexpected place. Finally, like humans in a zoo, they deemed the strange sight harmless and not worth further bother, and turned to carry on with the business of foraging and yawning and grooming one another.

Allurement, writes cosmologist Brian Swimme, is the dynamic, prospecting force that impels the universe to cohere:

> *The allurement we call gravitation, that of electromagnetic inter-actions, chemical attractors, allurements in the biological and human worlds...If we could snap our fingers and make these allurements — which we can't see or hear or taste anyway — disappear from the universe, what would happen?*
>
> *To begin with, the galaxies would break apart. The stars of the Milky Way would soar off in all directions, since they would no longer hold each other in the galactic dance....The Earth would break apart as well, all the minerals and chemical compounds dissolving, mountains evaporating like huge dark clouds under the noon sun.*[8]

The earth, out of which all living things arose, is constantly pulling its offspring close through the force of gravity. It allures them. Animals and birds attract prospective mates with displays of magnetism they hope will be irresistible: colorful feathers, strong antlers capable of forcing an opponent to his knees, a haunting song, a wonderful smell. We humans sponsor the good works of allurement even on the microscopic level. Biologist Candace Pert has shown that individual immune cells are not fixed in one place in the body, but travel, like busy doctors on call, throughout the organism to any area that needs them to repair damage or defend against a potential threat.9

We follow allurement all our lives. Even as babies lying in the crib we responded to what Wallace Stevens called the "particulars of rapture." We reached out our little hands to certain objects and cooed over them and cried when they were taken away, while other bits of the world whose center we commanded were not worth bothering with. As children we lost our hearts to a few pastimes or secret places so precious that we were loath to admit their existence even to our best friend. Allurement calls us to our favorite subjects in school and our occupations in adulthood. It defines our hobbies and the clothes we choose, tells us what dish to order in a restaurant, and determines which events reported in the newspaper will tug at our hearts. It makes us fall in love and picks our friends. It makes certain places on earth feel like home.

The power of allurement to alter our circumstances is so immense and so dominant that it can even rescue us, however momentarily, from grief, fear, and despair. Viktor Frankl, who was imprisoned by the Nazis in Auschwitz, recalls waking one morning and finding a stale crust of bread in his pocket. His misery, exacerbated by the moans of another prisoner close by, faded briefly when he put that bread into his mouth and "munched with absorbed delight."10 Rachel Carson, author of *Silent Spring* and fearless prognosticator of the fate of a planet drenched in pesticides, never lost her belief in the magic of allurement. The sense of wonder fostered in a child, she wrote, should be "so indestructible that it would last throughout life, as an unfailing antidote against the boredom and disenchantments of later years, the sterile preoccupation with things that are artificial, the alienation from the sources of our strength."11 A neighbor of mine, suffering through a painful divorce, told me that she always kept her bird feeder filled and would stop before her kitchen window many times throughout the day to watch the flurry of bright guests, the eager accommodating and the chasing away, the energetic life force — and feel hope for her own survival. Every day she set up the conditions of allurement, and every day, however briefly, she was lifted up and away.

BEING LIFTED UP AND AWAY is what happens to the mouse who's seized by a hawk or an owl, a raptor. The word *raptor* is related to *rapture*, and both nouns describe conditions in which a lesser thing is transported by the will and force of a greater thing: prey by predator, person by wonder. Allurement is answering the call; rapture is being picked up and carted away by the caller. We choose to respond to allurement; we are snatched by rapture, whether we want to be or not. Allurement is in the moment the hawk spots the mouse snuffling about in tall grasses far below. Rapture is in the instant sharp talons grip furry neck — and lift. Every now and then rapture seizes us when we're least expecting it and lifts us so high and far that it changes our life. That's what happened to Rousseau and to the quester who got a transfusion of mercy from a desert plant. Fortunately, though, we can also go courting rapture, as my neighbor did with birdseed, and so invite it to simply change our moment. That kind of rapture, which rises up in the midst of allurement, is what I call the embrace of the Beloved.

Many people are afraid to follow allurement. They think the rapture bird will take them so high they won't be able to get back. They fear they'll do dangerous, impetuous things: engage in sex with strangers, leave home and family to chase a daydream, give up a good job to pursue a better but financially unsound cause. They fear they'll end up like the legendary Irish poet Sweeney, who climbed a sacred peak to seek insight from "the god that kindles fire in the head" and was so shaken by the vision he received that he never recovered. He spent the rest of his days wandering helplessly over the hills, foraging for roots and babbling to the animals and birds.[12] A woman who gives herself uninhibitedly to sexual passion may resolutely avoid passion attained in a more metaphysical activity. Taking the first step to learn a long-desired skill or subject of study may strike an ordinarily courageous man as tantamount to going into debt to the mafia. In fact, my experience leading workshops on the Beloved was that many people are more afraid of the consequences of pursuing allurement than they are of staying stuck in ways of living that have no seductive power for them whatsoever. To get people comfortable with the pull of their own fascination, I have given workshop participants a sheet of notebook paper and asked them to write on each line one thing that was alluring them at that time in their lives: books they wanted to read, skills they wanted to learn, people they wished to meet, activities they'd like to pursue, projects that intrigued them, social and environmental causes they wished they had time to get involved in. In the process they discovered that their allurements were not only quite benign, but actually positive, constructive, and of potential service to others.

One woman, a former nun who attended a workshop in Ireland, remarked, "We're taught from the time we're young that we should fight temptation, and as a child I always interpreted that to mean I should fight desire. If you wanted something, you were bad. To think about deliberately following allurement feels wickedly delicious!" Following temptation is straying from the rightful track; following allurement — mindfully — is stepping onto the truest track of all.

ONE WAY TO TELL which is which is by looking for the path illuminated by Eros. Not some pseudo-Eros who tries to get you to take a peek at your Internet junk mail with PEN*!IS in the subject line, but the original Eros, daimon of love, the electrician who wires your allurement to the nodes most likely to light up the world.

Eros is that dynamic binding power between the desirer and the object of desire that Diotima told Socrates about. It's no accident that Eros is one of the few gods who have remained alive in the mythic pantheon of the modern psyche. We can't afford to let Eros die or be watered down into a symbol of something old and fusty; we need him too much. He excites us to the new and strange and urgent, and if we ignore him in our waking life, he grabs us in dreams and forces us to confront those desires and impulses we need to grapple with. Eros connects us with our future by opening us up to enchantment with what we must step closer to and hence pulls our steps in that direction. As author Thomas Moore has written, "It's common to point out the sexual nature of being forceful in a penetrating way, but we don't hear much about the sexuality of being open and receptive."[13]

And, as Diotima points out, Eros is working both sides of the fence — enticing us closer to the divine and the divine closer to us. This binding is more than sexual; it is moral, too, and intellectual, and aesthetic. Eros, writes Rollo May, "incites in man the yearning for knowledge and drives him passionately to seek union with the truth. Through eros we become not only poets and inventors but also achieve ethical goodness."[14] The perpetual drive to regenerate the self and grow more like the gods is the force of Eros at work in man and woman.

According to the third-century philosopher Plotinus, the true force of Eros — which is often misdirected — is the drive toward oneness. Eros, child of Aphrodite, who symbolizes the "Intellectual Principle," is the force of love that drives the soul to its "divinest" being: "The Soul directs its Act towards [the Highest] and holds closely towards him. . . . Love, thus, is ever intent upon that other loveliness, and exists to be the medium between desire and the object of desire."[15] That "other loveliness" is the higher goal, the good or moral act of the self realizing its Self. When we act in accordance with Eros we willingly become the moth that must fly toward the alluring flame. To live with Eros, however, does not mean being killed by what burns for us; it means giving ourselves body and soul to what we love.

Eros drives African American families living in once-fertile farmlands along the Mississippi River to fight relentlessly against the incursions of petrochemical companies, whose gigantic refineries squeeze out their communities, endanger their health, and poison their land. Eros sent Gauguin to Tahiti in search of the forms and colors he needed to express his creative hunger, and it sent Proust to his bed to delve relentlessly into the thick blankets of memory. The naturalist John Muir never left the company of Eros as he roamed through the Sierra Nevada Mountains in the summer of 1869, exclaiming over wildflowers and climbing high into a tall tree during a thunderstorm to get as close as possible to nature's delirium. Eros drove grieving parents who had lost their children in car accidents to found MADD, Mothers Against Drunk Driving. Eros moves in the men and women who volunteer on the fire and rescue teams in my rural community. Eros pierced the heart of geneticist Barbara McClintock, who received the 1983 Nobel Prize in Physiology or Medicine for her discovery that genes "jump" from one chromosome to another. As she worked, McClintock used to imagine herself walking among the kernels she examined under a microscope: "I was part of the system," she explained. "I was right down there with them.... As you look at these things, they become part of you. And you forget yourself. The main thing about it is you forget yourself."[16]

Forgetting oneself while in pursuit of the soul's thriving is falling into the embrace of the Beloved. This kind of rapture will not only *not* drive you insane, but it will engage you more fully in the now. Diane Ackerman calls this intense personal engagement "deep play," a state characterized by "clarity, wild enthusiasm, saturation in the moment, and wonder... [a] waking trance."[17] Following allurement aglow with Eros, we turn in the very direction where we're most likely to find ourselves by losing ourselves.

A MAN IN ONE WORKSHOP CHALLENGED the wisdom of this approach. Several years earlier he had been introduced to acupuncture and immediately felt sure that this was the work he had been born to do. Even as he kept his full-time job as a paralegal, he started taking classes in acupuncture and herbal medicine. After years of hard but joyful work, he received his certification. He rented office space, took care decorating it, and set out to attract clients. And found he couldn't make a living. A few people came to him, but his appointment book stayed depressingly blank. Although he remained convinced that this was his soul's path, two years later he was deep in debt and still fretting all day in an empty office. Finally he had no choice but to close the practice and get another job. "That was following my allurement," he said, still smarting over what felt like a betrayal by the universe. "I 'followed my bliss,' as Joseph Campbell used to say. And I got nothing from it."

There's no assurance that riches and fame, or even a decent income, will be ours once we put down that heavy old ax we've been hauling around and answer Huldra's sweet summons to head into the forest. We may get absolutely nothing for our pains — except a long walk to the Beloved with Eros powering our limbs. And this man took a walk that quenched a longing in his soul. All he could know in retrospect was that *not* to have embraced his passion would have been to stay stuck in what was predictable and safe and probably to spend the rest of his life regretting his failure to answer so clear a call to action. Perhaps in the future he will have another opportunity to be the acupuncturist he dreamed of being, or perhaps the skills he learned or the people he met during his training and practice will benefit his life in some other way. He dared, he did what he loved, and he is no more a fool than a writer I know who has written five novels, suffered the rejection of all of them by various publishers, and is now at work on a sixth. Answering the Beloved's call under the presumption that it is bound to lead to success is almost as misguided as refusing to heed that call for fear that nothing will come of it or even that something awful will happen to punish us for our temerity.

And the fact is that in many myths, fairy tales, and legends, this is precisely what does happen to those who follow their fascination: they get punished — at least at first. Sleeping Beauty pricks her finger on the forbidden spinning wheel. Pandora peeks in the box the gods have warned her not to open and lets loose all the ills of the world. The Navajo warrior Twins ignore their mothers' nervous caution and venture ever more boldly into the boyhood games that presage their destiny. Whereas poor Orpheus ruined his chance to lead Eurydice out of the Underworld by doing the one thing he had been warned not to do, it was fear, or distrust, that goaded him to that most ill-advised backward glance. In contrast, disobedient heroes and heroines like Sleeping Beauty and the Twins take their apparently rash actions against the counsel of their elders and the gods out of curiosity and fascination — and simply because they have to set in motion the forces that will shape them into the person the story needs them to be. Disobedience baptizes the merely curious into the heroine or hero and provides a lesson from that time forth to every girl and boy who sits enthralled at the storyteller's feet: by breaking the rules and then doing your best to clean up the mess you've made, you take on the larger self you hoped would be given you more freely and painlessly. Risking the anger of the authorities in order to peek, bite, marry, unlock a gate, or in some other way barge into an alluring place more timid souls avoid is to gain a prize far greater than security and approval: the boon of becoming the divinest self.

We will make mistakes. We will act imprudently, and we may not always get home in time for dinner. I have enthusiastically said yes to two or more most worthy allurements scheduled for the same day and then had to make a choice that hurt or angered somebody. The Beloved is not good with scheduling. And Eros is so persuasive that when we feel him move close we are likely to agree happily to anything he suggests. In the Welsh myth, Pwyll, an impulsive young man, makes the mistake of letting his hunting dogs take game brought down by the magical hounds of the otherworldly King Arawn. The trial Arawn devises as punishment is meant to force Pwyll to look long and hard at his tendency to snatch what he wants without considering the consequences: he must assume Arawn's form and sleep each night for one year beside the king's beautiful wife without ever succumbing to the temptation to touch her. Because he is determined to learn from his mistake, Pwyll manages to pass the test and by his success attracts the attention of another immortal, the wise, bold, and beautiful

Rhiannon, who falls in love with him. But as the epic tale unfolds, Pwyll, Rhiannon herself, and eventually their child face one adventure after another in which they take what they want unthinkingly and then must suffer the consequences. In her commentary on the myth, Moyra Caldecott writes that if we are not properly prepared to meet the challenges and manage the rewards of the spirit realm — or our own realized life — circumstances force us to take stock humbly, that we might learn from our mistakes and try again. We must "respect [the intuitive faculty] but not seduce or be seduced by it. This is a warning to some of us who are tempted to go off on wild tangents from reality, claiming that we are following our intuition."[18]

Some allurements, moreover, are no calls from the Beloved, but simply greed-driven distractions, excuses we use to talk ourselves into overlooking responsibility and feeding a personal hunger. The Beloved wants us to *be* and to *do*, not to *have*, and although it may be Eros who's made you fall in love with a new Porsche, it's probably glamour and glitz, not the Beloved, who's calling you to the driver's seat. Still, allurement beckons all over the place, and it is often difficult to differentiate between the call of the libido and that of the soul. Worthy people from Clytemnestra to President Bill Clinton have discovered how easy it is to rush with reckless glee into sexual escapades that end up having disastrously long-term consequences. It's the work of a lifetime to distinguish soulful yearning from possessive lust. According to the ancient Egyptians, it was even the work of the afterlife. In Egyptian myth, when a person died, the jackal-headed god Anubis weighed his heart on a balance scale whose other side held a feather. A heart filled with greedy desire could tip the scale. If that happened, Anubis tossed the body to the Grave Monster, who gobbled it up. The owner of a lighter heart joined Osiris in the Underworld. No doubt many of those heavy hearts belonged to people who had convinced themselves that they made their decisions for only the noblest reasons.

Righting the scale is an ongoing task. We must court the Beloved, follow Huldra through the forest, but we need to heed where we place our feet. When the Sufi dervishes whirl, they become part of the divine vortex of the cosmos. Every now and then, however, they deliberately bring themselves back from the brink of the trance by stopping and placing their hands on their shoulders to form the *alif*, the number 1, and in so doing make sober testimony to the oneness of God. The Maenads, followers of Dionysus, also attained spiritual rapture in dance. Ecstatic with primal energy, these women, who owed no allegiance to family or home, who made love with strangers in the villages they passed through, who offered their breasts to wild fawns and goats, and then at other times tore the flesh from these animals and devoured it raw — these Maenads flitted over the boundaries of civility and madness. Still, it is said, they maintained inner peace at all times. Even as we mortals must examine our allurements with enough dispassion to choose the ones that will lead us closer to the Beloved and our highest purpose, we also have to be willing to toss excessive caution to the winds, for we never know when allurement will usher us onto exciting, challenging, and creative new paths or fill us with ecstasy in the moment.

I learned a lesson in how to balance allurement and responsible good sense one morning on my way to meet a friend for breakfast on New York City's Upper East Side. It was a beautiful spring day, and the flowering plum trees in front of the brownstones on my friend's block blossomed purple and white. At the foot of each tree, in a small square of earth surrounded by a low, dog-proof fence, daffodils, hyacinths, and crocuses bloomed. I was just climbing the steps to my friend's brownstone when I noticed a father and his little girl across the street. The father was dressed in a well-tailored business suit and carried a briefcase. The little girl wore a dress and a French beret. I imagined he was taking her to school before catching a taxi to work. Suddenly the child pulled her hand from her father's, darted over to one of the tiny urban gardens, and bent down to smell the flowers. I held my breath, remembering how my own father had reacted to such breaches of the schedule: stop it, get over here, I have to get to work.

But this man was different; he simply waited, not watching his daughter, not looking at his watch or tapping his foot, just gazing around the block and giving his child her time. She finished with the flowers, ran back, and took his hand. A few steps down the street they came to another tree, another patch, more flowers. Once again she had to go and investigate. Once again he permitted it without any sign of impatience. This went on all the way down the block, and each time the man allowed the little girl her need for wonder.

And I thought, This is the discipline we must cultivate in ourselves, this twofold permission, first to lose ourselves in the flowers that seduce us, then to come back to the business at hand. The voice of the stern patriarch within us may butt in at first with practical objections to what looks like a waste of time, but if we keep practicing, the business of smelling flowers will become a practice as vital to our health as jogging or meditating. The presence of the good father is the same as our sense of what we must do and where we are in life, and by heeding it we pay homage to our conscious, rational mind that manages us so magnificently and prevents us from getting permanently lost in the world of wow, like a flower child on LSD. We won't go mad like poor Sweeney, because the mature and conscious adult of us is waiting, ready to take the hand of the wandering, wondering child and walk beside it down the street. And, so guided, we may give ourselves over time and again to rapture.

THE SOUL PAYS A PENALTY, moreover, when it ignores the call of allurement. Greek myth tells the cautionary tale of three sisters, Alcithoë, Leucippe, and Arsippe, who considered themselves above the ecstatic pleasures offered by Dionysus. Hard at work before their looms, they could hear the god of passionate engagement approaching with the Maenads, but, proud of their moral superiority, they would not even budge to glance out the door. They just sat there, weaving diligently and trying not to imagine the possibilities getting closer and closer.

Well, you can't ignore Dionysus and hope to survive unscathed. Vines from the grape, sacred plant of intoxicating transformation, began wrapping round their looms and then around their loins. The threads they tried to control came loose from the shuttle and turned into tendrils that twined with the vines. Terrified, the sisters fled as far to the back of the house as they could. They cowered in darkness, but they could not escape their own cockeyed upstandingness, and so they metamorphosed into bats, the creature who hangs upside down in the dark.

We ignore allurement at our peril. If we cannot stand outside ourselves in wild ecstasy (the Latin roots of *ecstasy* mean "to stand outside"), we will cower alone in fear. We will demand safety and security over freedom. We will frown on people who don't follow convention or who seem to be having too much fun or exhibiting too much sexuality. We will become conservative in crimped, unhealthy ways, preserving what has ceased to serve us, saying no to the naughty, the quirky, the weird. The quite possibly seductive. What we devote our life to, instead of liberating us, will tie us into knots.

And there are many flowers just waiting to tantalize us in the midst of our busy, focused adult lives. Which particular sights and sounds and concepts in a world filled with offerings will send us a personal invitation to enter into a tryst with them? Which convictions, trying to be heard, are whispering that there is important work we need to get on with, skills we need to learn, teachers and mentors we need to contact? Like the woodcutter in the northern forest, we must drop the tools that have grown to fit our hands so well and step into the seductive unknown. We must follow the path to the Beloved as our pounding heart hopes: any moment now, any step, she will stop and turn around and smile again....

And so she does, though not in the limited way we've probably hoped for. She turns around as the daffodil waving at your feet, or as the teenage boys doing acrobatics on skateboards in the supermarket parking lot, or as a heartfelt conversation with a good friend.

And then the Beloved turns his or her back again and continues on into the forest. For it is impossible, as we know, to stay for long in the arms of the divine.

Yet an extraordinary thing happens when reality once again settles around your shoulders. Following Huldra becomes what you do for a living. Like the lovers of Krishna, you watch the god dance away over the hills, and then you return to the cows, the loom, the children (the office, the phone, the children), and get on with the business of living without him and longing ever for him. Now, though, you find that the scent of the god clings to your hair. The divine touch tingles on your skin. That moment has swept you away and, sensible as you are once more, some part of you is still airborne, and you continue to feel the rapture in your blood. You are what you were before, but more so. You have known union with the Beloved, and nothing can ever be the same again. You go home and announce to your family that you are now a Cardinals fan, and left-handed to boot. You welcome yourself as the Woman Who Weeps Before Flowers as well as the Woman Relentlessly Climbing. You acknowledge that the river guide has escorted you to a wild and erotic part of yourself, and so you kiss your husband and children hello as if you have been away for a very long time, and pick up the phone and call the local gym to inquire about a class in rock climbing. You know yourself loved. Henceforth, you will not forget your ability to touch the sacred.

CHAPTER NINE

Beauty Tips from Myrna Loy

THE SHADOW, THE CRITIC,
AND OTHER OBSTACLES TO THE BELOVED

"You may not marry my daughter," thunders the king in the fairy tale, "until you have passed a test."

Every lover has heard those words. Though the tests vary from tale to tale, the theme bears repeating, because we can never learn the lesson too well: love is not enough. In order for a union to receive the blessings of the realm, the hero must prove himself worthy.

Of course he accepts the challenge. The resolute and smitten hero or heroine will do anything to win the hand of the beloved. Although he may quake with fear and doubt, off he goes to face the trials that have been set for him. And what trials they are! The lovers of myth and fairy tale must, for example, suck on seven loaves of iron bread and wear out seven pairs of iron shoes, climb a glass mountain, knit capes of nettles for seven swan brothers, bridle the horse that belongs to the wind, or slay a fire-breathing monster. As the Roman author Apuleius tells the tale, when repentant Psyche determines to win back Eros after he's fled from her betrayal, she must answer to Venus herself, goddess of love and Eros's mother, who assigns her such tasks as dividing a huge mound of diverse seeds into separate piles and making her way into the Underworld to steal a box containing the beauty secrets of Proserpine (in Greek, Persephone), the bride of the lord of that dark realm. Such tasks are impossible, and that is the point. The hand of the one true beloved cannot be won by just any mediocre hopeful.

But of course the hero succeeds, for love, mere scaffolding at the beginning of the tale, is a grand place to live once it is furnished with the virtues of courage, persistence, and ingenuity. The king or goddess who ordered the trial welcomes the hero into the realm with grudging respect. And the wedded pair, as every child knows, lives happily ever after. It could not have happened otherwise, for if monsters remain unslain, mountains unclimbed, and hidden treasures unclaimed, then the lovers will always be naïve and immature and the kingdom unsafe.

The trial of the mythic hero has its counterpart on the personal level. We must brave the underworld of ourselves, challenge the dragons lurking there, and bring back the gold they guard, or we will not be able to enjoy a stable partnership with the inner Beloved. Because these destructive energies lurk below our consciousness, we can spend years — sometimes an entire lifetime — devoting precious energy to tiptoeing around them. But until we face what's there and integrate it in a positive way into our conscious behavior, we remain fragmented, for how can we love and respect ourselves fully when we cannot even bear to acknowledge certain facets of who we are? We must confront the troublemakers within, or they will plot against us and foil our most virtuous acts.

MY OWN COURTSHIP OF THE BELOVED took a decisive turn after I reluctantly consented to accept beauty advice from Myrna Loy.

The actress, about whom I knew almost nothing, appeared in a dream about a year after I began seeking the Beloved. She was sitting in a high director's chair, wearing a pink satin robe and pink high-heeled slippers with angora pom-poms at the toes. Her long, shapely legs were crossed to their best photogenic advantage, and she was swinging the upper one impatiently. It seemed I was supposed to interview her, but now she wouldn't talk to me because I was late.

"Myrna Loy!" I exclaimed to Andy the next morning. "I hardly even know who she is. I know she was a movie star in the forties, but I wouldn't recognize her if I saw a picture of her."

"She was in *The Thin Man* movies with William Powell," Andy said.

"Myrna Loy!" I said to Barbara Vernovage the next time we had breakfast together. "Where on earth did she come from?"

"Why don't you ask her?" suggested my practical friend. "She's some aspect of yourself that you're late in coming to, but she obviously got all dressed up for the meeting."

For a couple of days, I simply considered my impression of Myrna Loy. The woman in the dream struck me as histrionic, glamorous, seductive, superficial, imperious, and not very bright. What could such a person possibly have to teach me? Eventually I settled back in the little chair in my study, closed my eyes, and let her image float up once again. There she was, perched on her director's chair, coquettishly swinging that leg. I asked her why she had come to my dream.

"It's you who were supposed to come to me," she said crossly. "A lot of people want to do interviews with me. I'm very popular, you know. And you were late."

Half-heartedly I apologized. I felt she was beneath my dignity. I asked her what she wanted to talk about in the interview.

"About my interesting life," she said, as if it should have been obvious. "About my career and how sought after I am."

"So tell me about your interesting life."

Now it became obvious that she was not fooled. She knew exactly how I felt about her, and she wasn't going to let me get away with it a minute longer. "The problem with you," she sighed, "is that you're afraid of being glamorous! Why are you ashamed to show your beauty? You should be more like me, for goodness sake!"

This was not advice I cared for at all. I didn't like this frivolous creature in her pink peignoir and her showy self-satisfaction. She represented a type of person I disdained: the pampered woman who cared only about how she looked. This was the woman who had nothing better to do in the morning than spend an hour putting on her makeup and trying on a lot of expensive outfits before choosing the one she would wear. She would spend the day shopping for more clothes, getting her nails done, scrutinizing and comparing different shades of lipstick at department store cosmetics counters, and sitting under a big domed hairdryer in the beauty parlor reading fashion magazines. She didn't have to think or work or try to prove to the world that she was smart and tough enough to do a man's job. I should be more like her? I had nothing but contempt for her.

THE TENACITY OF MY RESISTANCE to being influenced by a woman like that, or rather, by my impression of her — for my impression was the problem and had nothing to do with the real-life Myrna Loy — was a big clue that she represented a secret, shut-off part of me. She was the other, or the double. Many of Edgar Allan Poe's stories feature doubles, such as the suspicious stranger, the criminal, or the sickly twin who, we come to realize as the narrative unfolds, has all too much in common with the upright, respectable citizen who wants to kill him or lock him up. Jung called the inner personality that we are intent on denying the Shadow. By any name, it is the embodiment of some bundle of qualities we prefer to think ourselves superior to.

We like to see ourselves, and hope that others see us, in the most flattering terms possible. We are generous, loving, honest, hardworking, and full of noble intentions. But we are also miserly or envious or deceitful or lazy or obsessed with sex. Because we know that such a despised quality skulks somewhere inside us, we work very hard to keep it in exile. Secreted away, it has plenty of time to sit around thinking up mischief. The Shadow is the fairy in the attic who, because she was not invited to the royal christening, focuses all her vengeful energy on getting her spinning wheel ready for the day when the princess will find it and prick her finger on it. Until we deign to notice the scorned double, it makes its presence felt in covert ways, some embarrassing or shaming, some quite nefarious. For example, a man who is asked to give a testimonial speech for a colleague whose success he bitterly resents may unintentionally pepper his remarks with anecdotes that are more cruel than humorous. Or a conscientious environmental journalist and activist may morph into her own worst enemy. That's what happened to Elizabeth Brensinger, who has written about her painful encounter with Shadow during the Canyonlands vision quest she had such high hopes for. During her solo, Brensinger was beset by difficulties: cold and darkness (i.e., excessive shadow) in her north-facing solo spot, a case of hives that forced her to go back to base camp for help, menstrual cramps, and an escalating din of self-criticism about her competence to handle all these challenges. When an early winter storm forced the group to hike out of base camp a day early, she stomped up the trail so angry, bitter, and defeated that she could hardly bother to avoid trampling the fragile cryptobiotic soil. She felt "absolutely no connection to this supposedly sacred land, except for the emotional charge that was my desire to leave it. This rejection, too, I now recognized as metaphor: I had rejected my spot just like I'd historically rejected my own shadow, preferring to believe only in the 'nice' parts of myself and thereby denying half of what it meant to be human."[1]

Jung once remarked that he would rather be whole than good. That's not how most of us were brought up. ("Nice girls don't let boys know how much they like them," as my mother said.) We're rewarded for being "good," and we fight the "bad" impulses that threaten to come spurting out of us like smarmy goo: for example, keeping our fidgeting to a minimum and nodding politely when all the while we're boiling with resentment as a friend expounds interminably on some small personal drama. An example of how the suppressed double can wreak great damage in "good" people is the sex scandals that blistered out of the Catholic Church in the early years of the twenty-first century. Priests who had systematically tried to stanch any feelings of sexual desire in themselves, particularly homosexual feelings, had molested young people in their congregations for years, even after receiving all-too-inadequate warnings from Church authorities.

We all have a secret other, but it's usually hard to identify. As one psychologist remarked, you can't exactly get a good look at the big fish that's swimming just behind you and trying to swallow you. One surefire way to spot the nefarious double is by considering the people for whom we have a vehement, irrational hatred — and can't seem to stop thinking about. When I was a first-grader living in Springfield, Illinois, for example, my mother and her friends had what I now recognize as a group Shadow. They used to cluck disapprovingly about an attractive woman on the block who liked to sunbathe in a bright orange bikini. Her moral failing seemed to be less the act itself than where it took place — not in the privacy of her backyard, but on a chaise longue in the front yard, where everyone (and everyone's husband) could see her. What fearsome sexuality of their own might these women have been trying to push out of sight?

How our anti–role models see themselves, or what anyone else thinks about them, is irrelevant; it's the qualities we project onto them that cast the long black Shadow we fear to tread on. It mattered not at all to my unconscious that the real Myrna Loy, whose biography I bought in a secondhand bookstore shortly after I had the dream, not only had been a talented comedic actress but had served on the New York State Democratic Committee and been appointed as a UNESCO ambassador. The role my psyche cast her in was as much a fiction as any of the characters she played on screen (some of whom were actually very witty and clever, even though they wore peignoirs and could toss their hats on a sofa with artless grace). Robert Bly writes: "If we maintain eye contact with that person [we resent], we can damage him or her by our anger and hatred. If we break off eye contact and look down quickly to the right, we will see our own Shadow. Hatred then is very helpful."[2] Hating the other makes the ego feel smug: "I'm certainly glad *I'm* not like that!" In my aversion to the Pampered Woman, for example, I usually forbade myself the pleasure of reading *Vogue* magazine. But every now and then, when I was in some distant airport and unlikely to be spotted, I would buy it and devour it guiltily. If I saw anyone else reading a fashion magazine, I haughtily concluded that she was not anyone who could possibly be a friend of mine.

The shady double can cause problems when we start to build a relationship with the divine Beloved, for even as we begin to muster courage, trust allurement, and make more room in our heart for an inclusive, compassionate, and passionate way of living, we are still directing fear and hatred toward the inner villain. In so doing, we try to keep a secret from ourselves in much the same way as we would hide the existence of a lover from a husband or wife. We must blithely pretend that everything is open, clean, and aboveboard, while continuing to think up ways of passing judgment about the double onto somebody else, who not only possesses the same monster we do but has the temerity not to see this as a problem. ("Janet is so power hungry! Look at the way she curries favor with the boss. She has absolutely no modesty. I hate people like that!") The Beloved certainly isn't fooled. The Beloved knows all about our Shadow and wants us to get to know it, too, so it will stop coming between us lovers and what beckons us forth. As Melissa Werner observed when she and Barbara and I had dinner together, the Beloved "loves all the parts of me that come from my deep self." That includes those parts the ego has trouble loving. Besides, as I was to learn when I stopped shunning the Myrna Loy of myself, I could take advantage of her most prominent qualities to actually improve my relationship with the Beloved.

TO BECOME WHOLE ADULTS, able to face the trials of life and to bring our passion into the world in creative ways that range from how we treat our children when they misbehave to how we respond to an environmental threat to our community, we must pay attention to the secret other and find out what it wants from us. And it's not just the Shadow that can cause problems, it's any inner figure that seems to have a mind and a very strong will of its own and that sometimes refuses to cooperate with what we think of as our best self. The psychotherapeutic method known as psychosynthesis calls each of these aspects of the self a "subpersonality": "a semi-autonomous, 'structured constellation of attitudes, drives, habit patterns, logical elements which is organized in adaptation to forces in the internal and external environment.'"3 In other words, a force to be reckoned with. Until we deal with the subpersonalities face-to-face, they will continue to act out behind our back.

The Critic is one such troublemaker, and one that practically everybody can identify with because, unlike the Shadow, its influence is very hard to ignore. The Critic carps at us that we're not good enough or smart enough or pretty enough or clever enough, and we might as well give up. Sometimes the Critic mimics the voice of a parent or another early authority, but it can also have a tone and timbre all its own. The Critic wants us to be perfect, and nothing less than perfection will please this demanding taskmaster. We're lost, therefore, before we've hardly begun, for every lapse from perfection incites the Critic to berate us mercilessly. A strong inner Critic can quickly sabotage our relationship with the Beloved, for moving into the world as into the arms of a lover necessitates doing things that are new and untried and hence unlikely to turn out perfectly. If, for example, we fall hard for an Escort to the Beloved and get our hearts broken or fail to pull off a project we envisioned, the Critic gloats: *See, you idiot! You never should have tried. This Beloved stuff is not for you. You're not smart enough, creative enough,* and so on and so forth. The Critic stands behind us, digging its long fingernails into our shoulder and whispering cruel nothings into our ear; the Beloved stands ahead of us in the dappled sunlight, smiling beguilingly and beckoning us forth into allurement and passion.

Another stubborn subpersonality is one that psychologist and deep ecologist Molly Young Brown has called the Loyal Soldier, since its martial ways were formed during our childhood to help us survive confusing or dangerous situations, and it has never learned that the adult in whom it still stands vigilant guard is no longer at war with those old enemies. For example, a girl growing up in a chaotic, violent household with an alcoholic father might try to gain some control over the situation by turning into a strong caretaker who believes she needs nothing for herself and then, in adulthood, finds herself lapsing into the role of caretaker for the men in her life. Bill Plotkin writes:

> *The Loyal Soldier's approach to this task, was* — and continues to be — *to make us small or invisible, to suppress much of our natural exuberance, emotions, desires, and wildness so we might be sufficiently acceptable.... The Loyal Soldier learns to restrain another sub-personality we might call the Wild Child, our original sensual, magical, untamed self that has an essential relationship to the soul and is not interested in limiting itself in any way.*[4]

People often confuse the Critic and the Loyal Soldier, but they are not the same. The Critic is a judge; you can never do anything to please the Critic. The Loyal Soldier, however, is a protector who only wants you to stay small and safe so that nothing will harm you. The Critic tells you you're too stupid and worthless to walk into the arms of the Beloved. The Loyal Soldier tells you you'll be killed if you try it. Both try to hold you back, but their reasons for doing so and the attitudes behind their efforts differ greatly. As my friend and colleague Joe Woolley has pointed out, the Loyal Soldier actually loves you very much.

When people finally shine the spotlight on the insidious characters that inhabit them, their first reaction is often a determination to "kill" the Loyal Soldier or the Critic or Shadow so they can get on with their life. It doesn't work. These well-ensconced companions will simply hide out in some inner closet where we won't notice them for a while and then, just when we think the coast is clear and we're congratulating ourselves on our maturity and wisdom, they pop out and snare us all over again. Instead of trying to kill or banish them, we have to get to know them, find out what they want, and negotiate with them. "Identify with that which haunts you, not in order to fight it off, but to take it into your self; for it must represent some rejected element in you," wrote Rollo May. May described a ceremony enacted by the Yoruba people of southwestern Nigeria, who believe that illness is caused by witchcraft. To drive out the spirit that possesses them, they dress up as and dance the part of the person they believe has caused their sickness. In one instance, a man who was having trouble with impotence dresses up as his mother and, with the support of the whole tribe, "he not only confronts the devil toe to toe, but accepts her, welcomes her, identifies with her, assimilates and hopefully integrates her as a constructive part of himself — and becomes both more gentle and sensitive as a man as well as sexually assertive and potent."[5]

When I began presenting workshops on the Beloved, I was not surprised to discover that firmly entrenched subpersonalities could restrict a person's ability to embrace the Beloved, and I devised an exercise centered on giving voice to some of these underworld bosses. The Loyal Soldier voice was both fairly easy to tap and touching in its loyalty, but it could be persuaded to give up control once the conscious adult self felt the support of the Beloved. Jeffrey was a balding, middle-aged man of small stature. A few years earlier, he had been diagnosed with cancer and had suffered a great deal from the treatment. Now in remission, he nevertheless looked back on the whole ordeal with wonder and gratitude, for he felt it had inculcated in him a sense of the preciousness of life that he would never again take for granted. He dreamed of writing a book and developing a series of workshops for people with life-altering illnesses, so that others, too, could learn to use a frightening and debilitating experience as a springboard for transformation. His Loyal Soldier, however, resisted this idea mightily. In taking on the soldier's role, Jeffrey seemed to shrink as he crouched by the chair he had been sitting in and, wringing his hands, tried to warn his adult self that it was better to stay invisible, better not to call attention to himself. He wasn't big enough to fight back, the worried guardian warned; bullies would beat him up for sure. So persuasive was this old voice that, after hearing the words that had emanated from his own mouth, Jeffrey slumped back into his chair in abject discouragement. "That's what I deal with," he said flatly.

When everyone in the group had spoken the voice of the Loyal Soldier, it was time to take on the role of the Beloved. Once again Jeffrey leaped into character — literally. He walked over to the other side of the large, bright tent we were meeting in and then, bouncing around on the balls of his feet like a basketball pro showing off for the crowds, he waved his arms and beckoned to that shy, resistant self whom he had symbolically left sitting in the chair.

"Hey, Jeffie! Over here, Jeffie! Whatcha waitin' for? Have I got plans for us! Come on, man! You're the only one who can do this, my friend! You've been through hell and come out on the other side, and you've seen the light! Do you know how many other people would love to find what you found, Jeffie? The world *needs* you, my man! So get up off your ass and get on over here and let's get to work!"

It can be exhilarating to give voice and movement to these parts of ourselves that we have avoided for so long. We may be loath to face them at first. We may feel like a fool when we start speaking in their voice. But once we simply turn to them as semiautonomous beings and make an effort to pay attention to what they have to say, we find that they're not so bad after all. Moreover, they are usually more than willing to tell us about themselves — who they are, why we needed them, and what we must do to transform them. Jeffrey was thrilled with the brash, outgoing energy he discovered bubbling forth from his inner Beloved, and by the end of the workshop he was a very different man from the one who had arrived. He realized that he was no longer a small boy who had to protect himself from bullies and that, instead of making himself invisible, he now needed to be as visible as possible. He couldn't wait to get home and start on the projects that he and only he was capable of carrying out.

THE SHADOW IS HARDER TO ILLUMINATE than the Loyal Soldier. In the first place, we have invested a great deal of time, energy, and creativity in keeping the Shadow out of the way, and to acknowledge it is to risk seeing ourselves as the very monster we most hate and fear. Who wants to admit to the inner torturer, the pornographer, the intolerant bully, the lazy bum who would rather spend the evening reading a gothic romance than a professional journal? The entire house we live in could come crumbling down, and we would be left with nothing but dust and the sound of a terrible existential wind rushing through our ears. Moreover, as psychologist Marion Woodman has pointed out, receptivity itself, the state of willingness to let in the new and different, is a problem for many people: "Our society is geared to block reception. Children learn while still very young to block and to pretend.... Bombarded by trivia, and bombarded by heartbreaking images of famine, wars, desecrated nature, [adults] are obsessed with their own defenses."[6] Anything that threatens these defenses, even something that could liberate one and initiate her into a life of passionate involvement with the world, is to be regarded with suspicion by someone who sees a shift in the status quo as a psychic siege. Furthermore, we all have such different Shadows, with such idiosyncratic quirks, that we can't necessarily locate them with a particular tool, as we can often rout out the Loyal Soldier, say, by listening for the voice that wants us to stay small and safe. Looking for the Shadow in people we love to hate works — but only if we're willing to take on what shows up. We can also discover the Shadow in dreams if we're lucky enough to catch hold of some threatening or contemptible figure and brave enough to confront it in the waking world.

When we do make an effort to know the Shadow, we take a big step toward freeing ourselves from an old tyrant who prevents us from fully accepting ourselves and hence from following the path to the Beloved. James Hillman proposes that the "cure" of the Shadow is a twofold problem. First, it is a moral problem: we must recognize what we have repressed and how our repressions have damaged us and others. Second, it is a problem of love: "How far can our love extend to the broken and ruined parts of ourselves, the disgusting and perverse? . . . How far can we build an inner society on the principle of love, allowing a place for everyone?"[7] Once we've identified the dark double, in other words, how do we live with it? Can we, in fact, even make friends with it, so it becomes an ally instead of a terrorist?

It's not an easy task, by any means, but accomplishing it need not be arduous and a task full of pain. Bly suggests boldly reclaiming the Shadow qualities we wish to exile. For instance, a woman who fears the wicked witch of herself could determine which women she knows who may be holding her witch projection (often it's her mother) and then go to them and demand, "You have my witch! I want it back!"[8] Art therapist Linda Jacobson encourages her clients to draw or paint their Shadow from different perspectives, such as incorporating the Shadow into the rest of the persona as they see it or drawing themselves from the Shadow's point of view.[9] As a way not only of recognizing the weird and stifled in ourselves but of actually giving it a promotion, Marsha Sinetar, author of *Do What You Love, the Money Will Follow*, recommends identifying contrarian traits that we may have denied because they don't seem to conform and asking if we might instead take advantage of them. For example:

- Do you have work habits that you may rigidly have suppressed in an attempt to conform and be more like others?

- Do you have personality traits that you . . . initially struggled against, thought were wrong and tried to change or hide?

- Have you stopped trying to achieve something in some "nonsignificant" areas of life because you were once told these weren't important enough to warrant attention?

- Is there a "time-out" activity (like sleeping, watching TV, fishing, listening to music, daydreaming) that gives your work efforts renewed vigor, but which you feel you shouldn't do?[10]

Liz Brensinger, after her disappointing vision quest in the canyon, not only spent months scrutinizing the disdained part of herself, she also wrote a book about her experience and began offering workshops to help others face both personal and cultural Shadows.[11]

As a living symbol to help integrate self and Shadow Robert Johnson has proposed the image of the mandorla. A medieval Christian symbol meant to depict the separate spheres of heaven and earth and the meeting place between them that is the human heart, the mandorla is the almond-shaped segment at the place where two circles overlap. By inhabiting each circle in turn, or each side of two opposing constellations of our being, and then nosing into the place where the opposites join, Johnson suggests, we discover that there was only one circle all along.[12] Michael DeMaria, a psychologist and musician practicing in Pensacola, Florida, has designed an elaborate and effective group ceremonial dance using the image of the mandorla. It takes place at night, sometimes on the beach, and includes drums, candles, and ceremonial gateways to mark the beginning and end of the process. While the drummers (who will later participate in the dance themselves) pound out an incantatory beat, each participant enters one of the two huge, intersecting circles that DeMaria has formed out of rope or drawn in the sand. In each circle, people dance out an opposing part of themselves: the wild artist and the responsible parent, the sex goddess and the good girl, the victimized child and the adult yearning to be free. Only when they have fully explored the contraries in each circle, which often (and significantly) means moving back and forth between them several times, do they enter the mandorla, the place of unity, and dance the dance of resolution.

Bill Plotkin leaped into a transformative mandorla of his own

when he invited a few colleagues to help him confront some shady figures who had recently been besieging his dreams. As he recounts the
story in his book *Soulcraft*, he had had several dreams about thugs
who stole from him and bullied him and treated him with disdain. At
the time these dreams heated up, he was leading a group of men and
women on an underworld journey in the red-rock canyons of Utah.
He asked them to help him reenact the dream scenario and in the
process realized that the thugs actually possessed several qualities that
he admired: "a fierce, no-holds-barred genuineness and the ability to
look the other guy in the eye and speak the plain truth, regardless of
whether it might hurt; their words were from the heart." Bill realized
that he needed to befriend the loving thug of himself, which meant
taking the risk of telling the truth to people "to the best of my ability
and with as much love as I could muster. My job was to *become* that
loving thug, to assimilate him."[13]

As for me, I decided to take on the Pampered Woman who had
been primping and flirting inside my unconscious for so many years
and to spend a day with her. Actually, it was Myrna Loy herself who
gave me the idea.

SITTING THERE IN MY STUDY and attempting a dialogue with her, I
could not help feeling superior, even though I tried not to show it. But
when she told me I should be more like her, I stopped being polite. "I
don't want to be like you," I informed her. "I couldn't bear to be like
you. Look at you. You wear pink high heels with pom-poms, for
God's sake."

"What's wrong with you?" she asked. It was obvious that my
opinion mattered nothing to her. "My clothes are beautiful and sexy."

"Being beautiful is all you care about," I said. "You're shallow and
superficial. You only want to be looked at."

"What are you afraid of?" she demanded saucily. "Do you think
men might find you desirable?"

"I'm afraid they wouldn't know that I'm smart," I admitted. It was a problem I'd wrestled with when I was younger and very pretty. People, men and women both, tended to respond to my looks first; men were attracted to me, and women sometimes didn't like me. It seemed they assumed that a woman who was attractive had to be as preoccupied with her looks as they were. With my tough-guy demeanor and decisive way of speaking, I had tried to let everyone know right off the bat that I was no mere body, but a thinker and doer to be reckoned with.

Myrna laughed. "My goodness, you're silly. They'll find out soon enough that you're smart. A woman has to take advantage of how she looks. She has to take care of her appearance."

"I have better things to do with my time," I informed her.

"I *make* time," she declared. "I couldn't do without my facials and my manicures. I love being admired and noticed. You should try it."

It was a most distasteful suggestion — so I decided to follow it.

EVEN THOUGH I KNEW, both from my own experiments and those of scores of vision questers, the value of taking on aspects of the self as if they were roles in a play, I could not remember ever feeling as loath to do so as when I began to contemplate spending time with Myrna Loy, the Pampered Woman, the Glamorous Movie Star. The more I thought about it, however, the more I had to admit that my scorn hid a secret envy. The truth was that there were times when I wished that I, too, could be a Pampered Woman, with nothing to worry about all day long but looking beautiful and being fussed over, who had no need whatsoever to prove that she was smart and independent. It would be nice to get facials and massages, to enjoy being looked at instead of getting indignant if somebody's head turned my way. I would probably enjoy strolling along Madison Avenue and pausing to look at designer clothes in boutique windows without feeling that only the wares displayed in bookstores and art galleries were up to my standards.

I planned to be in New York the following week, so I decided that instead of filling my schedule as I usually did, by doing business and seeing friends, I would have a date with Myrna.

I arrived in late morning on the appointed day and went first to a friend's apartment, where I would be spending the night. She had left for work, so I had ample time and privacy to prepare for the big event. I had chosen an outfit my Hollywood mentor would have approved of: a 1940s-style forest green suit of smooth polished cotton, with a straight calf-length skirt that flared at the bottom and had a slit up the back. The fitted jacket had a high collar and many small buttons extending down the front. My shoes were high-heeled, lace-up Italian boots that I had bought on a whim and worn just once. I set my hair with rollers, a practice I had given up almost entirely about fifteen years earlier, after I stopped writing and producing multimedia shows, and wore it long with a big tortoiseshell clip. I was ready. I left the apartment and took a subway to Bloomingdale's, where I had made an appointment for a facial and makeup session.

And then, for an hour or more, I, who had always longed for metamorphosis, underwent one, of a kind I had never imagined. I permitted another person — my consultant, she was called; I never got her name — to regard me as nothing more than a face and neck that needed beautifying. In a quiet chrome and mirrored room away from the bustle of the department store, I removed my suit jacket and put on a short white robe. The consultant, a small, thin woman with very short black hair and a serious expression, helped me to lie back on a table covered in crisp white sheets, and then she took over. She slathered on me gooey creams, sandy exfoliants, hot mud, and then removed them with slick oils and warm cloths. She doused me with cool mist. Her hands were silken and firm. I had no idea what any of the potions were or what they were meant to do. I didn't care. I just reveled in them and believed in the magic they were performing. It felt, I confess, wonderful.

When the facial was over, I was helped to sit up, as though a woman of glamour could not be expected to exert herself in common ways. The consultant ushered me to a counter in the main part of the store and quickly departed after passing me along to a woman whose badge identified her as Janine and who sat before a glittering silver and glass display of bottles and jars. Janine was in her late thirties with blond hair and perfectly applied makeup. Her tone was friendly but distracted: she was already scrutinizing my face and plotting her strategy. It was at this point that I began to worry about being seen. What if one of my friends walked past? A client? How would I explain myself? "I don't usually do this sort of thing, but Myrna Loy insisted." Janine clipped a paper bib around my neck and got to work, dabbing and smoothing with concentration. I couldn't help thinking about how this frivolity was taking a lot of time. I should have been at my desk working. I should have been having lunch with an editor. I fought the urge to impress Janine with a witty reference to Psyche searching the Underworld for Proserpine's box of beauty.

At last she was finished. Holding my hair gently out of the way, she unclipped the bib and swiveled the stool dramatically toward the mirror. And then I understood why women spend so much time and money on cosmetics: it is because they make of us a thing to feast our own eyes on. "Beauty is truth," Keats wrote. In modern America, beauty is accreted layers of illusion, and we all know it, but when we see our familiar features so enhanced, we become someone different from the woman we were moments before. And as we step away from the mirror, we believe that the whole world will be just a little bit gladder to see us coming than it would otherwise have been.

I was aware, as I left Bloomingdale's and headed back to the subway, of people looking at me. I was fifty-one years old, and heads were turning my way as they had not done for five years. My old way was to ignore the attention or, if I could, to bury my head in a book. My instinct was to do that now, but I refrained. Instead, I summoned Myrna Loy and drew her up within me like a deep breath. I looked straight ahead. I acted as if I loved being looked at and knew how to handle a little limelight. And to tell the truth, the return of attention now, in my middle age, was a treat. Once, when the looker was a particularly attractive man, I looked back. Our eyes met, and possibilities flickered between us. That experiment was exhilarating. I was almost having fun. It was difficult walking in those high-heeled boots, but I swung along as if I were a model on a runway.

My next stop was the Metropolitan Museum of Art. I flashed my membership card and tapped off to what had always been one of my favorite areas, the medieval wing, with its inward-gazing Madonnas, tapestries of paradisal gardens, coats of armor, and religious icons in ivory, burnished wood, and gold. I had it in mind to indulge in a bit of metaphysical play. Having by this time learned about the code of courtly love between a lady and her knight, I wanted to walk my own inner figurehead, the lady in chrysanthemum yellow, back to her outer, historical setting. I had practiced her walk as well as I could, moving into my life as gracefully and passionately as if the world were my waiting lover. Today, having taken the extra trouble to make myself pleasing to that world, I half expected something magical to happen in the junction between symbolic and literal, past and present. I hoped for a grand synchronicity. It even occurred to me that I might meet, there among the hushed and dimly lit stone walls, a modern knight. An Escort to the Beloved, perhaps. Someone with an important message for me.

It was not to be. I was incapable of giving my full attention to the objects I loved because I was distracted by myself. I'd had to walk several blocks from the subway to the museum, and by this time my feet were killing me. Moreover, the layers of beautification on my face seemed to be hindering my perception. I felt as if my eyeballs themselves, not just my lids and lashes, had been tampered with. My skin longed for air. And I could not stop thinking about how I looked as I stood there, all dressed up and looking at art.

Disappointed, feeling as if I had betrayed something precious, I left the medieval wing and hobbled around the museum for a while, hoping that some other exhibit would capture my interest, but nothing did, and my feet hurt even more. Finally, admitting defeat, I left the museum and minced across the street to the Goethe Institut. In the library I sank into a chair, unlaced my boots, and slid my aching feet into the capacious air of freedom. I spent the next hour there, memorizing "Selige Sehnsucht," "Soulful Yearning," in the original German, and then I took a taxi back to my friend's apartment. By the time she got home from work, I had washed off the makeup and wore a loose summer dress and sandals.

AS PSYCHE AND THE BRAVE SUITORS of fairy tales realize in the course of accomplishing the tasks that will, they hope, win them the hand of their beloved, the willingness itself to undertake these trials is the first step toward making them worthy of their goal. The story of Psyche is a particularly sophisticated portrait of the *psyche*, Greek for soul, or, in psychological terms, the whole Self. At first, Psyche whines and complains as she begins each task: it's too much, it's too scary, she's all alone and helpless. It's as if she's dragged down by subpersonalities all her own. Gradually, however, with the help of allies from the natural world and a growing sense of accomplishment, she stops feeling sorry for herself and simply buckles down to do what must be done. She starts accepting responsibility for the predicament she's in and becomes, by the end of the tale, a mature woman. She realizes that she is a force to be reckoned with. And even she, who has outwitted killer sheep to gather their golden fleece and retrieved a flask of water from the treacherous River Styx, even she is allured off course by the desire to be beautiful. As she makes her way back from the Underworld with the box of beauty that she's managed to obtain from Proserpine, she simply cannot resist taking a peek. She even rationalizes the act she's about to take: she wants to look her best when she's reunited with her beloved, after all, and what does she have in her possession right now but the makeup kit that the goddess of love herself has demanded? So she opens the lid a crack, only to discover that it is not cosmetics in that box, but drugs. The fumes from a powerful sleeping potion waft up and wash over her, and she crumples to the ground. Has Psyche learned nothing? It was her insatiable need to pry that got her into all this trouble to begin with. As readers of the myth, we squirm with frustration when Psyche fumbles her near-success this way.

But we need her fallibility as much as we need her heroism, for none of us ever succeeds in freeing ourselves completely and permanently from those inner characters whose rampant ways cause us so much difficulty. We will fall back into old patterns, though less helplessly and with fewer destructive consequences, for we are infinitely complex mysteries, we humans, with ancient emotional supernovas flaring at the farthest rims of our being. Getting to know just a few of them, and perhaps making friends with them, is the work of a lifetime.

To me Psyche's final act of impetuousness — which, by the way, does not yield the result we might expect (more about that in the next chapter) — now brought a lesson I had never before gleaned in all the years I'd thought about the myth. I realized that, for Psyche, being a warrior does not preclude being a woman glad to seize an opportunity for self-beautification. She has faced all manner of supernatural tribulations, and still she dallies getting home, because she is sidetracked by a new and untried beauty product. Her counterparts meander dreamy-eyed around the sparkling cosmetics counters of Bloomingdale's and a thousand other department stores every day. All of them — all of *us* — are just seeking the magical outer beauty that will enhance the inner beauty we want our Beloved and the world to notice. Beauty and valor are not warring qualities in the mythic Psyche, and nor, from that time forth, would they be in my psyche.

My willingness to accept beauty tips from Myrna Loy did not turn me into an indolent woman addicted to facials, fittings, and perms. But the escapade with glamour had always been intended more as a gesture of reconciliation than as a new regimen to follow, and as such it succeeded. I had made a peace offering to the dark (or rather pink) double I perceived as the superficial female, and she had taught me that certain acts of beautifying the face and body provided sensual pleasure. More important, once I took an honest look at this long-denied aspect of the feminine, I did not have to relegate her back to the closet, along with my high-heeled boots, but instead became more and more fond of her and began to allow her to tutor me in her ways. In the process she shed the specific persona of Myrna Loy and became what I called the Hollywood Star. Like the Myrna of my dream and dialogue, she represented confident, sensuous, sophisticated femininity, but without the flighty imperiousness that the Shadow had exhibited.

My tutorials with the Hollywood Star had some surprising consequences. For one thing, I learned to flirt. When I lived in New York, I had often admired the way many young African American women received male attention: they took it as their due. I would watch them on the subway. Instead of trying to ignore a murmur of appreciation or a long, meaningful look, the way white women usually did, they would turn their heads leisurely to gaze directly at their admirer. Then they might smile, queenlike, in acknowledgment of their beauty and sexuality, or they'd roll their eyes in amused appreciation of the way an erotic charge could sizzle so suddenly between a man and a woman. When I had met and returned the gaze of the man on the street near Bloomingdale's, I'd realized that I, too, could join this harmless mating ritual. So I started allowing myself to exchange probing glances with men, including strangers, friends, and casual acquaintances. I realized that, in such moments, the erotic potential — which could mount so quickly that both of us had to look away — was often accompanied, or even superseded, by something else, a kind of curiosity or fascination. So I began trying out the look on women, too, although that was harder for both of us and could never be sustained as long. When the look endured, however, it was an exquisite thing. The rawness of a soul, fully concentrated in the outward-turning gaze, and meeting, just for an instant, another raw soul, revealed something both exotic and very intimate. The connection between these two ensouled gazes penetrated veils, so each could see the Beloved in the other. Then, in a naked instant of acceptance and desiring curiosity that people usually do not allow into their life, I saw my Beloved in them and their own Beloved shining forth around them.

With the help of the Hollywood Star I made friends with a form of sensuality that was not directly linked to — yet not entirely separate from — sexuality. Dancing to African drums at a large gathering, for example, I became aware that my whole body was engaged in the deep corporeal impulses of the music in a way I had hardly dared to imitate when I took African dance classes in my thirties. After another dance a few years later a drummer confided to me that he'd had a hard time concentrating on his music because he had been so captivated by my sensuous dancing. I had been dancing with the inner Beloved. Besides moving differently, I started dressing differently. I had always liked wearing dresses, but now I found that I was choosing clothes that were plainer and more formfitting, and then embellishing them with soft silk scarves. My style became less eccentric and more, well, not exactly glamorous, but more feminine. I bought *Vogue* when I felt like it. I found a massage therapist near my home and started going to her regularly, relishing the luxury of touch. In my fifties, I finally stopped worrying about proving that I was smart and tough and allowed myself to be beautiful. It should not have been surprising that, not long after confronting the dragon, I received a proposal from the Beloved.

CHAPTER TEN

COURTSHIP OF THE BELOVED

THE PRACTICE OF A PASSIONATE LIFE

A few weeks after my beauty date with Myrna Loy, I had a dream. I was riding in the passenger seat of a pickup truck driven by a young woman about twenty years old. She had a pretty face and long, wavy, dark brown hair. She wore jeans and a yellow sweater, and she had a curvaceous figure that her tight clothes emphasized. She was driving the truck down a long, steep hill, which was bare of trees and shrubbery, although patches of new green grass showed through the mud and the old, slightly dirty snow.

The young woman was driving fast and jinking the truck back and forth just for the fun of it. Anxiously I gripped the armrest on the door. She glanced over and asked, "Is my driving making you nervous?" I fibbed that it wasn't and in that moment realized it was true; I was completely confident that she would get us safely to where we were going. I leaned back to enjoy the ride, which now felt daring and exciting.

At the bottom of the hill preparations were under way for a festival. People were setting up tents of different colors, with banners flapping over them, as if for a medieval tournament. I saw a yellow tent with a blue banner, a white tent with a green and gold banner. There were hundreds, perhaps thousands, of people camping on a big field. We weren't stopping here, though; our destination lay farther ahead.

Then the young woman was no longer with me. A middle-aged man, possibly a cowboy, was driving. He followed a narrow dirt road through the middle of the field, and the crowd thinned until we had left all the people behind. The road ended at a large open meadow, at the edge of which rose a solitary mountain. A man was waiting for me, and I saw that it was Lucas. The truck stopped. I got out and slowly walked toward him. He smiled, happy to see me. When I reached him, I put my arms around him, and he enfolded me in his embrace. I was so relieved to see him, to hold him at last. Bliss flooded me. I needed absolutely nothing else whatsoever.

When the embrace ended, we stepped back to look at each other. In his eyes I saw bottomless love and complete knowledge of who I was, inside and out. This man loved no one but me, and I loved none but him. Joy surged through me, and suddenly I had to have more of him. I pulled him close again, and we both laughed with delight. I could have stayed in his arms forever.

When I awoke, the bliss lingered, for now my conscious awareness knew what my unconscious had gleaned when it produced this dream. I had embraced my Beloved. The dream betokened a coming together of formerly disparate parts of me, and on a level as fundamental as the cracking and locking of tectonic plates to make a continent. What a long journey this subterranean process had been. And yet it could not have happened without extensive above-ground, very conscious effort. The embrace had to be preceded by a long period of courtship. After all, any lover has to win the hand of the beloved.

THIS IS THE LESSON PSYCHE LEARNS. When she succumbed to nosiness by opening Proserpine's box on the way out of the Underworld, she did not lose everything, as we would expect. Instead, she received the favor of divine intervention. Just as she was sinking onto the ground, overcome by the fumes from the potent drugs, Eros himself came to her aid. He swooped down, took her in his arms, and flew off with her. It was as if he recognized that the time had come when perfect completion of the tasks Venus had assigned her was less important than the willingness and persistence she had already shown in her efforts. "Enough is enough," he seemed to say. "You love me and I love you, and now I shall end the separation that is hateful to both of us. I shall come to meet you." Or, as a friend of mine said when he first heard the story, "You never know when grace will suddenly befall you."

Eros took his beloved directly up to Olympus. There Jove (the Roman name for Zeus), ruler of the gods, interceded and persuaded Venus to accept this plucky woman as her son's bride. The gods understood that, in the course of her trials, Psyche had matured. No longer a helpless innocent who must not be permitted knowledge of the holy one in whose arms she lay, she had learned to see both Eros and herself more clearly and hence had become an equal in the partnership. Having accepted responsibility for her actions, she'd gained courage and resilience. Moving toward the life she wanted, she became worthy of that life.

This whole process is the point, writes Erich Neumann in his classic study of the tale, *Amor and Psyche*: "With Psyche's love that bursts forth when she 'sees Eros,' there comes into being within her an Eros who is no longer identical with the sleeping Eros outside her. . . . It is in the light of knowledge, her knowledge of Eros, that she begins to love."[1] The human being, in other words, cannot truly love a god until she becomes conscious of herself as a partner actively engaged in that love. She cannot love the god until she knows that they are two, and that she is the initiator of the acts she takes in relation to him. And then, when she attains that state, the god comes to meet her. Psyche has courted Eros for all she's worth, and he has been won over.

MYTHS ENDURE AND REQUIRE TELLING again and again, because their plots are only partly about the characters who love and fight and shapeshift in them. They are also about us, and the "us" is whoever hears the tales, at any time in any land and, nodding slowly, says, "Yes, that's me, and that's my predicament, and now I perceive how I am part of a greater pattern that was shaped long, long before my time, and in this pattern I can even begin to glimpse something of the course my own situation must take." On the psychospiritual level, the winning of the mythic god-lover symbolizes the blessed union of the ego with the divine self, a process that cannot take place, says Qualls-Corbett, unless one has first tried to understand his or her inner polarities and worked to reconcile them. The first half of our life is an ongoing experiment in discovering who we really are; in chipping away at the encumbrance of parental, cultural, and peer expectations that bind us; and in setting free the authentic self struggling for expression, much as Michelangelo imagined carving the waiting, perfect David from the block of marble that obstructed him. Until we know and accept these often contrary elements of ourselves, after all, we cannot draw them together. They would just mill about the house bickering and trying to manipulate one another like the characters in *All in the Family*.

As Psyche must court Eros for the Olympic union to cohere, so must the striving, soulful-yearning, longing-for-wholeness self court the inner Beloved so that healing and integration may occur. In psychological terms, what I am here calling the "courtship" is a lengthy process that entails fearless probing, honesty, willingness to face the Shadows and Loyal Soldiers, and, one hopes, eventually gathering the pieces of the fragmented self and uniting them into an individual grateful to be grounded in his or her own being. Whether one follows the path of psychotherapy alone, combines it with other forms of personal work, or chooses a more eclectic route to self-discovery, we all still need to court the Beloved. In other words, we need to stoke an active, burning impatience to reach that force that loves us out of our smallness and kisses us into our exuberance. We must constantly seek ways of knowing this being more deeply, expressing its vision more deliberately, and, always and forever, turning our face toward its warmth.

I KNEW A COUPLE, a Swiss woman who led camel caravan trips in the Sahara Desert and a man of the nomadic Tuareg tribe, one of the peoples indigenous to the rocky, windswept desert in what is now southern Algeria and northern Niger. When, after a few years of working together (for the Tuareg it is customary for men and women to have good friends of the opposite sex), they sensed a growing attraction to each other, they had to proceed correctly. They had to redefine their relationship, not by rushing into intimacy and moving in together, but by taking the slow, formal path of courtship that Tuareg culture demands. Each engaged in heart-to-heart conversations with their friends about the merits of the other. She accepted his praise of her beauty and courage as if it were her queenly due. He presented her with a saddle for her camel, the most prized of treasures for a Tuareg, a companion, provider of reliable transport in a challenging land, and, like women and the desert themselves, inspiration for many songs sung around a campfire under the stars. When he asked her to marry him and she accepted, both were entirely ready.

Even though we don't follow such formal courtship rituals in contemporary technological societies, we do court. In fact, courtship is a tactic practiced by anyone who wants to win the affection of another. A lover must be courted — that is, treated with the gallant *courtesy* that one member of a royal court extends to another. The practice of courting, or "wooing," the dove-tongued verb of the Romantic Age, lets the beloved know that the lover takes nothing, most of all the beloved's affections, for granted. The beloved needs to be persuaded of the lover's honor, attractiveness, strength, and charm and of his or her abundant possession of the characteristics most vital for making an ideal parent and helpmate. While unobtrusively emphasizing his or her own best qualities, the lover also dotes on the beloved in countless little ways. The lover prepares meals the beloved will like and gives gifts such as flowers, jewelry, or wine, indulgences to symbolize that the lover values the beloved in ways that far exceed the mundane and practical. In the lover's eyes, everything the beloved does is adorable because it is so new and fresh and original. Small flaws are overlooked, whims catered to. There is nothing the lover won't do to prove the enormity of her love, the respectability of his intentions. A character in one of Dostoyevsky's short novels compares the first ardor of courtship to a kind of bondage: "He probably would have been ready on the spot to do anything, however monstrous and senseless, to satisfy that woman's slightest caprice."[2] Eros streaks tirelessly between two courting lovers, infusing every act and word with magic, for passive loving would extinguish the fire, sure as rain.

THIS IS NO LESS TRUE in the relationship with the divine Beloved, whether we perceive the soul's faithful guide as deity, inner human, or energetic force. We mortals must roll up our sleeves and gather a bouquet of rosebuds to present with a curtsy to the god within, that we may win him or her over and prove that we are ready to dedicate ourselves to a lifetime partnership. However powerful the first encounter with the Beloved, however convinced we are that some ancient question that has vexed our souls is answered at last just by knowledge that the Beloved exists, we must, as Jean Houston insists, develop a solid, workable relationship with this force alluring us into our own authentic self. And that takes the kind of discipline not always welcomed in a culture that values quick satisfaction of its hunger pangs, spiritual as well as physical. The Beloved allures, half-hidden in the dappled shade or high up on the mountain, or she waits for us outside the bank with a violin held victoriously above her head. But if we only stand and hope for the Beloved to come close to us, we will never feel that blissful embrace. We must create ways to keep the bond strong.

Perhaps the best way to determine how to court the Beloved is to ask how we can devote ourselves to what tugs at our heart. Sometimes the tug is a moment's diversion, as it was for the little girl who wanted to stop and smell every daffodil on the block. Sometimes, however, the flowers in question will exude a more soporific perfume, in which case we must investigate if and how we will allow ourselves to fall more fully under their spell. Again, this does not mean being irresponsible or succumbing to excess. The traditional Navajos I spent time with in the late eighties, who were threatened with a law ordering them to vacate their homelands, would not have called what they did courting the Beloved, but they worked passionately and tirelessly to fight for the place that they insisted had been entrusted to them by the creator. Whether that meant hiding their sheep from government agents assigned to cull the herds, forming a human fence with their neighbors, or talking to a white journalist about spiritual beliefs they had previously kept private, they did what it took, because they were acting out of love.

Following allurement, whether it takes us off the path for a moment or a lifetime, often enables us to hear an inner voice that has been trying to get our attention for a very long time. A man I know who is usually very shy and excessively cautious about not making demands on others told me about a small yet bold foray he'd recently made into allurement. When a break had been called during a conference he was attending, he had uncharacteristically allowed himself to fall into conversation with the woman sitting next to him. An intense, honest, and inspiring dialogue unfolded over the next few minutes, unlike anything he had ever experienced. "This is the energy of the Beloved," he said excitedly. "There were a couple of times when we were talking when I almost held back, but then I thought, no, the Beloved would say go ahead, and so I did. I think this kind of union happens to me more now that I am carrying the energy of the Beloved."

To consciously carry this energy and to draw from it, as pure water from a deep well, is to court the Beloved. And as long as we maintain our footing in the real world and do not use the Beloved as a kind of emotional opium pipe, a source of endless fantasy to remove us from the concerns and responsibilities of life, we can tap into this energy whenever we wish. Contacting the Beloved regularly throughout the day, sometimes to ask advice, sometimes simply to evoke that erotic presence, is a way of wooing that has not only obvious short-term benefits (resolution of dilemmas, source of comfort) but also the long-range advantage of constantly reinforcing the bridge between us and our highest knowledge and wisdom. When I had difficulty making a decision or felt troubled by something, I often offered the problem to the Beloved, and the response was almost always immediate: whatever aroused a flare of passionate energy in me was the path I had to take. This was not always the option I would have preferred. Sometimes the Beloved said, "Be honest. Confront," when I would rather have heard, "Let it go, it's not that important." Or, considering whether I ought to stay at my desk and persevere with a writing project or drive an hour to Scranton to do volunteer work for a political campaign, I could feel in my body the magnetic pull of the need for activism, not at the expense of my other work, but in the midst of it, because it entailed acting on my beliefs.

Taking time to walk with the Beloved is an act of courtship. My college friend Melissa Werner walked every day with her Casizza, using the occasion to dialogue with her insightful, compassionate animus and to ask his advice about all manner of circumstances in her life. Melissa walked in a city park, following the trail and setting a brisk pace, her attention wholly focused on the labyrinthine twists of the dialogue itself. Another way of walking is to allow nature to provide the bends and byways. The magnetic force of allurement is constantly at work in the natural world. Setting out without a goal, emptying the mind of distractions, and simply paying attention to what provokes interest or curiosity along the way, we let our psyche know that we are willing to be seduced. Even if we consent to spending only a moment or two with the smooth stones, forked trees, purple wildflowers, shaggy coyote scat, or whatever forms, patterns, and sounds romance our attention, we close the gap between our own singular, blinkered agenda and the possibility of merging with the amazing and unpredictable other. When the conscious mind discovers how good we are at zeroing in on what beckons along a nature trail, it grasps that, yes, this human being really does know how to follow allurement. Suddenly we seem to have both the permission and the skill to start heeding invitations of the intellectual, social, and spiritual kinds as well.

Walking in the natural world not only brings us into alignment with allurement, it also subtly, and through the ploy of fascination, teaches us a fresh way of regarding others in this shared world. Rilke defined it as seeing as empathy, rather than seeing as inspection. To inspect a frog in a pond is to dissect it with the mind. Then the frog is a thing to be viewed only as some quantity isolated from the human, the imperial bystander who stands above and outside it. To see the frog with empathy is to fall under its spell. Then the frog, or whatever draws the attention, asks, in Rilke's words: "Are you free? Are you ready to dedicate your whole love to me?"[3] If we can honestly answer, *Yes!* then the imagination, the senses, and the heart accept the gesture of frog hospitality and happily enter frogdom. Rilke's contemporary, the French poet and chronicler of the inner life of *things*, Francis Ponge, wrote that we cannot truly see something until we approach it, not as a superior, but as an equal capable of startling us with the marvel of its selfhood. "It is necessary for things to disarrange you," says Ponge.[4]

Lillian, a sixty-seven-year-old sculptor and grandmother who attended one of the first Beloved workshops I offered, found herself rapturously disarranged by a meadow in June. During the imagery session to meet the Beloved, Lillian had encountered a sensuous man wearing a tuxedo and pressing close to her, like a partner in a waltz. When the group split up to take solo walks with the Beloved, she wandered down a country road and before long felt the urge to step off the macadam and into a meadow of wildflowers and long grasses. At first she resisted the impulse, afraid that someone would see her and assume that she was senile or crazy or merely a trespasser. However, this was a Beloved workshop, and so she followed the allurement. Immediately upon stepping off the road, she began to feel excited and daring. Trailing her fingers through the grasses, stooping to smell the flowers, she experienced an awakening of all her senses. She thought about how every summer, for more years than she could recall, she had yearned for a special companion who would lie in the grass with her, for this one act seemed to her the culminating expression of romance, sensuality, play, and the willingness to be deliciously lost. Her husband, a business executive, was not at all interested in the types of inner work Lillian thrived on, and, as she liked to joke, she had long since given up trying to convert him. Now, she realized, the Someone she had longed for had arrived, or rather, had been with her all along: it was her tuxedo-clad dance partner. She lowered herself down into the meadow. The grasses bent and bowed over her, the clouds bloomed and skimmed each other in the blue sky. Insects and birds sang all around her. To her surprise, erotic feelings rippled through her body. She realized that gratification of her need for a sensual engagement in nature did not depend on the company of her husband or anyone else, and that, from that time forth, she always had someone to lie with in a summer meadow.

Another woman I know courts the Beloved through an ever-changing altar that reflects the concerns waxing and waning in her life. During a cold, snowy February, for example, the altar was dedicated to the garden she would plant in the spring. She covered the surface in green velvet and on it arranged pictures from seed catalogs, a plan she'd drawn for the garden's design, a packet of seeds, and, in a small glass vase, a forsythia twig, its buds still tight with winter. Later she changed the focus to reflect her enthusiasm for her volunteer work in an animal shelter. Another time it was the focal point of her hopes and prayers for a friend undergoing chemotherapy. In this way she took her own passions seriously and sanctified them by offering them up as the center point of her spiritual life, symbolized by the altar where she prayed and meditated. Then, sanctified, they became even more serious.

We can consciously usher ourselves into a life of growing vitality and delight by respecting our bodies, by facing up to addictive, self-destructive behavior like smoking, drinking too much, eating junk food, or wasting long hours in front of the television. Caitlín

Matthews suggests several ways to nurture a relationship with a healthy daimon, including maintaining friendships with supportive people, taking care to distinguish between the human lover and the daimon, acknowledging and using personal power, and "letting go control and allowing passion to motivate creativity" in many and diverse ways.[5] Thomas Moore advocates drawing, writing, and keeping a journal as ways "to meet the soul, aflame with desire, on its own terms."[6]

NO MATTER HOW FIERY THE SOUL, however, no matter how ardent our acts to meet and fan it brighter still, we are all bound to suffer a drenching now and then. Some bold enterprise fails, a promising love withers, we have a bad day. Regular practices (taking walks, erecting altars) that were satisfying and meaningful when we first inaugurated them degenerate to rote. When the gestures become empty, it is easy to mistake the symptom for the ailment and to conclude that it is the Beloved him- or herself that has ceased to be of value. Infusing the courtship with fresh, creative approaches is the way to make it meaningful again, and also to keep ourselves enchanted with the process of becoming our most fully realized selves.

This makeover of the relationship with the soul companion need not be an expensive, demanding, or time-consuming process. Taking a different route to work, reversing the order of the morning routine, getting up half an hour earlier, or ordering something that we've never had off the menu jolts passivity into wide-eyed curiosity. Stepping away from the overly familiar, we come home to the extraordinary of ourselves and our world. Hasidic texts teach that although the soul is concentrated in the body, it is not restricted there but extends far and wide. Parts of the soul can be found in our belongings and even in places and objects that have not yet come into our life. Consider this as you go about a presumably ordinary day: perhaps a piece of your soul lies in wait for you somewhere. What if you left it behind because you weren't paying attention?

Another exercise, almost always guaranteed to produce interesting results, is to state to yourself, "Today I am going to have an important encounter with somebody." All day long you will be monitoring your meetings with friends, acquaintances, and strangers, wondering if this is It. You will be a bit more outgoing than usual, ask a few more questions, or reveal something that you might otherwise have kept to yourself. As you move through your tasks, your focus will be pointing here and there like sensitive antennae, gauging what is potentially juicy and delicious. By the end of the day you will probably have had that encounter; you will certainly have lived all your waking hours as a magician who coaxed wonder to burst from the ordinary.

A profound though sometimes difficult way to court the Beloved is to woo him through others. This does not mean flirting with everyone you meet; it simply means expanding the boundaries of the Beloved and actively seeking her or his manifestation in others. It is a two-way experiment, like perceiving yet another pane of glass embedded in that metaphysical mirror the troubadour gazed into to see both his own ideal face and the idealized face of his lady. For even as you attempt to glean a bit more of your own soulful radiance through your relationships with others, you are attentive to discerning ever new aspects of inner beauty and strength emerging in them. You are looking in their eyes, at their gestures and the way they sit, how they express themselves, and what they like to talk about, how they have chosen to spend their life for evidence of their own soulful yearning, or for what physicist Fred Alan Wolf calls God: "those parts of [their] world that are somehow transcendent or sublime."7

Neither of these exercises in compassionate scrutiny is easy, especially if the person in question is someone you really don't even want to like. These very people, however, may be the ones most worthy of the effort, for seeking the divine Beloved in them liberates your comprehension of who and what the Beloved is. And even people with whom you seem to have nothing in common, those with different spiritual or political values, different backgrounds or concerns, or, more personally, those who have hurt or angered you — even they long to be joyful, to be relieved of painful burdens and gifted with some blessing. Everyone has suffered and struggled throughout life and longs to be loved actively and sweetly. Morton T. Kelsey, an Episcopal priest and counselor, notes that the expanded outlook of love, in which the heart and the gaze are finely focused on the same object, leads to "a quiet ecstasy, in which we look at the world from God's perspective, and it has something of the quality of divine humor and joy about it."[8] Unlike some theologians, who see love moved by Eros as inferior to the God-centered love of agape, Kelsey believes that it is very hard to love generously and charitably until one has first burned with the longing and desire of Eros.

Valerie Wilkinson, a woman who took one of my workshops and with whom I began to correspond about this subject, believes that to truly incorporate the divine Beloved into life, one must "differentiate and articulate each individual relationship across the whole spectrum of luminous soulful energy, from the base to the subtle, and that this work will forge arcs of light between souls." The light of the Beloved would then be a palpable spiritual energy experienced by those in whom it shines. She wrote:

> *Many people feel there can only be one relationship — and maybe I think there can only be one physical (erotic) relationship — at least that is all I can or want to do. But real, interactive spiritual relationships that participate in the Divine Beloved can be multiple — and this is not virtual — all of the ones I have are with people whom I've met, shared a meal with, talked with, experienced as souls in some sense, like feeling their energy, knowing the sound of the voice. The Divine Beloved instructed me to expect to meet him, not only in my [human] beloved, but in others, known as Him by the inner recognition and the timing.*[9]

It takes daring to court the Beloved, no doubt about it. You must be prepared to go after what you want, what your whole soul knows holds the resonance it needs to make it sing. An extraordinary Inuit tale tells of a young woman who turned down one proposal of marriage after another, and finally, because she was all alone and contrary, moved off to the edge of the village to live in a tiny house by herself. One day, far across the snow, she saw a stranger walking, and her heart leapt. "That's him!" she thought, and took off after him. But as she chased him, the man walked faster. "Wait!" called the woman. "Wait!" He ran faster and faster until he was no longer a man at all, but a polar bear, a white streak gliding over white ice. "Wait!" called the woman. The polar bear dove into the sea, and the woman dove in after him. He emerged and kept on running. "Wait! Wait!" Once again he dove into the sea, and once again she followed. But this time, thousands of fish pulled her down and devoured her, and when she finally emerged, she was nothing but a skeleton. Once again, more alone than ever, she returned to her tiny house at the edge of the village.

The story ends happily. After many more days of loneliness and isolation, the skeleton woman receives a visit from a shaman who helps her to dance herself back into her body. The two of them then clasp hands and leap into his drum and, presumably, into a life of mutual respect for what makes each of them quirky, wonderful, and thoroughly lovable. For me, one of the many vital points of this rich feast of a story is the woman's determination to wait for the One who called to her soul and then to go to any lengths to get him. Is the shaman at the end of the story the same being as the stranger/polar bear? Was the woman being tested? Certainly she had to become unfleshed, to lose all her old ideas about who she was in order to be purified and pared down for the new, her true Beloved who guided her into the one dance she had been waiting all her life to move to.

COURTING THE BELOVED is courting your own engagement with life, no matter what your economic circumstances, state of health, marital status, or prior experience are. Courting the Beloved is ceasing to hold back out of fear and taking a risk to go for what you long for. If it doesn't work, it doesn't mean you failed or that the cause was wrong. Meanwhile, you have gotten yourself dressed up in all your finery for the Beloved, you have courted him or her, and you have declared yourself ready to engage fully in the partnership. Courting the Beloved blends opposites in the soul, as courting a real-life lover puts the assets of both in the best possible light. We discover, then, freedom in enthrallment, purity in wild passion, finding the self in the midst of getting lost in the Mystery. Courting the Beloved is choosing, over and over, to be more fully and gladly a part of the world. This is the path chosen by ascetic Jews who deliberately exile themselves to follow the Shechinah. Roaming as she roams, they devote their whole life to the search for the missing holy half that is God, the creator, the origin. The reunion will come, says the Kabbalah, only in the hour of redemption, but meanwhile, these rootless seekers know *hitlahavut*, ecstasy, for their souls are inflamed with love for God.[10]

AS WE MOVE *TOWARD* THE BELOVED, courting what allures, what evokes passion in us, what opens the heart to compassion and the soul to fearless joy, we *become* the one the Beloved loves. The journey, then, is a passage into becoming, as if we were constantly taking on a more and more delicately refined and luminous version of ourselves. We English speakers do not have a way of understanding this process that is innate to our culture. Our grammatical tenses leap like grasshoppers from past to present to future, so we tend to see movement as a series of discrete steps — 1, 2, 3, 4, and so on. The Hopis, however, have a tense with which to speak of the passage of things from one state to another. It is called *tunatya*, and it refers specifically to the process of something rounding into its fullness. I first heard about this subtle force of unfolding from a Hopi man who participated in the complex cycle of ceremonies enacted in his village throughout the agricultural year. "The kachinas that come from the San Francisco Peaks to the villages," he said, "come bringing the power of all that is germinating and coming to life. This power is in the clouds that hold the rain. It's in the seeds of the corn that we plant in the soil, and in the peaches growing on the tree. When you and I sit and talk right here in this house, that power of growth is in the words we haven't spoken yet. Everything the creator has given us is moving into its ripeness."[11] The kachinas, otherworldly figures who dance into the mesa-top villages wearing elaborate costumes and wooden masks, with turtle-shell rattles tied to their legs and bells on their deer-hide cloaks, and eagle plumes and sprigs of spruce on their headdresses, are manifestations of this *tunatya* energy of the cosmos, and they are bearers and spreaders of it throughout the village.

The Chinese martial art tai chi also exemplifies the flowering from potential to kinetic. In the moment before one begins to practice the form, he stands at the ready, in a state of *wu chi*. The instant he begins to move, possible becomes actual, becomes tai chi. We are all in this state of becoming at all times, on every level, cellular and circumstantial, physical and emotional. We are constantly plumping into the next phase of our ripeness, as the seed in the ground becomes the sprout, and the sprout becomes the stalk, becomes the flowering plant becomes the leaf enfolding the nubbin of a bud that rounds into the flower that falls to the ground to make room for the fruit. If we ever reached stasis, we would stagnate. That is why the Beloved must remain a dancing, elusive figure, always teasing us by calling us forth, only to step lightly out of our grasp as soon as we reach him. He must keep us germinating. If he stopped and waited for us to catch up and then just clasped us forever in his fond embrace, the essential fuse of our being would simply fizzle out.

Hence we court the Beloved, rather as the Hopis honor and evoke the subtle powers of the universe through their ceremonies, turning our energy in the direction of fruitfulness and growth. The effort itself waters the fertile ground. Furthermore, the transformation we perceive happens not just symbolically, but even on the physiological level. In fact, as Candace Pert and other scientists have shown, physiological states effect change in mental states, and vice versa. Peptides and the neurotransmitters they latch onto carry "informational chemicals" related to the whole vast range of emotions, from addiction to love of a child to a sense of victimhood. Habitual emotional responses to situations actually form entrenched pathways between neuronal transmitters and cells. However, when we break one pattern, such as the conviction that we must remain small and invisible, and begin to imprint a new one, such as behaving as if we are bigger and braver than we really believe we are, the chemistry of the body changes in response.[12]

This mind-body dialogue corresponds to the human-daimon feedback loop Apuleius perceived eighteen hundred years ago. Of one's ability to perceive the reality of the daimon, he wrote: "A divine nature is *immediately* present with all things but all things are not immediately present with it; because aptitude in the participant is here requisite to an union with that which is participable."[13] What this emphatic but somewhat slippery sentence means is that the daimon is right there, it exists, but you won't see it unless you take the time to look for it. And if you don't take the time to look for it and to seek out its companionship, to accept its bountiful gifts, then certainly you will have a poorer relationship, and fewer gifts. Hence, deliberate efforts to strengthen a relationship with the Beloved result in the presence of the Beloved becoming more tangible, the Beloved's direction clearer. Responding, we become more active participants in our lives, which inclines us to enhance our connection with the Beloved. Tohil, the one-legged Mayan fire deity who twirls around in his own sandal like a fire drill-stick, expressed this same truth when he remarked of the humans who were yearning for his gift: "Isn't it their heart's desire to embrace me? I, who am Tohil? But if there is no desire, then I'll not give them their fire."[14]

And when the desire of the person and the fire of the god come together, sacred union blazes.

CHAPTER ELEVEN

"Your Fullness Is My Delight"

THE CEREMONY OF SACRED MARRIAGE

One Saturday at the end of February, the first warm weekend after a long, cold, snowy winter, twenty-six men and women journeyed with the Beloved in a comfortable, spacious room in a stone retreat center outside Chicago. As the workshop participants sat in pairs around the room exploring their relationships with Escorts to the Beloved, walked over the prairie and adjoining woods with the Beloved, and shared their stories in a talking staff council, three wedding parties made their way up the hill to the nondenominational chapel nestled in the woods. Brides stepped delicately, self-conscious of their beauty and the extravaganza of lace and silk billowing around them. Bridesmaids, a colorful flow of giggles and importance, came next, with family and friends taking up the rear, smiling through the solemn, unfamiliar formality. It was a delightful accompaniment to our work.

For a culture that pays little heed to rites of passage, the wedding ceremony remains one of paramount importance. Even weddings performed by justices of the peace, featuring only the bride and groom in attendance and entailing little disruption of the daily routine, are remembered forever, and the choice to hold that kind of wedding over any other kind becomes part of the story that is told throughout the couple's life. Little girls dream about their wedding day long before they even begin to develop an interest in boys. Entire magazines are published about weddings and cover all the details of the event, from clothes, to catering, to etiquette, to suggestions for where to go on the honeymoon. Everyone imagines a wedding as a kind of salvation, when the inner, beautiful self will step forth into the warmest and most generous of all possible embraces. In Toni Morrison's novel *Beloved*, Sethe rallies from her disappointment after learning that an escaped slave girl is not entitled to any sort of wedding, and she makes up her mind that she will at least have a wedding gown:

> So I took to stealing fabric, and wound up with a dress you wouldn't believe. The top was from two pillow cases in [her employer's] mending basket. The front of the skirt was a dresser scarf a candle fell on and burnt a hole in, and one of her old sashes we used to test the flatiron on.... Finally I took the mosquito netting from a nail out the barn. We used it to strain jelly through. I washed it and soaked it the best I could and tacked it on for the back of the skirt. And there I was, in the worst-looking wedding gown you could imagine. Only my wool shawl kept me from looking like a haint peddling. I wasn't but fourteen years old, so I reckon that's why I was so proud of myself.[1]

We all recognize that a wedding betokens a permanent shift in the relationship between two individuals. From the time I was a teenager I had staunchly adhered to my position that marriage would inevitably lead to boredom and a stifling of my freedom. Nevertheless, from the moment Andy and I decided, nearly five years after we'd begun seeing each other, that we would get married, I never once regretted or doubted the decision. In fact, from that moment on, I felt a change in how I thought about the two of us. It was as if I had been spinning all my life around a sun in my own private universe and now, quite suddenly, a big orbital jolt had shot Andy and me together into the whirl of a common heavenly body, and that was the body of an Us. Couples who get married or hold ceremonies of commitment are stating that they honor and uphold the shared entity of the Us. This is a big event, which is why, as the minister or rabbi or justice of the peace is likely to remind the pair who stands there at the altar, it is "not to be entered into lightly." There was something tawdry about Britney Spears marrying her boyfriend "just for the hell of it" in Las Vegas and then, as if sobering up, taking steps to get the marriage annulled just hours later.

The wedding ceremony is sacred, it is "holy matrimony." When people marry, they do so before friends and loved ones, and the god of their understanding is asked to bless the union. The epithalamium, a poem written at least since Sappho's time to celebrate a wedding, includes supplications to the gods to bring their special favors to the event. The most famous epithalamium is that written by Edmund Spenser for his own wedding in 1595. In it the poet calls on the god of the sun and goddess of the moon; Hymen, god of marriage; and "great Juno, which with awful might / The lawes of wedlock still dost patronize," among a host of nymphs and other benevolent spirits, to bless the holy day and shower prosperity and happiness upon the couple. In D. H. Lawrence's novel *The Rainbow*, Tom Brangwen, a stolid man of the land who sometimes finds it difficult to express the magnitude of his feelings, tries to make a toast at his daughter's wedding that will convey his belief that a man needs a woman, and a woman needs a man, to be who they really are: "There's no marriage in heaven, but on earth there is marriage," he begins. Plowing along, he brings himself and the assembled guests to the touching conclusion that "a married couple makes one Angel. . . . If I am to become an Angel, it'll be my married soul, and not my single soul."[2]

Even if Brangwen is right, and "there is no marriage in heaven," we have always needed not only to invite the gods to our weddings, but to provide marriages for them in heaven as well. Indeed, humans have celebrated the ecstatic union of the gods long before anyone married for romantic love, and when women were but valuable property to be transferred from the keeping of their father to that of their husband for a good price. Some of the most beautiful words ever uttered or carved praise the union of divine forces coming together in love and desire. The story of Inanna, the Sumerian goddess of heaven and earth, the oldest written myth known, was inscribed beginning in the third millennium B.C.E. on clay tablets. It tells of the goddess's coming of age, empowerment, and, ultimately, her descent into the Underworld to attain her true queenly maturity. But it is the eroticism of the epic, suffusing the songs from the "Courtship" cycle, that has the power to moisten heavy clouds, birth healthy young from the wombs of sheep, tease green shoots out of dark soil, sweeten milk, make bread to rise, and move women and men to turn to each other with desire coursing through their blood. Inanna has sought her bridegroom in terms that unmistakably unite the sexual and agricultural:

Who will plow my vulva?
Who will plow my high field?
Who will plow my wet ground?

Her choice is Dumuzi the shepherd, and on their wedding night the fecund potential of growing things receives its potentiating spark as the goddess enters into lovemaking with the man of the earth and soil. Inanna sings:

Before my lord Dumuzi,
I poured out plants from my womb.
I placed plants before him,
I poured out plants before him.
I placed grain before him,
I poured out grain before him.
I poured out grain from my womb.

... My high priest is ready for the holy loins.
My lord Dumuzi is ready for the holy loins.
The plants and herbs in his field are ripe.
O Dumuzi! Your fullness is my delight!"[3]

Sumerian scholar Samuel Noah Kramer, who worked with story-teller Diane Wolkstein on the translation of the epic, says that the song was part of the sacred marriage rite in which the king of a Sumerian city symbolically wed the goddess Inanna, represented by the high priestess. The sacred marriage bed was ritually prepared, and the ceremony took place "to the accompaniment of merriment and such songs as those in 'The Courtship.' "4

The *Song of Songs*, written down in about 100 B.C.E., celebrates the union of Solomon, builder of the great temple in Jerusalem, and a beautiful, alluring woman who is a blend of goddess, sister, earth spirit, and bride to him. Sometimes the woman in the poem is said to be the Shechinah, or perhaps one of the local goddesses of the Middle East, who continued to make their influence felt among the early Jews even as monotheism gained hold. In any case, these verses link human eroticism not only with the flourishing of the natural world but also with the architectural and military vigor of a culture. The bridegroom sings:

Behold, you are beautiful, my love, you are beautiful. Your eyes are doves behind your veil. Your hair is like a flock of goats, moving down the slopes of Gilead.

Your teeth are like a flock of shorn ewes that have come up from the washing, all of which bear twins, and not one among them is bereaved.

Your lips are like a scarlet thread, and your mouth is lovely. Your cheeks are like halves of a pomegranate behind your veil.

Your neck is like the tower of David, built for an arsenal, whereon hang a thousand bucklers, all of them shields of warriors. (4:1–4)5

For millennia, worshipers have enacted sacred marriage ceremonies as a way of coaxing the cosmic generative forces to continue, at least for another season, and of implicating themselves in the whole pregnant process. Spring was the season for fecundity rites, for the fields and vineyards that had lain fallow over the winter now had to be seduced into blooming again. In Greece, Sumeria, Egypt, Turkey, Africa, and Britain, villagers gathered to plow the furrows and sow the seeds, offer prayers to the forces of germination, and celebrate the heavenly marriage. In this high holy ceremony, or *hieros gamos*, when a mortal man wed a manifestation of the goddess, or a mortal woman joined with a manifestation of the god, the moment of cosmic birth thundered forth once more, taking the whole world with it. Above seeded below. In Babylon, the daughters of noble families served as sacred prostitutes in the temple of Anahita, the moon goddess, to whom they dedicated the first fruits of their womanhood. In Lydia, initiates of Cybele, the great goddess of the Iron Age, received a ceremonial meal and drink, after which, according to ancient records, they "bore the sacred vessel" containing grains and fruits and symbolizing the womb of the Great Mother and then "entered into the bridal chamber," where they made love with a stranger.[6] Thus the woman dedicated her virginity to the goddess, and the man consummated his own yearning to become one with the divine feminine life force. This practice, which may strike modern people as degrading, was in fact a high honor, for the woman's purpose in the union, writes Nancy Qualls-Corbett, "was to worship the goddess in love-making, thereby bringing the goddess' love into the human sphere."[7] After serving her term as a novitiate to the goddess, the woman returned home and made a good marriage. Another kind of sacred marriage took place between the chief priestess of the temple, who had chosen not to be a wife in the conventional sense, but to give herself ritually and yearly in "marriage" to a king representing the potent male principle. In this act all opposites joined together in conjugal harmony: earth and heaven, male and female, death and rebirth, moist and dry, hard and soft, summer and winter.

ANY CEREMONY IS AN ACT OF CONCRETIZING one's movement from an existing state of being to another state of being that nears but is not yet at hand. A ceremony is like an intentional enactment of the Hopi principle of *tunatya*. It lassos our expectations of an imminent transformation with our current readiness to assume all the attendant responsibilities and powers of that transformation. Through ceremony, we call down into our whole being the altered state we feel drawing us on, and we do so in a manner that symbolically mimics the essential patterns of the new way. D. M. Dooling, cofounder and coeditor of *Parabola*, notes in the issue devoted to the theme of ceremony that when we are ready to make some big transition in life, we need all the help we can get. We need witnesses, intercessors, guides to the process. "Real help, real blessing," Dooling says, "can come only when what is real in the human reaches for the highest in himself and something higher than himself."[8]

That's why so many people choose to get married in a ceremonial way, so that as many loving, benevolent, joyful forces as possible can be mustered to usher the potential into the actual. When Andy and I got married, in an eclectic ceremony that took place in a Quaker meeting hall in New York City, officiated by a leader of the Ethical Culture Society from Teaneck, New Jersey, and comprised a mix of our own words and thoughts and the traditional wedding vows of the Episcopal Church I'd grown up in, we turned and spoke to the assembled group about our decision to have them present instead of simply getting married at City Hall, as we'd briefly discussed. Such an event was so important, we said, that we wanted to share it. It was too big for two people to contain. And we needed the support of those we loved and who loved us to bind us to the commitment we were making to each other. By creating a beautiful wedding, we, like billions of other couples around the world, hoped to create a beautiful marriage.

A ceremony — whether it be a sacred marriage ceremony or any other kind — need not be complicated to be profound. It doesn't even have to involve other people. Indeed, some of the most beautiful ceremonies I've ever heard of have been enacted by people who thought they knew nothing about ceremonies and who, on their vision quest or a solo walk during a workshop, suddenly knew not only that a ceremony was called for, but how they must enact it. Usually all it takes to get the process started is some idea of the transitional movement that is occurring or about to occur, the passage from one state to another — from childhood to adulthood, say, or from always following the dictates of others to claiming one's autonomy, the movement of entering a new phase of responsibility at work, closing the door to marriage and taking up the life of a single person, or beginning elderhood. In correspondence to the emotional or spiritual passage, the progress of the ceremony usually entails some kind of physical movement: walking from the darkness of the forest, say, to the light of a clearing; calling in a part of oneself, acting it out, and ushering in its transformation; or battling a demon and then, having triumphed, taking up a warrior's staff. In their preparation handbook for people embarking on vision quests, Steven Foster and Meredith Little list many symbolic acts that express an inner turning point: "burying, burning, smashing, changing name, bathing, crossing thresholds, masks, vows, cutting flesh or hair, heaping stones, aligning stones, chanting, use of sacred pipe, rattling, singing, being silent, changing clothes, use of candles or fire, nakedness, dancing, exchanging gifts, self-purification, tying or untying knots, smudging, sprinkling, playing an instrument, praying."[9]

Actual physical gestures seem to convey to the whole body, mind, and spirit that we are serious about this transition we're making. When a woman who had long hidden her homosexuality from her husband, friends, and grown children crawled out of the sharp, dense, brittle manzanita thicket she had chosen to represent the conditions of her existence and stood, tall and jubilant, to proclaim her identity in the midday sun, she felt years of silence, shame, and heartache fall away from her. The ceremony was bigger than the symbolic act she took; it recognized, reimagined, and intensified who she had been, how determined she was to change, and what she was going to feel like as a result. And even though we may plan the basic course the ceremony will take and have an idea of the desired outcome, we are often assisted in our efforts in surprising ways. A lizard sits still on a rock during the entire time that a woman unburdens herself of an old and painful secret that she has never revealed to any living being. In the midst of a man's private farewell to the woman he is divorcing, his walking stick cracks in two, and he is pierced by awareness of the unhealthy dependence on his soon-to-be-ex-wife that has propped him up for thirty years. A rainbow arcs through the sky at the end of a sacred marriage ceremony. We never know what serendipitous events will occur to indicate that the gods really are listening and enthusiastically applauding our efforts.

People sometimes enact sacred marriage ceremonies during their vision quest as a way of solidifying a more trusting relationship between soul and conscious self; to put behind them a real-life partnership that they have been unable to let go of, even though it has long since ceased to work; or simply because, at last, some small miracle has occurred and they have fallen in love with the divine in themselves. Wishing to solemnize the occasion and consecrate the union, they transform their solo spot to wedding chapel, trousseau, guest list, and reception hall, all in one. They adorn themselves with whatever finery they have on hand (one woman cut the straps off her lace chemise and draped it over her head as a bridal veil) and gather a bouquet of wildflowers. They invite the rivers and trees, the ravens and cicadas to be their guests and witnesses, and they might ask a tree or a particularly alluring rock to stand in as the bride or bridegroom. Many recite the traditional wedding vows or make up variations to suit the occasion. After the ceremony, there may be a celebration — pine needle confetti tossed into the air, a dance or song led by the newly joined pair, a water toast offered to the assembled guests, rooted, winged, and mineral. The woman who elevated her underwear to a bridal veil modified it further after the ceremony by cutting it up into small squares with her pocket knife, filling the squares with the petals from her wedding bouquet, tying them with cord, and presenting the little "medicine bundles" to her fellow vision questers and the guides upon her return to base camp.

Among the boons of a sacred marriage ceremony he performed during a vision fast in the California desert, a friend and colleague of mine, Peter Scanlan, discovered self-forgiveness, healthy self-love and acceptance, and the ability to love others (and express it to them) more readily. Peter had decided to take time to be alone with nature because he needed to resolve a conflict that was festering deep within himself. Two years earlier, he had fallen in love with a woman who had long been his friend and had kept the ensuing affair with her a secret from the woman who had been his partner for many years. Although he had finally told her the truth, and they were now in the process of separating, Peter's joy in his new relationship was sullied by feelings of guilt and shame for how he had treated his partner. Feedback from friends just before he set out for the fast and some important dreams told him clearly that the time had come to stop living the life of an immature boy unwilling to accept the consequences of his acts and to start embodying his mature masculine self, that only then would the goddess of himself, the divine Beloved, come to meet him.

During his time alone, Peter decided to hold a sacred marriage ceremony. He spent hours preparing: calling in the presence of women he knew and respected to serve the goddess, creating an altar, and dressing in symbolic clothing, including a soft scarf given him by a woman friend, medals representing both the goddess and his medicine name, his father's wedding ring, and a black flag printed with the word *Courage*, which he tucked into his belt. He smudged the altar with sage, wrote a poem to the goddess, and then simply waited nervously, like a bridegroom. "I knew that she was ready," he later wrote to me and his other friends, "when I saw the pink and blue hues of her gown in the sky and [the moon's] shining silver luminosity. I knew that the masculine sun energy was present in her reflected light, which softened it and made it possible to look at it."

Peter greeted the goddess in her celestial form, praised her many beauties, and thanked her for waiting so long for him. He read aloud to the goddess the poem he had written to her, and then they exchanged vows of commitment:

I, as goddess, to the mature adult masculine of myself; I, as the masculine, to the goddess dark feminine mystery of myself. I took my father's wedding ring, which I have worn on my little finger for a year, and placed it on the chain I wear around my neck that holds the two medals. The ring joins them in the circle of wholeness. Together we sang my song of the story of the love of the ancestors (a song I had received from the birds earlier in the fast). I thanked all who had come to witness. I called for the feast, throwing bits of dried fruit in all the directions after she and I had taken a tiny morsel of each: apple, apricot, and prune. It was a communion, representing nourishment of body, soul, and spirit and the joining of all of us as one.

Then it was time to party, to dance. First, a waltz, and we danced to the Tennessee Waltz. We boogied to the Rolling Stones: "Can't Get No Satisfaction," transforming the words to "Am getting a lot of satisfaction." Finally a polka to honor the request earlier in the day of my Slovenian maternal grandmother in the form of a barrel cactus.

Months after this beautiful ceremony, Peter continued to feel its impact. He was better able to deal with the conflicts of his life and to handle maturely the difficult emotional and legal responsibilities his separation entailed. He felt that he had accepted his part in the tangled story of love, desire, and deception and had finally stopped trying either to talk his former partner out of her anger or to view himself as a despicable human being unworthy of any love at all. At a birthday party for Jan, the woman who was by then his fiancée, he declared his love for her in front of a large gathering of their friends, family, students, and colleagues. He had taken into himself both the sacred feminine and the mature masculine and had ceremoniously joined them in marriage, and at last he could love fully. He said later, "I could not have married Jan until I had married my Beloved."

MARRIAGE WITH THE SACRED other bathes us in the full glow of our true self. Entering into this sublime union, we take on as a lifetime partner the most eternal, faithful, and luminous part of our being, whether we envision this aspect as angel, semidivine daimon, kundalini energy, psychological state, or deity. We become the one loved by the Beloved. And we bubble over with our own essence — not just our personality, as we have previously known it, but our full being, melted down, and turning to gold in the crucible of the divine. Assuming the mantle of what Jean Houston calls our own "godded potential," we begin the process of doing what can be done by no one else — living life authentically, creatively, and passionately as only we can live it.

I myself enacted a sacred marriage ceremony with the Beloved a few months after my dream of embracing Lucas. While participating in a training given by Bill Plotkin in a rocky canyon in Death Valley, I organized a small wedding to take place in the gap between the afternoon session and group dinner. My own wedding veil was the purple scarf printed with moons and stars that had featured in Lucas's dream; I tied it around my head gypsy-style. The ceremony took place at a large, flat boulder about a quarter mile up the broad wash that extended into the mountains from our camp, and it featured two good friends, Kerry Brady and Louden Kiracofe, as witnesses, and Bill, standing in as the bridegroom. Bill climbed onto the boulder with me, while Kerry and Louden stood side by side on the ground before us.

Addressing my Beloved, seeing the divine one, the alluring, erotic soul seducer, not my friend and co-guide, I thanked him for entering my life. "With love, my Beloved, you draw me to passion and delight in life," I said. "You seduce and enchant me. You animate my soul and send fire into my heart, my sexuality, my spirit. You will be my love forever."

Then Bill spoke as the Beloved. "My love, I couldn't live without you. My voice is your voice. My breath is your breath. My heartbeat is your heartbeat. I am the sparkle in your eyes. I am the laughter in your throat. We belong together. I am so glad that we have come into each other's lives. I will always be with you."

We embraced. I was surprised by the enormity of this act. I had imagined that it would simply feel like hugging my friend Bill at the end of a vision quest, but it did not. I was embracing the Beloved.

We stepped apart, and I grabbed him to me again, as the dream had scripted, and this time it was Bill I hugged, not an agent of the sacred world. Standing apart once more, we looked into each other's eyes and laughed with delight.

The entire ceremony had probably taken less than ten minutes and had faithfully followed the outline of my dream, yet the enactment of it had an effect much greater than the sum of the details. Bill's poignant words, the eager willingness of all three of them to attend my impromptu wedding, and even my own ability to let go of self-consciousness and claim the man before me as the divine Beloved himself filled this simple occasion with a radiance akin to that of the silver moonlight that was beginning to suffuse the stony valley. The dream had given the dreamer a message, and the dreamer had heeded it and translated the personal, inner invitation into a public and joyful milestone.

JOINING WITH THE SACRED BELOVED means allowing ourselves not only to love the world more fully and creatively, but also to be loved by it. We give up feeling unworthy and inferior, because we experience ourselves ripening into our authentic being. The Beloved loves us not because we are or hope to be famous, charitable, or rich, not because of some charismatic power that others project onto us, not for qualities of intelligence or a great management style or working-mom-superstardom that we try to make others see in us. The Beloved loves us because, as Bill so beautifully declared, that loving breath is our breath, that cosmic laughter emanates from our own throat, the heartbeat of the Beloved pounds in our chest. Knowing ourselves loved by the eternal and, at the same time, the very personal, we cannot help but give love back to ourselves and to the wide and potent world around us.

The sacred marriage with the divine Beloved, like marriage to a human beloved, cannot be rushed into prematurely. If disparate parts are not yet ready to come together, a rite of union may be a memorable event, but it is not likely to have lasting consequences. Marriage can confirm a union, but it can't create one. When the time and circumstances are right, however, and we do make the commitment to the inner Beloved, writes Qualls-Corbett, the sacred marriage has profound consequences:

> *On the intrapsychic level...when unconscious projections of the animus and anima are withdrawn and their qualities are integrated into consciousness, they are met with a mixture of fascination and fear, not unlike the feeling of meeting a potential lover for the first time. There is a feeling of ravishment, of breaking through....A sense of upheaval is experienced. One then begins to befriend the soul, the spirit. Rational and irrational functions become companions respecting and learning from one another. Seeds of creativity from the unconscious ripen to maturity in consciousness....*
>
> *On the transpersonal level, the sacred marriage extends beyond the boundaries of human understanding. One is united with the divine, the source and power of love. Through the mystical union a portion of divine love is received and contained within oneself. In the act of sacrifice to a greater authority, earthly values such as ego desires or identification with a power, are transformed into a capacity to love on a plane which surpasses human understanding.*[10]

A friend and mentor of mine, Jesse Zeller, says you practice divine love with your human beloved. I take this to mean that both partners mindfully and gladly attend to the fine-tuning of compassion, deep understanding, acceptance, curiosity, wonder, awe at the utter mystery of the other; freedom to explore and change oneself jubilantly; and loving care of the path the two of you walk together. You take care of the partnership together, while each of you takes care of your own partnership with the Beloved. Everybody knows that courtship precedes marriage. But it seems to me that these attitudes and attentions constitute a courting that must continue long after the happy couple says "I do." Emerson rather crankily opines that all the charms that first draw a couple together end up, after long years of marriage, to be "deciduous," but Andy and I found that, with mindfulness, we could remain evergreen. One way we kept the courtship going was by putting a stop to arguments as soon as they ceased to be important expressions of feelings and deteriorated into a tussle between two stubborn people who needed to win. At that point, we knew it was time to "start over." One of us — it didn't matter which — went out the front door, waited outside for a few moments, and then came back in, calling out, as if having just arrived home after a long day, "I'm home!" The other then hurried to greet the "returning" one with a welcoming hug and kiss, and we began the discussion all over again, amending the place where it had deviated into a fight. This simple exercise worked every time, even though we almost always resented having to give up our righteous anger to launch it.

Since I had begun to track desire, Andy had met his own Beloved and become fascinated with the subject. We had long discussions about who the Beloved was, how "higher lovemaking" was related or not related to the relationship with the human partner, what were calls of the Beloved and what greedy whims. In many ways the Beloved, or Beloveds, brought us even closer. So it was perhaps not surprising that, a year and a half after my sacred marriage ceremony in Death Valley, Andy and I had another wedding of our own. It was his idea. He'd had a bad case of flu that had lingered for weeks at the end of that winter, and he woke me up one morning to say from his side of the bed, "Life is too short. Let's get married again." When I readily agreed and began embellishing the proposal with plans for a wedding in our meadow with all our friends present, he surprised me further: "I was thinking we should go to Las Vegas." Andy had never even been to Las Vegas. Whereas I myself loved the outrageousness and flamboyance of the city, Andy was about the most un–Las Vegas–like person I knew.

Nevertheless, we had a June wedding in Las Vegas. The chapel we booked was Wee Kirk o' the Heather, in the old downtown, chosen to commemorate our trip to Scotland at the time of our original wedding. We stayed at the elegant Bellagio, with its dancing musical fountains, multiple swimming pools, galleries of original art, and lovely rooms with luxury bedding and big bathtubs. I even wore a real wedding gown. At our wedding fifteen years earlier, I had been too contrary to wear white, too tough to reveal the romantic feminine bride-side of myself, and had worn an eccentric twilight-blue linen dress from an artsy boutique in Santa Fe. But a month before the new big day, Kerry Brady and I were strolling through Durango after a vision quest when I spotted, in the window of a small dress shop, a Victorian-style wedding gown of lace and silk. When I tried it on, it fit as if it had been designed and tailored just for me. I bought it instantly.

The small staff at the Wee Kirk had their own ideas of what constituted a proper wedding, and they insisted that I make an entrance at the rear of the tiny chapel and walk toward Andy, who waited at the altar, with its bouquets of plastic flowers. I found the idea a bit banal, but I complied, and discovered that, as I approached my groom, neither of us could contain wide grins of joy. And when, during the nondenominational ceremony, the elderly minister delivered an apparently heartfelt analogy between marriage and an ocean whose depths one can never know, I could not hold back the tears. Afterward, holding hands, Andy and I walked to a nearby hotel to catch a taxi back up the Strip. Feeling the lovely silky dress swirl sensuously around my legs, the sun on my face, and the familiar rhythm of our shared pace, I could have walked for hours.

WE ALL WANT THE DEEP LOVE of a human partner, but even when we are so blessed, the partnership with the Beloved remains the most important of our life. Humans may abandon us through death or straying affections, but the Beloved is our heartbeat forever. The

Beloved will always remain faithful. And every day, including the last, sometimes excruciatingly painful hours of our time on earth, we have the opportunity to determine how we will move in tandem with the Beloved, how we will love him or her, how we will cross the space that separates us, how we will take on more compassion, creativity, beauty, and wildness on behalf of what we love. Stephen Levine, who works with people who are dying and has written extensively about the dying process, reports that it is not unusual for people close to death to find the peace, spiritual fulfillment, and bountiful love that have eluded them all their lives. It is never too late to embrace our passion and our connection with others. Nor is it ever too early. Those who have not undergone years of psychotherapy or had a profound dream or soulful encounter with the inner lover, and those who are still young enough to be struggling to define who they are, can nevertheless court the Beloved, for by doing so, they evoke what beckons them into their own becoming. They water the unfolding flower of themselves even as they weed the garden of their present condition by being as honest with themselves as possible, confronting the Shadows and Loyal Soldiers that get in their way, diverting judgment of others into compassion, and taking risks when something deep and true inside of them demands it. The effort we put into the relationship with the Beloved is always worth whatever difficulties or obstacles we encounter, moreover, for we come to understand that, in the darkest of times as well as the brightest, we will know love, connection with the great cosmic mystery, and even joy. The human search for wholeness, claims John P. Dourley, is actually a quest for the divine, for in the effort one moves "toward a state of consciousness in which the individual draws progressively nearer to an inner source, at once the source of all consciousness and so of whatever meaning exists in the universe.... In this process the individual comes to a more residual experience of that point at which one's personal being intersects with the divine, and through it with all that is and can be in the human and natural world. This process of self-discovery entails the discovery of one's native divinity, experienced as a greater appropriation of one's personal wholeness."[11]

When we embrace the Beloved and know ourselves to be one with him or her, an essential part of us, previously unconscious, awakens to life, as Sleeping Beauty awoke to the kiss of the handsome prince. The prince, like any warrior-lover worth his salt, has bushwhacked through the thorny brush surrounding the kingdom, has climbed the stairs of the silent, dust-furred castle, has looked upon the sleeping princess, and has kissed her awake. Each of these two united partners now gazes into the eyes of the true redeemer. If, as developmental psychologist Bruno Bettelheim believed, the story of Sleeping Beauty reaches the hearer at many ages, enabling a young child to grasp her autonomous selfhood and an adolescent to recognize the possibilities of living in harmony with another, then for the adult the tale can impart yet another meaning: the significance of union between a person and her or his sacred other. We have been waiting so long for this moment! The prince has been trudging so bravely and so alone through the broken kingdom that sank into obliviousness when all the good citizens fell asleep with their princess. He moved toward his beloved as if all the world depended on it. (It did.) As for the princess, she has been unconscious, unable to attend to, or even to perceive, the needs of her people or her own blossoming female body. With that kiss, that first tentative engagement of male and female, all that has been somnolent comes alert, healthy sexuality stirs, what has been separate is united, and the kingdom, freed of imprisoning numbness, quickens to life.

And of course, as in any marriage made on earth or on the mount of the gods, there is much to accomplish after the ceremony if one would live happily — or, better, passionately — ever after.

CHAPTER TWELVE

How Big Love Can Be

BRINGING THE BELOVED INTO THE WORLD

"There are so many ways to think about love," Meredith Little said thoughtfully. She had listened to my story, as she always listened, attending to it with her whole body. You could see her listening. She sat very still, leaning forward slightly, and her blue gaze broadened, as if to spread beyond the teller, over the whole personal watershed out of which the story was emerging. With her husband, Steven Foster, Meredith had sat in California deserts and listened to the stories of thousands of vision questers for nearly thirty years, and her features were etched by sun, wind, and concentration. The intensity of her focus was lightened by the one piece of jewelry she wore, a single arrowhead earring carved by Steven out of blue desert glass.

We were sitting over dinner at a long table on the last night of the annual Wilderness Guides Council meeting, held that year — just six months after I had met Lucas — at the Stovepipe Wells Campground in Death Valley. Every year in late February, sixty to eighty people who lead vision quests and other wilderness rites-of-passage programs gathered to reconnect, share tales, and discuss the business of the council that provided a network for the guides and kept track of the public lands where they took their groups so that no place would be overused. For the first two nights of the meeting we did our own cooking in the campground, but on the final night we all ate together. This year the event was a "banquet" catered by the restaurant at the Stovepipe Wells motel. It was the typical, unremarkable big-group meal — chicken, mashed potatoes, and broccoli, with fluffy white rolls and a salad of iceberg lettuce — and it was served in an equally unremarkable room, a long, rectangular space around whose walls marched a line of uniformly sized portraits of Death Valley park rangers smiling in front of desert landscapes.

Making my way from the buffet table with my plate, I'd spied the empty chair next to Meredith. As the creators of the contemporary vision quest and as the teachers, or even grand-teachers of all of us, a couple who exuded almost as much love for all the people who had sat in circles with them as they did for each other after almost three decades of marriage, Meredith and Steven were always in high demand at the council meetings. Every now and then, though, a kind of guilty concern for the privacy of this very private couple seemed to seize everybody all at once, and then you would see either or both of the founders of the movement enisled in the midst of the crowd.

This, apparently, was one of those moments, so I slid in beside Meredith, and we dove into talk, ensconced in the kind of protected space I had learned from her how to create for an intimate conversation in a public setting: blocking everything else out and zeroing in on the high points without any waste of time. My big news item, of course, was having fallen for a young man who'd apprenticed on a vision quest and trying to learn how that passion could propel me to the true Beloved. "It's only been a few months," I told Meredith. "I have no idea where it will lead. But it seems to me that there's something wonderful and big and important about tapping this source of longing and allurement. I mean, what do you *do* with something like this that just swoops down and snatches you up? How can you use it to guide your life? How would life be different if we acted because we were seduced forward by the world instead of pushed into it as if by a little dog barking and nipping at our heels? Countries all over the world have myths about the search for the divine lover. People of every religion write poems to God as the Beloved. We have dreams about the lover whose embrace we want never to leave. What can all this teach us about how we live, or could live?"

Meredith sat for a while, gazing, tasting the story. Then she said, "There are so many ways to think about love."

I waited expectantly. She was a friend, but she had been my teacher first, and she had the ability to perceive in a story many truths previously unknown to the teller herself.

In her husky outdoor voice, she went on, "You know, when something like what you're describing happens, you can respond in several different ways. One way is just to go right into it. You could say, 'Well, this is a very strong force, and I'm just going to abandon myself to it and give up whatever I've built up previously in my life, because this is so big. I need to be with this person and consummate this powerful love that's calling me.' So, *Pow!* You have a love affair. Or you can look at it as projection: 'This is a person who is learning from me, the teacher, the vision quest guide. He doesn't love me so much as he loves some aspect of himself. And I love him as some aspect of myself.' And that may be true. We're constantly projecting onto other people something that is forming in ourselves. Or, you can do what you're doing: you can say to yourself, 'Isn't it wonderful how big love can be!' Then this love becomes something you can take back home with you and give to the people."

IN THEIR BOOKS ON THE VISION QUEST and in their programs, Meredith and Steven were emphatic that the quest is not simply about personal growth or healing an old wound or learning to bond with nature, essential as any of these experiences may be in enabling the whole process to unfold. On the vision quest, as on every mythic journey, there is a vital Something that has to be found and brought back home. The Hero Who Returns is a far different person from the Hero Who Went Away. Stamped, signatured, tried, tired, bashed, beaten, triumphant, bashed again, embraced by the god or goddess, a pilgrim with sore feet and a new, clear understanding of what he must do in the world, the Hero Who Returns comes bearing something that is all his — and much too precious to be kept to himself. This is the gift, or "giveaway," a life task that is both noun and verb, a treasure whose brightness increases the more the bearer bestows it on others. The prince kisses Sleeping Beauty, and the whole somnolent kingdom stirs to life. The plucky monkey Hanuman, by recalling his own true self, leaps across the ocean in one bound, rescues Sita, and returns her to Rama, her prince. The young Lakota man who sets off on a desperate hunt for meat to feed his starving people returns home with instructions to prepare the way for the holy White Buffalo Calf Woman, who comes to give the people the ceremonies that will define their place on earth. The Ten Oxherding Pictures, which depict the stages of Buddhist enlightenment as a simple country narrative, culminate with the seeker, having found and mounted his ox — having discovered his true Self, his Buddha-nature — returning home in a picture entitled "The Oxherder Enters the City with Bliss-Bestowing Hands." There is no sacred journey without the gift upon return.

When we introduced this idea at the end of a vision quest, there were always some people who worried. *I don't have a gift*, they thought. They assumed that a gift was something you could define concisely, like a healing touch or a clear soprano voice. They leaped to the conclusion that giving a gift of self meant ministering to the poor and sick in the Calcutta slums or performing some other large, saintly task that they themselves would abhor and the world greatly admire. But the gift is both simpler and more demanding. Not some ornate but impossibly heavy rarity, the gift, wrote P. L. Travers, is the very true self: "Perhaps the myths are telling us that these [quests] are not so much voyages of discovery as of rediscovery; that the hero is seeking not for something new but for something old, a treasure that was lost and has to be found, his own self, his identity."[1] For Marilyn, the quester who dragged herself to the top of a mesa in search of a panorama and found instead a clump of wildflowers, the identity-treasure was awareness that a soft and delicate part of her had to be given room to grow. For Jeffrey, the formerly invisible boy, the treasure was the realization that his dream could only be realized by a confident and visible man. For another vision quester, it was the openhearted, charismatic person who emerged during ten days in the canyons, after he had spent fifty years believing himself a victim of fate.

Overjoyed to have glimpsed this precious rediscovered self at last, some questers balked. "But I've been giving to people all my life," they protested. "Can't I have something just for myself for once?" Not this, we told them, not the fullness of your being. Without some way to actualize it, the vision of the authentic self would never be anything more than a dream, beautiful but useless, even to the dreamer. Giving it out to the world, on the other hand, magnifies rather than diminishes it. Besides, the giving away is not a choice, it is an imperative. "Nephew!" an old medicine man says firmly to Black Elk, after the boy tells him about the vision he had years earlier and has kept to himself ever since. "You must do your duty and perform this vision for your people upon the earth. . . . Then the fear will leave you; but if you do not do this, something very bad will happen to you."[2] Kept within, the burgeoning, visionary self has no air and light to grow, and fear, like that suffered by Black Elk, or depression, or a sickening sense of self-betrayal begins to fester. Once freed, the self takes wing.

And when the hero or heroine takes on the true self, Travers adds, "he takes part in the one task, the essential mythical requirement: the reinstatement of the fallen world." It is a simple matter of cause and effect. By holding up to the light his long-buried treasure, the triumphant seeker casts glittering prisms on the path for anyone else to use as stepping-stone or guiding lamp to their own buried riches. If the hero radiates the joy of coming into ever fuller relationship with the divine, rediscovered self, others cannot help but be warmed.

AS MEREDITH IMPLIED, following the path toward the Beloved also requires a giving away of the self. The Beloved is an exclusive lover, but not a jealous one. The Beloved wants the affections of the one who loves him or her to spread wide and to touch many, for the enlargement of the self is, after all, the Beloved's goal, and love, by its nature, is a giving impulse. If we only stay at home, curled up in an easy chair and engaging in long, intimate dialogues with the inner lover, all the while becoming withdrawn and oversensitive and ignoring the world's invitations, we are not following the way of the Beloved; we are simply being self-indulgent. The way of the Beloved is to take the mythic journey every day, to get out of the bedchamber of bliss and into the vast, crowded waiting room of the planet.

Then there's absolutely no telling who'll benefit.

One man, for example, discovered that the skill of intuition, which he had previously overlooked, was the treasure both he and others needed. At the time he encountered the Beloved, Jim Samanen had recently left his job as a chemist at the pharmaceutical company where he had worked for twenty years and had accepted a management position there. Although he felt prepared for the change in responsibilities and was excited about bringing different skills to his work, the Beloved made him aware that he was missing one vital ingredient: "All during the workshop I had a sense of the Beloved standing over my right shoulder," Jim said later. "He was very close, very loving, and I could feel him whispering directions to me. I didn't used to trust my intuition. I thought that my rational, logical way of knowing was the only one I could rely on. But I began to pay attention whenever I heard that whisper. The consequence is that I find myself making decisions fairly spontaneously. I increasingly trust my intuition, which, to me, is the voice of the Beloved." In his new job, Jim found that the burgeoning voice of intuition was invaluable in helping him to speak extemporaneously at meetings, answer questions honestly and thoughtfully, deal with conflicts, and treat people, from his bosses to his staff, with respect and interest. After a year or so, he was deeply moved when he learned that he had gained a reputation as someone who could be trusted. Developing his intuition also helped him to improve his relationship with his teenage son, since the constant presence of the Beloved, he said, reminded him "of the higher good, the nobler act. So when I am in a heated situation with my son, I am responding not as a stern disciplinarian, or worse, as an older sibling, but as a mentor."

Like the Ancestors of the Australian aboriginal Dreamtime, who sang the mountains, watering holes, and rocks into being as they walked over the uncreated world, the lover of the Beloved brings a new landscape into being with every step. Allurement beckons. Passion, seeking to embrace the beckoning one, responds. A moment of compassion, "deep play" concentration, conscience, or aesthetic ecstasy — a moment of falling in love — could occur at any time. Knowing this, the lover moves with excitement and heightened awareness. The void beneath the foot before each new step is cushioned with potency. All is uncreated. With every movement the seeker-lover makes, he or she sets a course on ground that is temple, honeymoon suite, laboratory, and garden all in one. This is so whether the site of that ground is a studio, a classroom, a mountain trail, a clear-cut forest, the AIDS wing of a hospital, or a refugee camp in Sudan. Any place that calls the longing soul forth to embrace and be embraced is a blessed place.

When Eros and Psyche settled down together with the gods, they had a daughter they called Pleasure, but whose name Erich Neumann equates with mystical joy, produced when winged divine love and the human determination to experience that love come together.3 For the Sufis, ecstasy is the discovery (*wajd*) of true being (*wûjûd*). As we begin to take our passion for the Beloved into the world, we can expect to discover and fall in love with our own true being in countless aspects and circumstances of our lives. I remember a man who had received the medicine name Lion King on his vision quest, exclaiming during one of our reincorporation talks, "I want to know everything there is to know about Lion King! I want to know how Lion King makes love. I want to know how Lion King unpacks his suitcase when he gets home after this quest. I want to know how Lion King buys birthday presents. I want to be Lion King in everything I do." The lover of the Beloved could say, similarly, "I want to love the Beloved in all I do."

THEOLOGIAN FREDERICK BUECHNER WROTE, "The place God calls you to is the place where your deep gladness and the world's deep hunger meet."4 Hunger and gladness: this is a startling pair of conceptual allies — not hunger and eating, or hunger and satiation, not gladness and sorrow. Buechner implies that a hunger, however and wherever it arises, is a need that is best satisfied not by those with certain credentials and provisions, but by those with the most ardent *desire* to respond. To respond as one is deeply and personally urged to do is to answer not just the one in need, but to answer God — or the sense of divine principle, or the Beloved — as well. This is the meaning of the "call," a summons so direct and specific that the one who hears it has no doubt that it comes from a sacred source and no choice (at least if she knows what's good for her) but to follow the direction it compels. The result is a sense of fulfillment that extends to giver and recipient — and presumably to God, the caller — alike.

Often people imagine that when they set out to find their treasure and embrace their Beloved, they will set sail on a swift river that will buoy them rapidly toward their rightful future. They want confirmation of their purpose on earth, a preview of the Big Picture, a holy news flash about their true, right livelihood. Every now and then, that is actually what happens, but even then, what is revealed is nothing less than what was there all along — and we still have to do the work to realize the vision. Sam Martinborough was an outgoing, irrepressible Guyanese musician who came on a four-day quest in Pennsylvania's Endless Mountains at a time when his future was uncertain in many respects. He had recently lost a job he loved, teaching choir to inner-city children, and on the morning he set out to drive to Pennsylvania, he'd had to stop first at Goodwill to drop off boxes of furnishings and clothes from the apartment he was forced to vacate. When he returned home, he would be sleeping on friends' couches and looking for a new job. There was one beam of light in this dim picture. Sam's wide travels had fueled his fascination with the musical traditions of many different cultures, and he had an idea for how to use that interest to take his work in a new direction.

Nevertheless, he was not at all sure he was up to the task. "I'm a black man. I'm a musician. I'm gay. I live in a conservative, staid city," he told the group as we huddled under a large tarp in a hemlock forest while a rainstorm pounded the slate-gray afternoon. "The days of Martin Luther King are over," Sam went on. "If I take on this work, it will affect a lot of people's lives. There'll probably be as many people mad at me as thanking me. Most of my friends think that what I want to do is impossible. Maybe it is. Maybe I should just lay low and find another safe teaching job." Nevertheless, he was intrigued by the concept of a Beloved who beckoned to him, and the next morning, when he stepped over the ceremonial gateway made of stones, he declared his intention for the twenty-four-hour solo: "To fuse with my Beloved."

The quest was held in a large nature preserve, and Sam had chosen his solo spot at the very back end, where the preserve bordered a farm whose boundary line the owner had pugnaciously defined at the end of a trail with a row of thick, four-foot-tall pylons driven into the earth, each painted with one dripping Day-Glo orange letter to form the words NO TRESPASSI. The final N and G were slathered on two adjacent trees. As he slowly approached the boundary, Sam began to play with the letters on their individual posts. He realized that they included, for instance, the French word *NOTRE* (our), *PASS*, and *SING*. On reaching the sign he sidled between two of the pylons and stood defiantly on the other, forbidden side of the demarcation line, then stuck out his tongue and chanted with boyish impertinence, "Nyah, nyah, nyah!" The first thing he did after setting his backpack down in his solo place was to follow the boundary line past the pylons and into the woods, past the remains of a deer, a rock wall, and a barbed-wire fence. He put up his tarp, then returned, compelled to continue his exploration of this formidable barrier and what it had to do with him. This time he sat before the dead deer, contemplating the consequences of boundaries and how this one might have affected the life of the deer. Again he went back to his solo spot. The hours passed. Sam lay in the sun and felt its warmth on his skin. Considering the deer, he thought about the dying aspects of his life. In the evening he returned yet again to the no tresspassing sign. Now it seemed that more was demanded of him than simply contemplating or even defying this prohibition. What was required was some act of recognition of boundaries and what could be done with them — what he could do with them.

Using a tree to hoist himself up, he climbed onto the first pylon and balanced there. Then, like a tightrope walker, he made his way step by step across the entire length of the barrier until he reached the other side. He jumped triumphantly down. And in that moment he realized what, in his heart, he had known all along: that his gift was the ability to straddle boundaries. As he told the group the next day, "The Beloved said to me: 'You are the one who can cross between the worlds. You can teach Gospel music to white people and bring blacks into the symphony orchestra. You can bring joy to your uptight city by making everyone feel included. Only you can do this, because you understand what it is to belong to many different, polarized worlds at once.'" Sam returned home to found MSSNG LNKS, an organization that brought together the musical styles of different cultures and blended them in innovative ways in performances created for children.

THE HUNGER PANG THAT SAM PERCEIVED in the world was the need of musical people from different cultures to express themselves exuberantly and innovatively, and his own gladness was to play with and redefine boundaries to bring those diverse strains together. The gift he acknowledged by tightroping across those forbidding pylons would change his life and those of thousands of others as well. Thankfully, though, the world's hungers make themselves known in infinite ways, most of them smaller and more temporal.

I witnessed one brief moment of falling in love many years ago in a New York City subway. Entering a nearly empty car one afternoon and seating myself on a long bench, I could not help but notice that the shabby, unkempt man opposite me, whether drunk or just exhausted, had slumped so far over in his seat that a sharp turn around a curve in the rails would probably have dumped him on the floor. I noted this, I say, then I turned my attention to my book, for I did not regard it as my concern. The train moved ahead, stopped at a station, moved ahead, stopped. A man got on. The newcomer was middle-aged, tall, and gangly, with thin hair. He was the kind of nondescript person who would never be noticed in a crowd. He walked with his shoulders hunched forward. His unfashionable, ill-fitting brown suit might have come from a thrift shop. He carried no packages, briefcase, or brisk attitude to indicate that he, like most New Yorkers, had important places to get to. And as he started down the aisle past the slumped man, he went no farther. He stopped, took note, and turned back. Then he slipped his hands under the man's armpits and very gently righted him. It was an act that took only seconds to complete, and the recipient of the attention never awoke. When the man in the brown suit turned around again, I saw on his face a small, fond smile. I could not miss the point, though it had nothing to do with me, that there had been some kind of love in that gesture he'd made. The image never left me, though the incident happened long before I began to think about the Beloved, long, even, before I knew that a twentieth-century white woman could go on a vision quest. But later, whenever I thought about the many ways possible to follow allurement and to court the Beloved by being the lover the Beloved loves, I thought about that act. A certain thing needed to be done, the plain man in the brown suit had known that it was his to do, and he did it with joy.

Hiding no part of our being from ourselves, accepting what we have lived through, how we see the world, and what we love as essential components of our divine nature, we are more able to take in the complexity of all life, not just in good times, but also in those steeped in grief, anxiety, and fear. For example, Mary Morgan, a psychotherapist living and practicing in New York City, was, like all New Yorkers, deeply saddened and shaken by the terrorist attacks on September 11, 2001, and she wanted to do something to help. Immediately she contacted the emergency aid center and volunteered to do counseling for survivors and the relatives of victims. However, so responsive were so many people to the crisis and so overworked were the volunteers trying to deal with an emergency of this magnitude, that her calls went unanswered, and eventually, feeling discouraged and helpless, she gave up.

A few weeks later, Mary heard someone casually refer to the World Trade Center by its familiar name, the "Twin Towers," and she felt as if a bolt of lightning had sizzled through her. Suddenly she knew what she had to do. As a young woman in her twenties, she had been devastated when her twin brother was killed in an accident. Now she began to wonder how many twins had lost their own closest sibling in the terrorist attack. With diligence and determination, she set out to investigate. This time no delay, unanswered call, or long moments spent on hold with the phone pressed against her ear could discourage her; she was fired with purpose. Finally she was able to obtain the names of the surviving twins, and she contacted them and set up a support group. The group met once a week for several months, and Mary introduced practices such as deep imagery and the telling of life stories, as well as more conventional methods of group therapy. The "twinless twins" formed a close bond with one another, and Mary was able to bring together members of a grieving community in a way that she, and only she, with her life's experience, professional training, and unique sensibility could have done.

A dominant theme of eco-philosopher Joanna Macy's work is that it is only by facing our deep despair over the looming dangers and real devastation threatening the planet that we can kindle our greatest compassion. The effort it takes to block out deep-seated concern about poverty, the extinction of thousands of animal and plant species, the spread of incurable AIDS, radioactivity in the soil, uranium mining in the fragile desert, the likelihood of repeated acts of terrorism, destruction of ancient forests, pollution of rivers and soils and skies, genocide as a tactic of war, and countless other cataclysms and potential cataclysms not only fails to keep these horrors at bay but stuffs away the feelings we dread to feel. When fear, outrage, and sorrow remain unexpressed, we may release them in inappropriate, involuntary ways, such as blaming others, becoming politically passive, or hardening ourselves to the needs of even the people closest to us. We may feel fragmented, guilty, or listless.

In contrast, acknowledging despair about the state of the world is actually healthy. It does not make the despair worse; it liberates and then transforms it. It enables us to remember that we are part of all life, it strengthens compassion, reduces dichotomies that divide people, and empowers us to bring about change. What occurs after we have reached through the pain to touch the tensile web of life beneath it is "*beyond* catharsis," Macy says. "By recognizing our capacity to suffer with our world, we dawn to wider dimensions of being. In those dimensions there is pain still, but a lot more. There is wonder, even joy, as we come home to our mutual belonging — *and* there is a new kind of power."[5] Besides, say the Sufis, pain opens as many doors to the divine as pleasure does, since every hammer blow the heart receives cracks it open wider for the Beloved to occupy. It is only by facing the pain, lying down at its feet, and then climbing out of it by rechanneling the dammed-up energy released in the process that we can transform both ourselves and the source of the suffering. Then we become for others what the figure of the Beloved is for each of us — a presence who offers love, support, and even joy in any and all circumstances.

"YOU CAN TAKE THAT LOVE," Meredith had said, "and bring it back to the people." Who, then, are these "people" she spoke of? The term may evoke an image of a queen riding in an open car and waving with regal detachment to the anonymous crowds of her subjects. Do we all have "people"? I used to think that one's people must consist of a static, identifiable clump that had to be located before it could be served: a doctor's patients, say, or an actor's audience. Instead, I have come to believe that the people, quite simply, are the souls we touch as we make our way to the Beloved. For Mary Morgan and for the man in the plain brown suit, the people were strangers with a need that they, and only they, could meet and out of whose lives they then passed. For Jim Samanen, the people included both the employees at work and his son. The people are the recipients of our fully expressed being, and we find them by heading toward what tugs at our heart. They are children and women and men whose circumstances, every day or once in a lifetime, reach out and grab us and invite us to offer ourselves with generous eagerness, unafraid of being judged — or, more likely, especially at first, acting despite that fear. They are students or teachers or a waiter in a restaurant or the harried airline attendant trying to assist frustrated travelers after thunderstorms have shut down an airport. They are the CEO of the corporation and the person who cleans the office late at night. They are the spouse who needs our attention and comfort about some problem at work and the stranger at the church social who looks shy and out of place. Perhaps our people are not even human beings, but injured wild animals or an old family farm tagged to be bulldozed into a housing development. When we perceive the Beloved in many forms, we realize how many and genuine are the ways of loving back.

We may tell ourselves we don't have the proper gear for pursuing the path of passionate engagement. "You couldn't talk about this stuff to women from the East End of London," sniffed a friend of mine who lives in England. "They haven't got the time or the income or the wherewithal to follow their allurement." But time and income and wherewithal are not what the Beloved wants from us. And if we're honest with ourselves, we can tell where the hidden treasure of the self lies as surely as if a metal detector loudly beeped its location. In the early spring of 2004, for example, forty women ranging in age from late forties to late seventies sat in a circle of folding chairs in the meeting room of the Unitarian-Universalist church in Valparaiso, Florida. Small votive candles set around the outside of the circle cast a soft, intimate glow over the darkened space. It was the monthly meeting of the Crones' Circle, and I had been speaking about the imperative of giving the gift of self. A big gray-haired woman had been sitting back in her chair, ankles crossed in front of her, arms folded over her ample chest. Her body language bespoke separation from the rest of the group, perhaps even a separation she was determined to uphold. But toward the end of the meeting, she began to speak.

She laughingly told the group that she knew little about allurement. She wasn't even sure what it meant. Recently, she said, she had impulsively set off for the laundry room in her apartment complex in her bare feet, and her husband had "gone on about it" to such an extent that she simply sighed resignedly and slipped on her shoes to avoid further commotion. She wasn't sure if a sudden whimsy to walk barefooted was allurement; maybe it was just plain craziness. "I had five children in twelve years. I didn't have time to follow any passion. Now they're gone, the grandchildren are okay, well, most of them are, but there's nothing I can do about the ones that aren't. I'm seventy-two years old. I don't know about allurement," she said yet again. She paused. "But talk about things in the news that grab you, there's this priest in Haiti. I just know I have to contact him...." She didn't go into any detail, but as her voice trailed off, her face took on a look of beatitude. She was there with him, not in that room, where a chorus of approving murmurs and words of encouragement were arising from the other women in the circle. A week earlier, Haitian president Jean-Bertrand Aristide had been deposed, the country was in chaos, and something about an unknown priest had touched this woman, who thought she knew little about allurement. Urged to do so by the group, she promised that she would contact him.

How strange and marvelous it is that we are each beckoned so specifically by certain hungers of the world, even though the threads that attach us to them are so slender it's easy simply to brush them aside as cobwebs. Yet to seize hold of these threads and follow them demands no special training or economic privileges, as people prove every day when they follow life's invitations large and small and hence move closer to the Beloved. Any of us can forge a dynamic, erotic connection with the world around us and become what Thomas Moore, in *The Soul of Sex*, calls "persons of deep affection":

> *Like the monk in his or her monastery, we can find ways to make our affection visible and felt. We can be affectionate toward our friends and neighbors and in such simple ways sexualize the neighborhood. We can be outrageously affectionate toward our lovers and spouses and thus give the world the model it needs for living from the heart. We can nurture our affection for animals, things, and places. All of this affection brings into human community a vision, a point of view, and a philosophy discovered in our most sublime meditations and readings. It is the anima soul to the animus intellect, the heart-spouse to the mind-lover, the visible body to the hidden spirit.[6]*

Some seekers of the Beloved are not as interested in this, the outer-directed phase of the journey, as they are in the earlier ones. The perfume they wish ever to be enchanted by is the one that envelops them in those intimate moments of rapture with the soul guide. They could happily meditate for hours on the Beloved. They can't get enough of that warm, loving, erotic presence. They hurry to lock themselves in their bedroom to seek counsel from the Beloved after an argument with their spouse, but they won't engage in an honest, if difficult, conversation with the real person who, at that very moment, sits slumped and stewing in the other room. They love the sense of intimacy they feel as they walk with the Beloved, but they shy away from any suggestion that a real expression of this intimacy might necessitate their getting involved in the policies of the public school system, or finally, after thirty years of dreaming about it, signing up for tango lessons, or initiating a frank conversation with a friend who has hurt them. They want to immerse themselves in the great sea of oneness with sacred mystery and don't want to be bothered with negotiating around all the flotsam and jetsam strewn about the beach.

Caitlín Matthews identifies such an attitude as a sign of an unhealthy relationship with the daimon: a preoccupation with the inner lover to the exclusion of the world at large.7 It was the state that Eros originally counted on Psyche to loll in, dark and intimate and barring all intruders from the dreamy private play of the two lovers. It is a refusal of the possibilities of our nature that is just as likely to obstruct a relationship with the Beloved as ignoring that compelling presence would be. Love breaches us. Love expands our heart, opens our eyes, shows us the world glistening as if after a rain shower. If we refuse to step into this new world, in all its complexity, beauty, diversity, and need, we pervert love. We simply turn our back on the Beloved and go to sleep.

And the power of love, wrote Apuleius, is "exciting [one] to wakefulness."8 Like Psyche, we must throw off the temptation to remain in blissful darkness and shine the lamp on the very embrace that enfolds us. We must wake up with our whole being. Often fear is the godly voice that holds us down in some dark and cozy trap. We fear we are not ready for a bigger world. We believe we need more training, more education, more preparation, a different personality. We worry about what might happen if we do step into the world as into the arms of a waiting lover. Suppose everyone bursts out laughing? Suppose we send out invitations to the unveiling of the True Self and no one shows up? Suppose we exceed our own slim expectations, only to discover that even more is expected of us? Suppose we just get so full of ourselves that our friends no longer want anything to do with us? And of course we are all, already, way too busy. But, like Psyche, if we are to make this relationship work, we have no choice but to insist on seeing the whole picture. The myth depends on Psyche's refusal to remain content and uncurious in the tangle of bedding and empyreal sweet talk that Eros has set up for her. She has to bring light, or consciousness, to her love. She has to lean back from those loving arms long enough to see how she herself fits into them, and she must use her own erotic love to power her journey to maturity. The lesson, no less apt for contemporary seekers of the Beloved, is that we will not be mature lovers until we are willing to be bigger lovers. Hence we must constantly seek opportunities to introduce our divinely directed self to others.

Jesus, after all, left the desert, where he had retreated after his baptism, and went forth to preach the word of God that he had tried for years to ignore, believing that he was not up to the task. The Buddha, emerging from deep immersion in nirvana, touched the ground before him and declared, "The earth is my witness," and then set out for the Deer Park to teach the Four Noble Truths. The great Lakota warrior Crazy Horse rode out to isolated, sacred peaks time and again to fast and pray as the U.S. cavalry closed in on him and his band of resisters to the reservation system. He would sit alone, facing the sun and praying for guidance in serving his people in those desperate times. Cherishing others through a personal love of God is a spiritual duty, says Morton T. Kelsey. He stresses the need for Christians to transform themselves into their own image of the powerful force he calls the "Divine Lover" or the "motivating and creative core of the universe," since "we cannot remain in relation to that love...unless we begin to express the same kind of love to others."9 Buddhism has a similar aim of expanding love with the practice of *metta*, loving-kindness. In the meditation of the *Tevija Sutta*, one envisions her love stretching out to embrace, first one-quarter of the world, then half, then three-quarters, until the whole planet is suffused in love, "far-reaching and beyond measure." Buddhist scholar Christmas Humphreys elaborates: "He who realizes to the full the oneness of his life with all its other forms will find his consciousness expand proportionately, and as he understands, so will he love, until his heartbeat is the heartbeat of the universe, his consciousness coincident with all that lives."[10]

"TAKE ME TO EARTH," a goddess Beloved told the woman who sat curled up in a wicker chair on a screened porch overlooking the sapphire surf of Cape Cod. We had come to the point in the weekend workshop when the group focused on the Beloved and asked what needed to be done to strengthen the partnership. This goddess phrased well the step all Beloveds need their mortal person to help them take: she wanted to be taken down from her lofty domain on a celestial mountaintop and put to work. She needed to be actualized. After the meditation, borrowing a practice Bill used at the end of each vision quest, I concluded this workshop, as I always did, by asking participants to make a commitment to undertake one concrete and specific act within the next week to "take the Beloved to earth." The vows were creative and diverse, demonstrating that each person had a Beloved with exquisitely good sense in guiding the lover to the act most appropriate for him or her. People declared that they would: make amends to a sister-in-law with whom they had been on frosty terms for a decade, quit a hated part-time job and enroll in massage school, introduce the talking staff council to a family in struggle with three teenagers, take up painting again — and for the first picture paint the tree the artist had sat beneath during her walk with the Beloved — leave energy-draining social events early in the evening and go home to write poetry, give a backrub to a husband, learn Spanish, sit down for a talk with a boss, repair an old family heirloom, and make time each week for a date with the Beloved.

Vincent Rossi, theologian and director of the Religious Partnership for Forest Conservation, has said, "Human nature only finds its true meaning in the Divine nature, which is to say that human nature only fulfills itself when it transcends itself."[11] Nevertheless, despite the best of plans and intentions, despite the conviction that we follow a journey full of meaning, passion, and serendipity, giving away the gift of self can, like any big undertaking, be arduous at times. Even the Buddha felt some resistance to doing what he knew he had to do. After attaining enlightenment, he remained in a state of solitary bliss for several weeks. Then, when it began to occur to him how difficult it was going be to communicate to others the truths that he had realized, he found himself wishing that he could just live out his life in the wilderness, alone and at peace, unattached to the strife and sorrow of the world. Such a choice was really never an option, though, and he knew it, for the first of the Four Noble Truths he had understood was that life is suffering. To remain in solitude, as if he could ignore the pain of the world, would have been to betray the very path that had been revealed to him. And so he deliberately delayed his own liberation and chose instead to rebind himself to the endless wheel of earthly suffering for the benefit of others. This is the true meaning of compassion, an openness to all of life in all its forms. (Personally, I think the Buddha's small moment of reluctance to take on the gigantic task he knows is his alone gives the rest of us the opportunity to feel a special jolt of compassion for him.)

Foster and Little point out that the feelings of discouragement and powerlessness that beset someone setting out on a new path, particularly after a powerful transformative experience, are entirely natural, for "the inevitability, even the *necessity* of the darkness" must follow the brilliant flare of truth:

> The hero/ine learns to live in two worlds. This is perhaps the most important teaching of the Vision Quest. One world is sacred, spiritual, eternal.... The other world is mortal, material and subject to change.
>
> When the Vision Quest ends, the vision quest of life begins. The terms of this quest are that one learns to walk in balance between two worlds, that one seeks to conceive and then to give birth to vision. The willingness to be a channel of vision takes great

courage and endurance and is not lightly assumed. There will be
times when you stumble and fall. Then you will want to crawl
away to the sacred mountains. These are the times of the greatest
potential, when you are looking the dragons square in the eye.[12]

Even Mother Teresa, who often described her passion for her work in
the slums of Calcutta as stemming from being "in love" with Jesus,
succumbed occasionally to despair over her inability to do more
to help.

Overriding the discouragement, however, is the force that moti-
vated the action in the first place: love. If we court the Beloved regularly, we will come to fall in love with what we are doing, how we are
doing it, and whom we do it for, and this pervasive sense of love taps
out the rhythm of how we proceed. Every step takes us closer to the
arms of the Beloved, and every step is a venture onto hallowed ground.

Discouragement, even despair, may accompany the passage, but
they need not stymie it. For thirty years a Long Island, New York,
native, Pete Maniscalco, has been undertaking periodic retreats of
fasting and prayer in a tent he pitches on the beach in front of the
Shoreham nuclear power plant. At first Pete's activism was meant to
protest the construction of the plant. Later he wanted to call attention
to serious flaws in its safety regulations. Now his intention is to elicit
support for his vision of creating an educational and spiritual center in
the wooded area behind the plant, which both his extensive historical
research and his personal experience have led him to believe has been
a sacred site for at least 4,500 years. Knowing that one cannot truly
inhabit the sacred until one has stared into the face of the profane, this
gray-haired grandfather sits in front of his little tent beneath the
looming turquoise cooling towers as if they were holy icons. His
efforts, and those of the other activists he's collaborated with, have
succeeded in bringing about significant change: the plant has been
decommissioned, and ratepayers won $40 million in a class-action
lawsuit against the local power company. But for Pete there is still

work to be done, and he is compelled to bring it about through his singular path of sacrifice, solitude, meticulous study, and activism. Through his vigils before the nuclear facility he performs what Kant called a "beautiful act." A beautiful act is different from a strictly "moral act," although certainly they can be one and the same. One performs a moral act because he has to, Kant argued, but takes a beautiful act because he is compelled to do so out of love. Under such circumstances, nothing is too difficult.

And, in the undertaking, we find we gain strength, inspiration, and courage where we did not know they existed. I was guiding a vision quest in Scotland on September 11, and our group did not even learn the terrible news until four days later, when, dirty and jubilant, we surged into a tea shop overlooking the green, undulant bens, the mountains of the highlands. That night, back at the yoga center where we had begun the quest, we sat before a blazing fire in the hearth, and each person in the group — a mix of Scottish, Irish, Swiss, and American — imagined how they would take their vision home to their people under the weight of this new and unmistakable evidence that, truly, the world was in desperate need of compassionate authenticity. I, too, took part in the exercise and immediately saw myself leading a ceremony at Ground Zero for everyone who loved the city of New York. The event, held two months after the attacks, was called Attending the City. One feature of it was a commitment, made by each person present, to bring an act of beauty and compassion to the city within one week. One man decided to bake lasagna and take it to his district fire department, which had lost several men when the World Trade Center collapsed. Another would go out to dinner with friends at a neighborhood Afghani restaurant and make a point of letting the owners know that they continued to be a valued part of the community. A woman who had written a poem about the city after the attacks said she would distribute it as widely as she could — on streetlights, walls, and in the impromptu memorials that had sprung up all over the city since the attacks. Another woman would adopt a pet whose owner had been killed. Who knows how many people those acts of love and beauty, laid down in a storm of sorrow, touched? As for me, the organizing of that event demanded that I negotiate paths I had never before had to travel: renting audio equipment, getting permits from the Parks Department and the local police precinct, asking the Hilton Hotel to donate pens so people could write prayers on the red ribbons I then begged from a merchandiser in the Fashion District, distributing flyers all over the city. But for once my ignorance of what questions I needed to ask did not deter me. I was fired with the need to do this thing and convinced that people would want to help me out. And so they did, so they did.

In the company of the Beloved, we are not depleted by the outpouring of self, but energized by it. Then we can make choices about what matters to us and willingly sacrifice anything that would get in the way of our movement toward it. We modern Westerners do not like the notion of sacrifice. We want what we want when we want it, and we don't care to give anything up to get it. But the Latin roots of the word *sacrifice* actually mean "to make sacred," so letting go of something we value makes it sacred, for the void it leaves will, we hope, be filled with something of even greater value. Hence sacrifice becomes a choice we gladly make. And even though one gives with the anticipation that what is offered will be received and replaced with something else, the giving itself is an act of love. Sacrifice is not asceticism, Rumi pointed out, but love. The Norse god Odin sacrificed his right eye in exchange for the more sublime visionary powers of memory and premonition. Later, seeking an even greater trade of human for divine, he hung himself like an ornament for nine days and nights upon the World Tree, Yggdrasil, that he might be granted the highest mystical wisdom. Majnun gave up social acceptance, rank, and the comfortable mores of the tribe to pursue his beloved Layla with all the wild passion his soul demanded. Vision questers voluntarily sacrifice food, shelter, company, and diversion for three days and nights in order to be empty and available for intensified dialogues between outer and inner nature. A woman I know, Marcelle Martin, whose life centers on writing and leading prayer gatherings for Quakers, has chosen to rent out rooms in her home, take public transportation instead of driving a car, and buy her clothes in thrift shops, that she might have the time and independence to pursue the callings she loves and that do not pay much. Such sacrifices are not deprivations; they are clearings-out of the inessential, so that the mega-essential might pour in.

According to Hopi myth, the creator endowed each person with a miniscule hole at the top of their head, a doorway through which they might receive the guidance of spirit. I like to imagine that we also have tiny vents at the tips of our fingers out of which this abundant guidance, after getting heated up in the furnace of the soul, can radiate forth to others. If we hold inspiration's bounty within, we lose touch with reality and become self-obsessed. Giving it away indiscriminately, we get depleted. But by leaving both doors open, we welcome the love and guidance of the Beloved and sluice it forth, and the result is a constant stream of engagement with the one and the many, the divine and the ordinary, the giver and the receiver. Writing ecstatically of her soul's rendezvous with the young Christ who came to her in visions, Mechtilde of Magdeburg described the sense of renewal she experienced with each ardent encounter: "The more He gives her, the more she spends, the more she has.... The more the fire burns, the more her light increases. The more love consumes her, the brighter she shines."[13]

"WHAT I PRAISE IS WHAT'S WILD FOR LIFE," Goethe wrote in the poem "Soulful Yearning," "What longs for death by fire." Like the butterfly that is compelled to cast itself into the beguiling flame that will annihilate it, so must we, aching with holy longing, dive into the soul's great attractions, knowing that — willing that — they may consume us. This is not the annihilation of drug addiction, but immersion in what we love. It is not enough to flit around this flame; we must plunge into it, even though there's no guarantee we'll recognize ourselves afterward. We must risk losing our wings, our old agenda, our well-developed sense of self, our fear and our self-doubt, that we may truly fly. In the course of a human life, there will be many such flames, dancing and flickering, seducing and then swallowing us, yet if we avoid them, we only deny our passion and deaden our life. We become what Goethe, later in the poem, calls mere "dull visitors" on the earth, ill at ease in our surroundings, frightened of the judgment of others, holding back. Expressing ourselves with the flame that licks our heart and animates our body, we are holy lovemakers. Teachings in Hinduism, Sufism, and the Jewish Kabbalah declare that it is the heartfelt desire of each person to make love with God. Since that is impossible, we love God through others. By manifesting the inner light, our soul is drawn forth, more and more, to that which it most loves and which knows exactly why we were born and how we can manifest it — the radiant flame of the godded self.

A Jewish tale recounts the metamorphosis beautifully. It seems that a lowly man from the slums caught sight of a princess passing by in her carriage and was captivated by her beauty. His attraction quickly turned into obsession, and he finally managed to obtain an audience with her in the palace. Clumsily yet passionately, he confessed his love and begged her to marry him. Touched by his earnestness and wishing not to hurt his feelings, the princess told him gently that only in the cemetery could they be together. She spoke philosophically, of course, meaning that only death, the great leveler, would unite them, but the poor man knew nothing of euphemisms and allowed himself to believe that she was proposing a rendezvous. Off he went to the cemetery to wait for her.

There he sat, day after day, year after year, staying put, so as not to miss the arrival of his beloved. At first he amused himself with fantasies about what their life would be like as husband and wife. As time went on, however, he could not help but pay attention to the ceremonies of death that occurred all around him. He began to consider the transitory nature of his own and his princess's life. That led him to wonder what qualities of her beauty might survive old age, illness, and death. He contemplated what was lasting in the world and what ephemeral. He thought about love: the love of humans for one another and for God, the love of God for people.

As the man's reflections turned increasingly toward spiritual love, he slowly underwent a transformation. No longer a poor man from the slums with a foolish lust for a princess, he became a soul filled with love for God and all creation. He became what is called in Hebrew a *Tzaddik*, a God-realized person. Word spread about the wise man who sat praying in the cemetery, and people came to seek counsel with him. One day the princess herself visited, for she had married some years before and despaired that she had been unable to conceive a child. The *tzaddik* greeted her and thanked her with all his heart for inspiring his great journey of love.[14]

This story contains all the vital elements of the journey to the Beloved: the lust, at first concentrated on a human being and later converted to soulful yearning; the willingness, even in those early stages, to change one's life completely for the sake of the beloved; the expansion of the heart to include other people and the divine; the realization that questions of life and love and beauty, and how these exalted concepts touch the reality of death and sorrow, are the universal forces that bind people together; and the magnification of the soul, not by force of will, but through love. And, always, the memory of where it all began.

What, along this journey is *not* divine? The imponderable nature of the universe and the wonder of our own miraculous ensouled bodies falling in love, witnessing acts of compassion and bravery, and, on occasion, enacting them ourselves make of us the moth that seeks the flame. The Imponderable cannot be known, but it can and must be pondered, and so we do as the moth does: we buzz around that curious, enchanting flame, exploring it, daring ourselves to dance closer and closer to the light we cannot live without — until, finally, unable to control ourselves any longer, we dive into the flame and lovingly lose ourselves. In touching others we are transformed; in transforming ourselves, we touch others. Loving the Beloved, we become the beloved. We realize how big love can be.

CHAPTER THIRTEEN

The Lover Who Came By Staying Away

BECOMING THE GOD WITHIN

How such a phenomenon of rock could have ended up here, even in the middle of the Sahara Desert, where rock prevailed, was a bafflement. As far as the eye could see, the mountains were black, tinged now and then with a vaguely rusty sheen like that which smudges old black silk, but dominantly, decisively black. Millennia ago, the Hoggar Mountains had boiled out of the sand, their black basalt bubbles hardening into boulders that made up the slopes. The mountains slithered across the land, then seemed to slip underground, only to emerge again miles farther on. Yet here, into a clearing at the cul-de-sac where two black ridges had merged, one red, enormous boulder somehow had dropped. The red was oxidized iron, and you could sometimes turn over a black stone on the desert floor to see its red heart, but this was an entire red sandstone complex in the midst of shiny black walls. For crashing onto the sand, the boulder had split apart into several large pieces to form a rough circle about thirty feet in diameter. The pieces ranged from billboard size to kingsize-bed size to coffee-table size. Ages of wind and blowing sand and, every now and then, rainwater, had pumiced the edges and scooped out hollows, so the rocks were sensuous and inviting to the touch. The place was a labyrinth, a natural wonder, a sculpture garden, and a playhouse. I called it the Red Temple. It was my solo place.

I had come to the Sahara in southern Algeria to participate in a vision quest led by my friend and colleague Sabina Wyss and her friend Marianne Roth Mellakh. Marianne had been leading camel caravan trips with the nomadic Tuareg for fifteen years, and Sabina had had the idea of combining the adventure travel with a vision quest. The Sahara was one of the places I'd fantasized about as a young girl, when I rehearsed my exit from Omaha by reading about exotic locales in the *World Book Encyclopedia*, then wandering around my backyard pretending I was there. (Parting the dangling strands of the willow tree, I stepped through a beaded curtain into a Tangiers tearoom; surveying the white expanse of the yard from underneath snow-laden pine boughs, I contemplated the Arctic wilderness I was about to cross.) The moment Sabina had told me about the Sahara quest, I'd wanted to go. And so, four and a half years after I began my journey to the Beloved and four days away from the southern Algerian village of Tamanrasset, one by Land Rover and three by camel, I had set out to find the spot where I would spend my solo and had come upon this anomalous, whimsical place.

I AWOKE TO THE DEEP GOLD DAWN of my third day there. It was the day, traditionally, of the all-night vigil. Crawling out of my sleeping bag, I put on my clothes, a loose-fitting cotton suit of tunic and trousers, called a *gandora*, and rewound my *shesh* around my head. This long turban, folded and looped artfully by the Tuareg and much less so by us questers, kept the sun off the face and could be adjusted in a hurry to prevent windblown sand from infiltrating the nose, mouth, and eyes. Today was the fourth day of the fast, and I was very weak. Moving slowly in the cool dawn, I walked the half mile or so around the curve of the mountains to the stone pile, which Dayeb, my "buddy," an elderly, weathered Tuareg man, had visited the previous evening. Dayeb, like most older Tuareg, had spent many years traveling on camel caravan trips of up to fifteen hundred miles to collect and trade salt harvested from the desert floor. The salt was then mixed with water and poured into cone-shaped molds about the size of the orange "nuns" set up around highway work sites. Because the salt brought higher prices when it was whole and peaked than when it had crumbled, and because loading and unloading it from the backs of the baggage camels risked damaging it, men and camels would trudge on and on for most of the day and night, resting only during the hottest hours of midday. One member of the group carried a small brazier attached to a cord around his neck and in it nursed precious live coals on which he would make the ceremonial tea that our own group drank three times daily. Dayeb had blue-black skin and bright dark eyes. When, after I had found the Red Temple and he had pointed out — with sweeps of his hands and the universal sign for *sleep*, two hands pressed together and pillowed under the cheek — where I could shelter from the afternoon sun, we had walked around the mountain in search of a stone pile site. Our gestures had concurred that this open area before a black niche of rock would do well, and Dayeb had picked up an enormous triangular rock that must have weighed thirty pounds and, hefting it aloft with both hands, declared it into the sand. Each morning I set a second stone to sit like a child at the big one's foot, and in the evening Dayeb moved it aside.

I made my contribution and started slowly back. As I returned to my red rock, the sky was firing up, and though the sun had not yet risen over the mountain, light was suffusing the desert to the south. I climbed up on what I thought of as the "veranda" rock, a large, flat stone that jutted straight out of the southern side of the stony configuration, and settled down to watch morning penetrate the most inviting vista in my immediate landscape. Beyond the black arms of the two ranges, the land fanned away into the distance: a sweep of white sand in which a few low, black islands of rock drifted on the surface. Watching the light pour down the mountains like honey, I thought about the sunrise I would be witnessing in twenty-four hours, after my vigil. On previous fasts, I had always looked forward to the vigil, but this time I felt only a sense of duty. I had no clear idea what my intention would be, and, furthermore, I did not look forward to spending an entire long March night facing east, symbolically the direction of fresh beginnings and dawning vision, but here a gigantic dead end of a black wall just a few hundred feet away. Far more enchanting was the landscape to the south. Jumbo, the Tuareg medicine man who accompanied us on the trip, had told us questers that that was the one area we were not to go into for our solo, since the camels would be grazing there and also because it provided the only access to the outside world. I had come to think of it as the land of the Beloved — elusive and alluring, beckoning and forbidden, present and distant all at once. Now, watching the sun slink down the black range to the west, painting the rocks purple and blue and magenta, it occurred to me that I could break the rules.

"Who says I have to face east?" I asked aloud.

The southern expanse shrugged its shoulders.

"I'll do my vigil facing south," I announced. And instantly felt excited.

Then, as if to confirm this wise decision, two small birds arrived and perched on a tall plinth of rock just behind my shoulder. One began to sing, and on and on it sang, a long, trilling lyric that rose and fell, expounding and imploring, for several seconds. Finally the bird fell silent. Its mate responded with one small chirp, as if to offer encouragement or perhaps ask for more information. The first bird obliged with another round of song. Listening to them with sensibilities honed by days of fasting, solitude, and desert extremity to accept all events as portentous, I had no doubt but that the singer was a male bird and that he was courting his beloved. And then I understood that the birds had come with instructions for how I was to spend my vigil: I would sit facing the enchanting landscape of the south and singing to the Beloved, imploring him to come to me.

Throughout the day, except during the searing hours of the afternoon, when my activities were limited to creeping from one scrap of rock shade to another, I prepared. I brushed my hair, took a sponge bath, and dressed in a clean *gandora* and *shesh*. I had planned to put on clean clothes after the vigil, but I was getting ready for a tryst with the Beloved, and it was clear that, for such an occasion, one had to beautify herself before, not afterward. I prepared the veranda rock, brushing it clean of sand with my hands and carefully choosing four stones, which I arranged on it at each of the cardinal directions. This would be my purpose circle, the sacred navel of the universe, where I would sit and focus on my prayer of meeting the Beloved. In the circle I placed my sleeping bag, a rattle, plenty of water. Anticipation and eagerness tickled me, as if a rendezvous really was nearing.

And at dusk, at that precise moment when you cannot tell from the sky whether it is day or night, and the gate between the worlds of the known and the enticing unknowable creaks open, I stepped over the threshold.

"Greetings, my Beloved," I called out. In the south, the white sand fan, with its black islands of rock, smelted in the twilight. Behind me and to my sides the mountains pressed close. The desert, at least, was paying attention.

"Beloved! Companion! Guide! Seducer! You who beckons me forth into the mystery of the earth, the mystery of life, the mystery of all that invites my participation! Bold one who makes me bold, calling me into what is mine alone to do! Lover who entices my being! Soul guide leading me to the cave on the mountain, I summon you tonight! Be with me! Force of alluring love! Inviting one! Enchanter! You who stand on the far side of what is difficult and even impossible and crook your finger across those abysses I fear to cross! Beloved! Come! Show yourself to me!"

I sat down on the rock and began to shake my little rattle as I called out as many names and terms of praise as I could think of, or rather, that poured out of me in a stream as fluid as the song of the bird to his mate. The more I implored, the more fervently I wanted the Beloved to reveal himself to me as he never had before.

It had been two or three years since I had called the Beloved "Ascends to the Dark" or pictured him as a man resembling Lucas.

Over a period of several months he had gradually lost form and gained in energetic presence. Now his countenance was vague, as if hidden behind one of those watery patches TV news editors put over the face of someone whose anonymity they want to protect. At first I had resisted this transformation: I wanted my handsome imaginal lover back. But the new incarnation, or rather disincarnation, was determined to remain. And although the Beloved was mostly bodiless now, he certainly did not lack substance. Indeed, his presence was palpable, exciting, heated, and erotic. Just thinking about evoking the Beloved, I felt that blast of a response: a surge of erotic energy that shot through my groin to my belly, then spread to my heart, throat, sometimes all the way to the top of my head or down the backs of my thighs and knees, to puddle beneath my feet. Since this transformation had occurred, I made it a point to remind the people who took my workshops that the Beloved was an elusive suitor, and it was not necessary to pin him or her down into some recognizable form. Indeed, the Beloved probably needed both his fugitive and his seductive aspects in order to excite us forth into life at its most arousing. If we tried to hold the Beloved still, I said, even in the form of a particular image, he or she could not slip off into the very direction we most needed to go.

That's what I said. Tonight, though, I wanted concreteness. I wanted a revelation, a new image, a message, a suffusion of rapture. Something big. I knew very well that one can't dictate what one gets on a vision quest, but, as Rumi said, "You must ask for what you really want," and so I did. Repeatedly.

"Come to me, my Beloved," I called out into the night. "Show yourself to me! You are the great and seductive and empowering force of my life. You have changed me utterly over these past few years. Now enter me! Teach me! I want to know you even more fully."

I knew that the Beloved, if he did come, could take hours about it, and I didn't want to fall asleep and miss something important. Yet even after just an hour or two or three — there was no way of telling

— I was already getting stiff and impatient. The stars revolved too slowly around the sky. The moon would not rise until nearly morning, so the light on the land was fixed. I wondered how fast the stars moved and briefly wished I had a watch so I could occupy some time by figuring out the ratio between star progress and watch-hand progress.

I decided to give thanks. That would be a good thing to do on a vigil, and besides, it would show the Beloved that I had learned a thing or two about love. So I picked up my rattle again and began to speak aloud the names of all those whom I loved or liked or admired or who had touched me in some way. I started with Andy. Then I named the other questers and our guides, European and Tuareg. My camel. After that, I spoke, in a spirit of gratitude, loved names in no particular order, simply acknowledging whoever appeared in my mind's eye: family living and dead, friends, teachers, idols, questers, famous writers, animals, neighbors, lovers. What had started as a ploy for passing time gained momentum until I felt I was being blessed by each of those people who rose up before me, reminding me of their contribution to my life.

After I had given thanks for those I loved, it occurred to me to turn to the unlikable black mountain in the east and offer prayers for those who had hurt or disappointed me, and so I did that, in the same spirit, and was gratified to discover that the list was quite short. I wondered if it might have been longer before the Beloved entered my life and stretched my heart in so many new directions. And, although I had included him in my paean of gratitude, I thought again of Lucas, who had started me on this journey. Then I turned back to the south and settled down once more to watch the caravan of stars trudge across their ancient terrain.

ABOUT A YEAR AND A HALF EARLIER, I'd had the opportunity to sit with Lucas on a carpet of autumn oak and beech leaves in Rocky Mountain National Park and to tell him what had happened to me as a result of his dream and his words of love. I had not seen him since Bill and I drove away from the ranch under Shandoka's shadow, and we had not communicated since the day I had phoned him. Now we had both been asked to give talks at a gathering of eco-psychologists and educators whose work focused on providing transformative experiences in nature. I was to talk about personal ceremony; Lucas would discuss his wilderness programs for teenagers. When I had received the brochure about the conference and seen his name on the list of presenters, I had almost changed my mind about participating. I told Andy why.

"You can handle it," Andy said. "You need to go and take advantage of this opportunity to talk about your work."

So I had gone, anxious about what might happen to my allegedly quieted heart, for the strange yet irrefutable fact remained that I had never been smitten with Lucas in his presence, but only after his declaration of love finally turned me on like a house full of lamps set on timers to light by themselves when the owners are on vacation.

When I spotted Lucas in the meeting room on the first night of the conference, my heart skipped. He was bending his tall frame over three or four people, talking intently. I looked away, then looked back. He would not focus in my mind. He was half blurry recollection of the man I'd met on the mountain more than three years earlier, half distorted fantasy lover. I could not conceive of any course of action to resolve the two, so I impulsively made my way over to the group and interrupted them with my arrival. Lucas and I greeted each other as old friends and made a date to take a walk before breakfast the following morning.

So we sat facing each other on golden leaves, our backs against two white aspens, a tree that always struck me as omniscient because of its multiple kohl-rimmed, almond-shaped eyes, an effect created each time the bark healed over a wound made when a branch broke off. And finally I had the chance to tell him the whole story: the first longing; the sense that what truly longed to be loved was the divine itself; my reunion with Melissa and how that led me to Ascends to the Dark; beginning the workshops; confronting the Pampered Woman; weddings in the desert with the Beloved and in Las Vegas with Andy; the ceremony at Ground Zero that the Beloved called me to — in short, the revolution of my life into passion, compassion, and engaged eroticism. I left nothing out. "And," I added, as if it were an afterthought. "I climbed to the cave."

I HAD CLIMBED TO THE CAVE. The year after I met Lucas, I'd returned to Shandoka with Bill for another vision quest. And realized that in order to complete the dream, I, too, had to make that journey.

It had been an arduous ascent, all of it supervised by Bill, who stood at the edge of the meadow, watching me through his binoculars. When I had assured him that such close monitoring would not be necessary, he informed me that he would be doing it anyway. He was worried about the loose rocks, which would be even more hazardous slicked with the rain that had fallen that morning. "As a guide, I'd advise you against doing this," he told me. "As your friend, I know you have to do it."

So there he stood, watching, watching. I was acutely conscious of him and how long it seemed to be taking me to make any progress, but I would not turn around to see how he was taking it. The day before, as I'd stared up at the slope, contemplating this journey, I realized that I could not look back once I had started. I would maintain my connection with the mountain, focus on what was drawing me up. I would not examine where I was coming from. That included, I now realized, the prickling refrain of doubt that I was too old for this journey, not fit enough, and foolish besides, and that Bill, the superathlete, must be impatient with my pace. I decided to liberate myself from my rain gear. Although the sky was still overcast, the rain had stopped, so I tore off my jacket, peeled my rain pants over my boots, and stuffed the bundle into my daypack. Then I shook my hair out and scooped it up into a barrette to get it out of my face. Immediately a breeze rushed to cool my skin. Now that I was unhindered by the rustle of Gore-Tex, silence rushed to surround me. Gradually my heart quieted. And with the physical stripping away, the anxiety dissolved as well. I stopped worrying about whether Bill might be restless and instead felt the sweetness of his support. Besides, age had nothing to do with it: I had to go to the cave on the mountain.

At the lower third of the slope, the hike was almost pleasant. The hill, covered in long green grass, sloped gently up. A few small spruces grew amid bright spots of orange Indian paintbrush, indigo gentian, and lemon-yellow portulaca. I felt almost whimsical about my little adventure. I felt as if I were playing a game of hide-and-seek with Lucas's dream image of me. Was there a Trebbe in the cave? Heading up there toward her, would I pass a point where I felt more like me — the ideal me, the future me — than I had a step earlier? Crisscrossing this game was another: I was following in the footsteps of a guide from the other world. At first he had been Lucas, but then, like a hero in any tale undergoing time and many tellings, he had metamorphosed into a mythic figure. One had split into two. The path I walked was blazed by my Escort to the Beloved. I headed toward the Beloved himself.

The difficulty of the journey became apparent as the angle of the slope sharpened. I realized with a start what had escaped me during three years of camping in the meadow and gazing up at this mountain: that the reason all the trees were so small was because they stood directly in the path of rock- and snow-slides and never got a chance to reach maturity. Then the trees ceased altogether, and rocks alone proliferated in the grass. And then there was no grass, just layer upon layer of rock. Now I had to stop after every step to choose my next step: small stones were treacherously unstable, boulders were too big to get on or over. I was clambering about when I heard an anomalous sound, which at first I took for the rush of wind. But this sound came from a particular place, and it did not crest and fade, as wind sounds would. Unmistakably, it was water. Several minutes later, a few vertical feet higher, the sound coalesced into an image. It was a waterfall, toward the east, where Shandoka's long shoulder began to slope up toward the summit. It plunged down from a black rock overhang, fell about sixty feet in a straight, narrow, silver jet, then vanished into the black tumble of scree. It was a creature of the heights, this waterfall, like a rare species of mountain goat or a wilderness nymph, beings who thrive in certain wild, remote niches and never venture anywhere else. Unknown to ground-dwelling life-forms, such beings could be witnessed only by those who braved the heights, like the raven, who croaked now as it beat its heavy wings through the gray, misty air, crossing between the waterfall and me. Like me. Starting on again, I felt reassured that I was on the right track.

So steep was the slope now that I could not even see the cave above me. On I went. The cave appeared again. It vanished, it appeared. The rain started again, and I stopped to pull on my waterproof gear, grateful for an excuse to rest. Shortly after I set off again, not even my slow two-legged approach would suffice; I had to hunker down and creep like an animal over the jagged, wobbly field of rock. The cave vanished once more. And reemerged. Finally, with each step, a little more of the opening rose up, a black orb emerging over a rocky horizon.

And suddenly I was there and gasped aloud. Blooming right outside the entrance to the cave was a huge clump of columbine — lavender, blue, and white, in full bloom and in such profusion that the plants looked less like individual stalks than a bush, deliberately planted by some high-altitude gardener to grace the doorway to a sacred place. I took off my pack, set it on the ground, then sat before the entrance, waiting for my heart to steady. The cave was smaller than I had imagined, a roundish shape less than six feet in diameter and a few inches less in height. The walls were black, rough, and slick with the water that seeped and dripped continuously over them. The ground was covered with damp moss of a brilliant kelly green. When I could breathe normally, I asked permission to enter, waited a moment, and stepped through the opening.

The place was exquisite, a tiny, moist, fecund grotto at the top of a stony mountain. It was a gem in a big, rough setting. It was gentle, feminine, and welcoming. I greeted it, and the success of the journey, in the only way that seemed appropriate, by lying down on my stomach on the wet moss. I breathed in the pure mineral sweetness of the soil and spread my arms out to the sides, so the fingertips of both hands touched liquid rock. I knelt then and raised my face to the roof. Droplets of water fell onto my head, neck, shoulders. I tipped my head back, and they fell on my face. The earth was constantly bestowing its blessings on the lives of all us humans, I thought, and would, if only we opened ourselves to them, anoint us. I cupped my hands and the water blessings flowed into them, opened my fingers and the blessings dripped out of my hands onto the moss. I was a pipeline for earth's blessings. I leaned my head back and opened my mouth, and the very first drop that fell from the roof plopped right in. I laughed out loud. I ate the food of the earth. The next one fell into my mouth as well, and all the others, though I did not move, missed, to slide and drip over my face and hair. Kneeling on moss, I gave myself over to a radical baptism by the earth.

Then was time to put on the dream. I leaned out of the cave and from my daypack pulled out the purple scarf with the moons and stars and tied it around my head. I stood and stepped to the entrance of the cave and surveyed the land below for the first time. The meadow was very far away, my tarp a tiny smudge of green I could not even locate at first. I felt a nostalgic fondness for what was below, as if it represented not just distance in space but in time as well, as if I looked down at the whole journey to the Beloved.

Until I opened my mouth, I did not know what I would sing. The song, however, was ready. It was on my tongue, and out it flowed. I will not record it here, for it has always felt like something that must be sung to be communicated, sung to fulfill its purpose, which is to invite. Suffice it to say that it was a song of invitation to people to come to the earth, to receive her blessings, to pass them on, and on and on.

While I was singing I saw a black sliver emerge from a swatch of trees, moving with purpose. Bill. He paused. Probably he lifted his binoculars to his eyes and saw me standing there in my purple scarf, singing, for he turned immediately and the trees took him up again.

When I had sung the song several times, I entered the cave for the last time. I bowed and thanked the place for the ways in which it had beckoned Lucas and then beckoned me. Then I took off my scarf, put it in my daypack, and stepped outside. I turned once more to bow, then started down. Moments later, a light fog rolled in from the west and completely obscured both the cave and the green land below. I picked my way back to base camp enshrouded, like those journeyers in the myths whose passage is sealed from prying eyes.

"SO YOU SEE," I said to Lucas, who leaned against an aspen about three hundred miles northeast of Shandoka, "what has happened to me because of you. A dream that took — what? — a minute to get dreamed in you, words that took three or four seconds for you to speak to me — they have completely changed my life. I feel like I was a little mouse foraging in a field, quite content, believing I knew where I was going and what my life was all about. Then — whoosh! — an eagle swooped out of the sky and scooped me up and set me down in a whole new landscape. The eagle was you, and the Beloved is what you flew me to."

It had taken a while to tell the whole story, and I paused at last. I realized I was shivering, and it was only partly because of the chill in the Rocky Mountain morning air. I suddenly felt as if I had dredged the whole of me out of myself, all the fire and import, and that it would take a while for my heart to pump up enough warmth for replenishment.

Lucas smiled. And when he responded, his tone was — well, *supportive* would be the best description. Caring yet professional, he congratulated me on the good work I had done.

I felt like a disappointed child. I'd expected more: acknowledgment of the shared journey, maybe a narrative of his own, eagerly launched, about how our meeting had changed his life, too. Instead, he distanced himself from the tale and spoke as if to one of his therapy clients who had bravely gone through a tough time and come out ahead. And then he launched into an account of his own life. He had read the conclusion of my story as an invitation to respond in kind — not with a narrative on how his life had been changed by me, but with news of what had occurred since we'd last seen each other. As I struggled to put on a listening face, inwardly I brewed with resentment. Then, as he detailed challenges with his partners, his clients, his children, his health, I realized what I was doing. I was still hoping for a payoff. How quickly my lofty yearning could plummet into greedy, mundane desire. And then I realized that of course Lucas had to detach himself from the story now, as he'd always had to do, for the Escort can only lead us to the divine Beloved and then must slip away.

I adjusted my focus on the man who sat across from me and saw a person I had known once and liked, years ago, before his dream-self stole my heart. I saw a good-looking man with a vision of what he wanted to do in the world. He was accustomed to spending his days counseling others and now, finding himself before an elder he trusted and admired, sought only a little sympathy, perhaps some guidance about the messy, important conundrums of his life. I realized I was glad to be that person for him. I got more comfortable against the trunk of the wide-eyed aspen and gave him my full attention.

IN THE SAHARA, I JERKED. I had fallen asleep. Quickly, I checked the stars, which seemed not to have moved. Good. I hadn't slept long. Nevertheless, I was sure the night had turned colder, though that might have been due more to the relaxing of my metabolism than to a drop in the temperature. Eager to call attention to myself, in case the lapse in consciousness might have knocked me out of the Beloved's radar, I stood and beseeched into the night: "O, my Beloved, I'm only human! I can't help falling asleep! I wish I could stay awake for a thousand nights singing to you, dancing for you, calling out to you, but I am only a human woman. Come to me, oh, you seductive one, you who knows me better than any, you who smiles alluringly in the path between where I am and where I don't even know I need to get to, come to me! Show yourself to me. Ravish me!"

I sat down again, wrapped myself up in my sleeping bag, and tried to focus on the movement of the stars. I would stare and stare, trying not to blink as one diamond of light hovered over the peak of a mountain, almost holding my breath in hopes of seeing it drop in. My attention invariably veered, and when I looked back, the star had vanished, sucked up into whatever subterranean passage it would follow until it had circled back on the following night to its portal into the sky. I wondered if the Beloved might appear in the stars, coalesce into some new constellation. Or maybe he was a mountain. Was watching mountains swallow stars as important a task as it now seemed, or was it a distraction? The Beloved could be anywhere. But where, where? How could I coax him forth?

I thought of a story from the Benin tradition of eastern Africa. Before the birth of their child, a king and queen consulted a soothsayer and learned that their son must never know the love of a woman, or he would die. Anxious to protect him, they built him a complex to live in, beautiful and completely inaccessible, surrounded by seven rings of walls, each guarded by a ferocious dog. At the innermost door stood a bodyguard, heavily armed, who also kept an eye on the prince whenever he had to leave the palace. But one day when they were in the market, a beautiful young woman, Ahla, glimpsed the young man and made up her mind to win his love. With determination and cleverness she penetrated the very center of his prison sanctuary. The prince saw her, fell into desire, and the two spent the night in passionate embrace. In the morning, as it was foretold, the young man died.

But myth cannot allow love to kill. Shortly before the prince was to be cremated, a stranger to the village informed the grieving parents that he might live again if one person could walk through the flames of the funeral pyre and take his hand. Both the king and queen, each eagerly confident in their ability at first, failed even to penetrate the edge of the raging pyre. Ahla, of course, succeeded. It was love that guided her through the fire, and she never stumbled. She walked right through the heat of death to take her beloved's hand, he opened his eyes to her gaze, and they were reunited for life.

"Haven't I been through the fire for you, my Beloved?" I called. "Won't you come alive for me now?"

I recalled how afraid and ashamed I had once been of desire, more ashamed still to admit it. Now I taught workshops in which I encouraged people to track their desire to its source, then channel it into contributions to the world that only they could make. I chose the courses of my own life according to what seduced, from traveling to the Sahara, to jumping up from my desk and rushing outside to throw myself into an autumn wind that was frothing up everything in its path, to volunteering to investigate how our small village could get a grant to plant some trees. I no longer feared people or new situations. My human beloved, Andy, and I had discovered both a shared interest in the divine Beloved, which guided our individual avocations, and a rekindled erotic passion for each other in our late middle age. Andy had built a wood-fired kiln and a pottery studio at our house and was part of an active network of other full-time potters and artists whom some stroke of extraordinary synchronicity had moved, independently and for a variety of reasons, from all over the country to our remote corner of Pennsylvania. I taught workshops on the Beloved and led vision quests around the world and was writing a book on the Beloved and the path of erotic engagement that he had beguiled me along and helped me to understand.

I had stopped needing Andy's approval for my ideas and acts, because the Beloved had taught me to pick up my chrysanthemum-yellow skirts and step into every concern as if into the arms of my troubadour. As a guide, a teacher, and a writer, I was bolder, more impassioned, and more creative now, in my mid-fifties, than I had ever been. In all my works and days I sensed the Beloved's ardor as he slipped in and out of dappled sunlight just ahead of me, teasing me to translate into two-dimensional words and three-dimensional practices his multidimensional magnetism. Sometimes I felt I was flying faster than I could manage. I felt like the masthead on a ship, a female form pinned to the bow as if by gale-force winds and huge waves, and gaping in wide-eyed, shrieking disbelief as she plowed into the maelstrom. I was holding on, all right, but sometimes I wasn't sure if I would survive the ride. There was no other way to go, of course, so on I went. And I had never felt so alive.

THE SKY WAS DEFINITELY LIGHTENING. At first I'd thought it was just my imagination, but no, paleness had begun to infiltrate the black night to the east, and a few stars seemed to have been captured in it. There had been moments during the past eight or ten hours when I had feared, as the ancients surely did, that on this night the most dire of all things had occurred in the heavens, and the sun would not reappear to warm the land. On the tail of my relief, however, came anxiety. If dawn was close, the Beloved did not have much time left. At sunrise I would rise, step out of my circle of stones, pack up, thank this desert home, and start the slow trek back to base camp for breakfast. I pleaded once again, more desperately this time: "Beloved! Come to me! Enter me! Please!" I felt the presence of the Beloved always, but now I wanted him more vivid than ever. I wanted him manifest. I wanted him passionate like Krishna, resolute with love for me like Majnun, one step ahead like Huldra. I wanted him as sexy as Eros and as ecstatic as Dionysus. I wanted him at the end of the flames, like Ahla's prince.

But dawn would not be delayed. The paleness that had been almost indiscernible fortified and spread, and the black islands in the sandy expanse before me were once again assuming their shapes. Then the truth hit. The Beloved would not be coming. It was as simple as that. The sun would rise, and there would be no big encounter, no mystical revelation, no divine kundalini orgasm. I had forced myself to stay awake, had prayed and called and praised for hours — and the Beloved was not going to come.

And then something amazing happened. I had no sooner accepted that cold, disappointing knowledge than I was flooded with joy. I gasped out loud, and tears filled my eyes. I clutched my hands to my heart as gratitude seized me as in a great embrace. I could not get over my good fortune. That body, soul, biography, and circumstance had so fused into a person who would think it a good idea to spend a long night sitting on a rock in the Sahara Desert and calling out for the Beloved, and that that person happened to be me, struck me as miraculous. I could have thanked all holy forces, ordained and fringe, celestial and earthly, big and small for such a generous blessing.

"TO CARRY A GOD WITHIN ONESELF is practically the same as being God oneself," Jung wrote. He was reflecting on Mechtilde of Magdeburg, that ecstatic lover of Jesus, and asking himself if the force she described as "my soul roar[ing] with the voice of a hungry lion" had anything in common with the spiritual hunger of a patient of his. This woman had recently begun to consider Jung as a kind of divine "father-lover," and he wanted to help her peel away the projection. Then it occurred to him that the hunger for intimacy with the divine that was shared by his twentieth-century analysand and the thirteenth-century Christian mystic might actually be a powerful independent force that transcended the ages and had important implications for personal transformation. "Could the longing for a god be a *passion*," Jung wondered, betraying his excitement with italics, "welling up from our darkest, instinctual nature, a passion unswayed by any outside influences, deeper and stronger perhaps than the love for a human person?" Working with his patient and observing how she gradually took upon herself the charismatic energy she had originally perceived in him, he was persuaded that the quest for sacred intimacy is a fundamental human drive. It impels the seeker to grope, usually in instinctive, unconscious ways, for some known person upon whom to direct a deeply buried, yet forcefully bubbling font of soulful longing, passion, and creativity. Brought to consciousness, then mindfully activated, it can engender "the most immediate experience of the Divine which it is psychologically possible to imagine."[1]

This "being a God oneself" is no delusional, self-important elevation of oneself above others, no exertion of power *over* other people, but a confident, curious, delighted wielding of all the possibilities of one's being. It is an ongoing creative experiment that is not limited, as people commonly assume, to masters of painting and music, but is the malleable stuff that life tosses before all of us all the time. Like Ahla in love, we are the creators, destroyers, and resurrectors of our own fate, and, like her, when the love of the Beloved beckons us, we can walk through flames with grace and confidence. Seeking the divine Beloved, we become the lover the Beloved loves. Or, as physicist Fred Alan Wolf would put it, "the electron dances with the cloud of possibilities by following its lead as if the cloud were *real*."[2] Turning to the flame that calls us, we become incandescent ourselves. We shoulder our own divinity and set off up the trail to the mountain cave where our possibility beckons. Pursuing the Beloved, we move into the world as into the arms of a waiting lover.

IN OUR SAHARA BASE CAMP that day I told the story of my vigil to the guides and the other questers, and then, when I got home, I told it to Andy, and as the weeks went on, to some of my closest friends. It was Andy who discerned the true meaning of the experience.

When I had finished describing that moment of joy that unexpectedly followed a night in which the divine visitation I'd so longed for did not occur, he exclaimed, "That *was* the Beloved. You've been saying all along that it's the seeking that's important, not the finding. We never know when the Beloved will come, or even if, but that doesn't stop us from following what calls to us. You were following the Beloved that night. And when you felt that joy at the end of your vigil, that was the Beloved coming to you."

I jumped up and gave him a big kiss.

My deep gratitude goes, above all, to my husband, Andy Gardner, whose love and trust of me, combined with his own inexhaustibly curious mind, enabled him to take an active, supportive interest in a path that began for me with a seismic infatuation with another man. I could not have done any of this without him. As a friend of mine remarked, "He belongs in the Husbands Hall of Fame."

I thank:

Bill Plotkin, who was there at some of the most important junctions along the way;

Barbara Vernovage, for the winding, searching, and honest talks about the Beloved over dozens of breakfasts in the diners of Susquehanna County;

Kerry Brady, for abundant insight and friendship;

The friends and colleagues who shared their own stories and theories of the Beloved and whose excitement about this subject kept me excited, especially Liz Brensinger, Michael DeMaria, Chuck Dorris, Anneliese Heurich, Cynthia Keyworth, Meredith Little, Nancy Qualls-Corbett, Peter Scanlan, Jeannette Samanen, Phil Sims, Marcy Vaughn, Melissa Werner, Joe Woolley, and the Woodstock Group;

Those who organized or sponsored workshops on the Beloved — Joan Brady, Vickie Cunningham, Ellen Weaver, Lauren Chambliss, Kate Fitzpatrick, Valerie Reilly and John Sparks, Mike Beck, Audrey Dickson, Jim Samanen, Stuart Woodin, Kelly Ransom, Temenos Conference and Retreat Center, Rowe Camp and Conference Center, Shoal Sanctuary, Hope Springs Institute, Hollyhock, Bridgit's Place, and the Burren Holistic Centre — and all the people who attended those workshops, who wrote and phoned and emailed me to tell me their own stories of how the Beloved came into their lives. You helped me to find ever deeper meaning in this fascinating subject;

My agent, Anne Depue, and my editor, Georgia Hughes, at New World Library, for their excitement about this book, for their astuteness as readers of the manuscript, and for their inspired suggestions;

Parabola, that extraordinary magazine of myth and tradition, that has informed and ignited so much of my thinking, introduced me to new myths, and honored me by publishing my work;

And to "Lucas": thank you for the dream.

PROLOGUE. THE EMBRACE OF THE GOD

1. Myths, like the one of Krishna and his lovers, provide a wonderful context for finding our way through the wide and baffling world around us. Many people have defined myth in many ways (and far more accurately than the current popular usage, which means, simply, "false belief"), but none has captured the essence better than the child who said, "A myth is something that's make-believe on the outside and true on the inside." Myths, says author Max Oelschlaeger, "make intelligible what would otherwise remain incomprehensible" (*The Idea of Wilderness* [New Haven: Yale University Press, 1991], 10). Myths are narrative tapestries that depict the universal soul story. Although they relate cosmic problems and earth-shifting solutions, the motivations, dilemmas, solutions, and passageways they describe give us clues about how to approach our own most human dilemmas. All that befalls the characters of myth through magic, metamorphosis, and the interventions of gods is happening to us today through the mysteries of desire, fear, competitiveness, self-discovery, and the infinite doings of the world around us; myth offers us a map by which we can find our way.

CHAPTER 1. THE LEAP OF THE FLAME

1. Quoted in Freya Matthews, "Conservation and Self-Realization: A Deep Ecology Perspective," in *The Deep Ecology Movement: An Introductory Anthology*, ed. Alan Drengston and Yuichi Inoue (Berkeley: North Atlantic Books, 1995), 129. Matthews discusses the Latin term *conatus*, used by medieval philosophers and meaning "the impulse, not only for self-preservation or

self-maintenance, but also for self-increase or self-perfection — an impulse that is present in all living beings."

2. I had met Bill Plotkin in 1998, when I went on a vision quest led by him and three other guides in the San Juan Mountains. At the time I was immersed in writing about Native American issues, and Bill had impressed me as a person who seemed to embody both a practical knowledge and a deep, soulful connection with wild nature in a way I had never encountered in a white person. A few years later I began to apprentice with him and started working as his coguide in 1996. Although I had founded my own guide organization, Vision Arrow, in 1997, I also continued to work with AVI and, on occasion, to partner up with other vision quest guides as well.

3. Quoted in Gay Wilson Allen, *Waldo Emerson: A Biography* (New York: Viking Press, 1981), 269–70.

CHAPTER 2. DESIRE, OR THE FALL

1. Riane Eisler, *Sacred Pleasure: Sex, Myth, and the Politics of the Body* (San Francisco: HarperCollins, 1996), 174.

2. Chrétien de Troyes, "The Story of the Grail (Perceval)," *Arthurian Romances* (London: Penguin, 1991), 420.

3. Albert Camus, "Love of Life," in *Lyrical and Critical Essays*, ed. Philip Thody, trans. Ellen Conroy Kennedy (New York: Vintage Books, 1968), 57.

CHAPTER 3. THE LOVE WOLF

1. Izumi Shikibu, "My black hair tangled," in *The Erotic Spirit*, ed. Sam Hamill (Boston: Shambhala, 1996), 62.

2. Anonymous Egyptian, "He is the love-wolf," *Love Lyrics of Ancient Egypt*, trans. Barbara Hughes Fowler (Chapel Hill: University of North Carolina Press, 1994), 80.

3. Roland Barthes, *A Lover's Discourse: Fragments*, trans. Richard Howard (New York: Hill and Wang, 1979), 13.

4. Anton Chekhov, "The Boa Constrictor and the Rabbit," in *The Unknown Chekhov: Stories and Other Writings*, trans. Avrahm Yarmolinsky (New York: Ecco Press, 1987), 131–36.

5. Walt Whitman, "An American Primer," reprinted in *Parabola* 8, no. 3 (Summer 1983): 6.

CHAPTER 5. SOULFUL YEARNING

1. David Williams, *A Naturalist's Guide to Canyon Country* (Helena, MT: Falcon Publishing, 2000), 22–23.

2. Quoted in Irina Tweedie, *Daughter of Fire: A Diary of a Spiritual Training with a Sufi Master* (Nevada City, CA: Dolphin Publishing, 1986), 84–85.

3. The German-Jewish theologian Franz Rosenzweig has called this the only pure commandment, the one that issued forth as a directive from the realm of spiritual experience and could not have originated as a civic law. The human soul, in agreeing to this imperative, acknowledges itself as the lover of God and affirms its willingness to give that love. "In the lover's faith in her lover the soul becomes a truly human being," Rosenzweig writes, speaking of the soul as the feminine principle of the supreme being. "The Lover of God, the Love of Man," *Parabola* 20, no. 4 (Winter 1995): 64.

4. Al Gore, *Earth in the Balance: Ecology and the Human Spirit* (New York: Penguin, 1993), 220–21.

5. Julian Jaynes, *The Origin of Consciousness in the Breakdown of the Bicameral Mind* (Boston: Houghton Mifflin, 1976), 84.

6. Jaynes, *Origin of Consciousness*, 442–45.

7. P. L. Travers, *What the Bee Knows: Reflections on Myth, Symbol, and Story* (London: Penguin, 1993), 167.

8. Paul G. Zolbrod, *Diné bahane': The Navajo Creation Story* (Albuquerque: University of New Mexico Press, 1985), 180–81.

9. Jelaluddin Rumi, "Some Kiss We Want," *The Soul of Rumi: A New Collection of Ecstatic Poems*, trans. Coleman Barks (San Francisco: HarperSanFrancisco, 2001), 127.

10. Kabir, *The Kabir Book: Forty-Four of the Ecstatic Poems of Kabir*, versions by Robert Bly (Boston: Beacon Press, 1977), 8.

11. St. Teresa of Avila, *The Life of Teresa of Jesus: The Autobiography of St. Teresa of Avila*, trans. E. Allison Peers (Garden City, NY: Image Books, 1960), 111.

12. Quoted in Dr. Javad Nurbakhsh, *Sufi Women* (New York: Khaniqah-Nimatullahi Publications, 1983), 73.

13. John Donne, "Sonnet 14," in *John Donne: The Complete English Poems* (New York: Penguin, 1986), 314.

14. Uvavnuk, "The great sea," in *Women in Praise of the Sacred*, ed. Jane Hirshfield (New York: HarperCollins, 1995), 193.

15. Christopher Sandford, *Clapton: Edge of Darkness* (New York: Da Capo Press, 1999), 121.

16. Johann Wolfgang von Goethe, "Soulful Yearning," trans. Trebbe Johnson, with guidance and insight from Anneliese Heurich. The poem, in its entirety, is as follows:

Tell no one, only the very wise,
For the masses will surely mock you.

What I praise is what's wild for life,
What longs for death by fire.

In the calm wake of the lovenights
That conceived you, where you conceived,
A strange feeling overcomes you
As the quiet candle glows.

No more are you hounded
By gloom and dark limitations,
And a longing for a higher lovemaking
Grabs you and sweeps you up.

Distance matters nothing now.
Flying you come, flying and spellbound,
And at last, seduced by the light,
You, butterfly, are burned alive.

And as long as you haven't lived this:
Just this: to die and so to become,
You are only a dull visitor
On the dark earth.

17. Quoted in Jean Houston, *The Search for the Beloved: Journeys in Mythology and Sacred Psychology* (New York: Tarcher/Putnam, 1987), 124.
18. Houston, *Search for the Beloved*, 125.

CHAPTER 6. THE BELOVED

1. Hazrat Inayat Khan, *The Heart of Sufism* (Boston: Shambhala, 1999), 225.
2. Quoted in Peter A. Kwasniewski, "Wise and Foolish Virgins," *Parabola* 23, no. 2 (Summer 1998): 23.
3. Alain Danielou, *The Hindu Temple: Deification of Eroticism* (Rochester, VT: Inner Traditions, 1999), 8, 86. Danielou, who spent twenty years studying Indian music, art, and philosophy, demonstrates the utter inevitability of spirituality and eroticism in Indian art: "All means of contact between the individual and the universal being are of a voluptuous nature....Consequently, whatever causes a more intense pleasure on the erotic level brings us closer to absolute voluptuousness, which is in its essence divine and is both desirable and important for the development of the spiritual being. It is a thousand times easier to reach inner perfection through the experience of voluptuousness in bodily union — the image of the state of divine union — than by practicing austere virtues" (104–5).

4. Quoted in Elaine Pagels, *The Gnostic Gospels* (New York: Random House, 1979), 55.

5. Barbara G. Walker, *The Woman's Encyclopedia of Myths and Secrets* (New York: HarperCollins, 1983), 932.

6. Adolf Holl, *The Left Hand of God: A Biography of the Holy Spirit* (New York: Image Books, 1996), 20.

7. Samuel L. Lewis, *Sufi Vision and Initiation: Meetings with Remarkable Beings* (San Francisco: Sufi Islamia/Prophecy Publications, 1986), 35.

8. The Ojibwa relate the story of a young man who dreams of an elegant figure in golden clothing and a green plumed headdress, embodiment of the corn plant, who instructs him how to plant and cultivate that core crop of the Americas. A Lakota tale describes how Woodpecker brings the first Indian flute and its haunting love melody to a lovesick man desperate for some way to make known to his sweetheart the feelings he cannot speak.

9. John P. Dourley, *Love, Celibacy and the Inner Marriage* (Toronto: Inner City Books, 1987), 32.

10. Quoted in Dourley, *Love, Celibacy and the Inner Marriage*, 33.

11. Gertrude of Helfta, *The Herald of Divine Love* (New York: Paulist Press, 1993), 105, 175, 187.

12. Holl, *The Left Hand of God*, 22.

13. Plato, "The Symposium," in *Great Dialogues of Plato*, trans. W. H. D. Rouse (New York: New American Library, 1956), 98.

14. Apuleius, *On the God of Socrates*, trans. Thomas Taylor (Edmonds, WA: Holmes Publishing, 2001), 11.

15. Apuleius, *On the God of Socrates*, 12.

16. Marie-Louise von Franz, "Daimons and the Inner Companion," *Parabola* 6, no. 4 (Fall 1991): 41–42. Von Franz notes that, in its original form in Egypt and pre-Hellenic Greece, the *daimon* was "a momentarily perceptible divine activity, such as a startled horse, a failure in work, illnesses, madness, terror in certain natural spots."

17. Mircea Eliade, *Myth and Reality* (New York: Harper & Row, 1963), 120. Eliade quotes J. P. Vernant in this section: "The Muses sing . . . the first appearance of the world, the genesis of the gods, the birth of humanity. The past thus revealed is much more than the antecedent of the present; it is its source."

18. Interview with Terry Gross on *Fresh Air*, National Public Radio, October 10, 2000.

19. Anna Akhmatova, "The Muse," in *The Complete Poems*, trans. Judith Hemschemeyer (Boston: Zephyr Press, 1992), 374.

20. Margaret Fuller, "Woman in the Nineteenth Century," in *The Woman and the Myth: Margaret Fuller's Life and Writings*, ed. Bell Gale Chevigny (Old Westbury, NY: Feminist Press, 1968), 264. Fuller goes on to say that

although it was currently more native to a woman's character to serve as the inspiration for art than to create it herself, she looked forward to the day when there might be "one creative energy, one incessant revelation" flowing in both men and women.

21. Diane Ackerman, "Who's There?" in *Origami Bridges: Poems* (New York: HarperCollins, 2002), 243.

22. Robert Graves, *The White Goddess* (New York: Farrar, Straus and Giroux, 1978), 448–49.

23. Sylvia Browne, *Book of Angels* (Carlsbad, CA: Hay House, 2003), 29.

24. Giuseppe Tomasi di Lampedusa, *The Leopard*, trans. Archibald Colquhoun (New York: Pantheon Books, 1988), 291–92.

25. C. G. Jung, *Memories, Dreams, Reflections*, trans. Richard and Clara Winston (New York: Vintage Books, 1965), 336–37.

26. Jung, *Memories, Dreams, Reflections*, 182. Jung described Philemon as a "pagan" who "brought with him an Egypto-Hellenistic atmosphere with a Gnostic coloration."

27. Jung, *Memories, Dreams, Reflections*, 183.

28. Jean Houston, *The Search for the Beloved: Journeys in Mythology and Sacred Psychology* (New York: Tarcher/Putnam, 1987), 235.

29. Caitlín Matthews, *In Search of Woman's Passionate Soul* (Rockport, ME: Element Books, 1997), 20. In researching her book, Matthews corresponded with many women. She discovered that several had long enjoyed a robust relationship with the "regulator of the reservoir of passion." Some respondents expressed their relief that the inner lover was to be the subject of a book; they had believed that they alone harbored such a presence in their heart, and they had never spoken of him to anyone. The secret wasn't as shameful as masturbation, one woman observed, but it came close. Several women referred to the daimon as a being intimate with yet separate from them. He influenced every aspect of their life, drawing out the fullest expression of each: "He knows us intimately, and wants us to bring all our inner riches into the daylight of the everyday world," one stated (15). Another used the word *lifeline* to describe her daimon: "If I'm on the edge of an emotional cliff, he holds me and prevents me from falling as surely as if he were there" (152). Thrilled with the burst of creativity that a strengthened relationship with the daimon had fostered in her, yet another reported: "I feel I am merely the hands and voice of something that lies at my core, at the core of all being, the Beloved who wears different faces and transcends all form, time and place" (191).

30. Dourley, *Love, Celibacy and the Inner Marriage*, 8.

31. Nancy Qualls-Corbett, *The Sacred Prostitute: Eternal Aspect of the Feminine* (Toronto: Inner City Books, 1988), 141.

32. For more information about this process, see Eligio Stephen Gallegos, *The Personal Totem Pole Process* (Velarde, NM: Moon Bear Press, 1996) and Trebbe Johnson, "Finding Your Animal Guides," *Yoga Journal* (March/April 1993): 26–32.

33. Houston, *Search for the Beloved*, 130.

34. Quoted in Annemarie Schimmel, *Mystical Dimensions of Islam* (Chapel Hill: University of North Carolina Press, 1975).

35. Matthews, *In Search of Woman's Passionate Soul*, 104–5.

36. Veronica Goodchild, *Eros and Chaos* (York Beach, ME: Nicholas-Hays, Inc., 2001), 149, 150.

37. Fred Alan Wolf, *The Spiritual Universe: One Physicist's Vision of Spirit, Soul, Matter, and Self* (Needham, MA: Moment Point Press, 1999), 244–58.

CHAPTER 7. ESCORTS TO THE BELOVED

1. Walter F. Otto, *Dionysus: Myth and Cult* (Bloomington: Indiana University Press, 1965), 181.

2. Robert A. Johnson, *We: Understanding the Psychology of Romantic Love* (San Francisco: HarperCollins, 1983), 52.

3. Irina Tweedie, *Daughter of Fire: A Diary of a Spiritual Training with a Sufi Master* (Nevada City, CA: Dolphin Publishing, 1986), 81.

4. For more about the exploitation of sexuality in spiritual communities, see Katy Butler, "Encountering the Shadow in Buddhist America" and W. Brugh Joy, "A Heretic in a New Age Community," in *Meeting the Shadow: The Hidden Power of the Dark Side of Human Nature*, ed. Connie Zweig and Jeremy Abrams (New York: Tarcher/Putnam, 1991), 137–47, 150–53.

5. Laurence Rosenthal, "Confronting the 'Next Impossible': Musical Studies with Nadia Boulanger," *Parabola* 14, no. 1 (Spring 1989): 81.

6. From Linda Paterson, "*Fin'amor* and the Development of the Courtly *Canso*," in *The Troubadours: An Introduction*, ed. Simon Gaunt and Sarah Kay (Cambridge: Cambridge University Press, 1999), 39.

7. Paterson, "*Fin'amor*," 31.

8. The Countess of Die, like some other *trobairitz* poets, was able to articulate on paper what status and modesty would have prevented her from proclaiming out loud. The countess continues:

How I would like to hold him
one night in my naked arms
and see him joyfully use my body
as a pillow...
and offer him my heart, my love,
my mind, my eyes and my life.

My handsome friend, gracious and charming,
when will I hold you in my power?
Oh that I might lie with you
one night and kiss you lovingly!
Know how great is my desire
to treat you as a husband;
but you must promise me to do
whatever I may wish.

("A Certain Knight," trans. Anthony Bonner, in *The Soul Is Here for Its Own Joy*, ed. Robert Bly [Hopewell, NJ: Ecco Press, 1995], 142.) Another translator, Tilde Sankovitch, renders the lines in the last stanza as "Know that I would very much wish to have you in the husband's place," an even more forthrightly sexual allusion. See Tilde Sankovitch, "The Trobairitz," in *The Troubadours*, 120–21.

9. Marina Warner, *Alone of All Her Sex: The Myth and Cult of the Virgin Mary* (New York: Vintage Books, 1976), 134–48.

10. Frederick Goldin, *The Mirror of Narcissus in the Courtly Love Lyric* (Ithaca: Cornell University Press, 1967), 92.

11. Sylvia Plath, *Letters Home: Correspondence 1950–1963*, ed. Aurelia Schober Plath (New York: Bantam Books, 1977), 300, 298.

12. Quoted in Caitlín Matthews, *In Search of Woman's Passionate Soul* (Rockport, ME: Element Books, 1997), 49.

13. Kate Fitzpatrick, a teacher, musician, and dramatherapist from Donegal, Ireland, has written that if Cuchullain had chosen both Fand *and* Emer and found a way to love both fully and with integrity, then the male warrior spirit would have been integrated with its feminine side and hence would have attained the spiritual balance it sorely needed. "Celtic Myths in Healing Process: A Journey to the Warrior of Heart," in *Celtic Threads*, ed. Padraigín Clancy (Dublin: Veritas Publications, 1999).

14. Quoted in Matthews, *In Search of Woman's Passionate Soul*, 198.

15. Rabindranath Tagore, "They have no caste," in *Later Poems of Rabindranath Tagore*, trans. Aurobindo Bose (New York: Minerva Press, 1974), 62.

CHAPTER 8. SEIZED BY THE RAPTURE BIRD

1. Trebbe Johnson, "Wedding Night with the God," *Parabola* 29, no. 1 (Spring 2004): 80–89.

2. Clayton Eshelman, *Juniper Fuse: Upper Paleolithic Imagination and the Construction of the Underworld* (Middletown, CT: Wesleyan University Press, 2003), xxi.

3. William James, *The Varieties of Religious Experience* (1902; repr., New York: New American Library, 1958), 293.

4. James Swan, *Sacred Places: How the Living Earth Seeks Our Friendship* (Santa Fe: Bear & Company, 1990), 77. Abraham Maslow identified five stages in a peak experience: "emotional arousal and a sense of being guided by a higher force,...a trigger in the environment...feelings of energy, bliss, wonder, joy, awe, and love...manifestations of power, such as visions, prophecies, interspecies communication, the hearing of music, etc....a return to normal reality, feeling inspired and deeply touched."

5. Jean-Jacques Rousseau, *Confessions*, trans. Angela Scholar (New York: Oxford University Press, 2000), 342.

6. Elemire Zolla, *Archetypes: The Persistence of Unifying Patterns* (New York: Harcourt Brace Jovanovich, 1981), 50.

7. Alexander F. Skutch, *The Minds of Birds* (College Station: Texas A & M University Press, 1996), 44–45, 47.

8. Brian Swimme, *The Universe Is a Green Dragon* (Santa Fe: Bear & Company, 1984), 48. An interesting aside: Swimme identifies allurement as one of the ten powers of the universe, drives inherent in physical forces from galaxies to humans. Other powers include radiance, emergence, and transmutation. Allurement was the first power Swimme identified in a moment of revelation. As one of the world's foremost experts on gravity, he was stunned one day by the realization that gravity's essential principal, the power to allure, had been the very force that drew him to it (conversation with author, Estes Park, Colorado, June 23, 2004).

9. Candace Pert, *Molecules of Emotion* (New York: Touchstone, 1999), 181–82.

10. Viktor Frankl, *Man's Search for Meaning* (Boston: Beacon Press, 1992), 44.

11. Rachel Carson, *The Sense of Wonder* (New York: Harper & Row, 1956), 43.

12. Mara Freeman, "The Wide-Spun Moment," *Parabola* 23, no. 2 (Summer 1998): 29. Freeman points out that the Gaelic word *filidh* means both "poet" and "seer," since both vision and poetry fill one with the "rapture of illumination." The *fili* was trained in mantic arts — how to leave the body and ascend to the sky, how to communicate with the dead and the spirits. Irish poet-seers were mediators between the human and spirit realms. The trance journeys they undertook were to gain *imbas* — "knowledge that enlightens," seen as a gift from "the god that kindles fire in the head." The treasures they brought back could be either poetry or prophecy.

13. Thomas Moore, *The Soul of Sex: Cultivating Life as an Act of Love* (New York: HarperCollins, 1998), 139.

14. Rollo May, *Love and Will* (New York: Dell, 1969), 76.

15. Plotinus, *The Enneads*, III.5.2, trans. Stephen McKenna (London: Penguin, 1991), 177.

16. Quoted in Evelyn Fox Keller, *A Feeling for the Organism: The Life and Work of Barbara McClintock* (San Francisco: Freeman, 1983), 117.

17. Diane Ackerman, *Deep Play* (New York: Vintage Books, 1999), xiii.

18. Moyra Caldecott, *Women in Celtic Myth: Tales of Extraordinary Women from the Ancient Celtic Tradition* (Rochester, VT: Destiny Books, 1988), 33. Caldecott also shows how the heroines and heroes of this myth take advantage of their mistakes to learn how to act more appropriately in the future. A big part of enlightenment, both for the mortals and the immortals, is figuring out subtleties of behavior when in the company of people from the other world.

CHAPTER 9. BEAUTY TIPS FROM MYRNA LOY

1. Elizabeth Brensinger, *Earth Dreams* (New Tripoli, PA: Red Road Press, 2002), 73.

2. Robert Bly, *A Little Book on the Human Shadow* (San Francisco: Harper & Row, 1988), 47–48.

3. Martha Crampton, quoted in Molly Young Brown, *Growing Whole* (Center City, MN: Hazelden Educational Materials, 1993), 238.

4. Bill Plotkin, *Soulcraft: Crossing into the Mysteries of Nature and Psyche* (Novato, CA: New World Library, 2003), 92. See 91–96 for suggestions on "Welcoming Home the Loyal Soldier."

5. Rollo May, *Love and Will* (New York: Norton, 1969), 131.

6. Marion Woodman, *The Pregnant Virgin: A Process of Psychological Transformation* (Toronto: Inner City Books, 1985), 129.

7. James Hillman, "The Cure of the Shadow," in *Meeting the Shadow: The Hidden Power of the Dark Side of Human Nature*, ed. Connie Zweig and Jeremy Abrams (New York: Tarcher/Putnam, 1991), 242.

8. Bly, *Little Book on the Human Shadow*, 42.

9. Linda Jacobson, "Drawing the Shadow," in Zweig and Abrams, 297–99.

10. Marsha Sinetar, "Using Our Flaws and Faults," in Zweig and Abrams, 117–18.

11. For information about Liz Brensinger's Shadow workshops, see her website: www.redroadenterprises.com.

12. Robert A. Johnson, *Owning Your Own Shadow: Understanding the Dark Side of the Psyche* (San Francisco: HarperCollins, 1991), 97–118.

13. Plotkin, *Soulcraft*, 270–71.

CHAPTER 10. COURTSHIP OF THE BELOVED

1. Erich Neumann, *Amor and Psyche* (New York: Bollingen Foundation, 1956), 80, 81.
2. Fyodor Dostoyevsky, "The Eternal Husband," in *Three Short Novels of Dostoyevsky*, trans. Constance Garrett, ed. Avrahm Yarmolinsky (Garden City, NY: Anchor Books, 1960), 330–31.
3. Quoted in Nancy Willard, *Testimony of the Invisible Man: William Carlos Williams, Francis Ponge, Rainer Maria Rilke, Pablo Neruda* (Columbia: University of Missouri Press, 1970), 7.
4. Quoted in Willard, *Testimony of the Invisible Man*, 6.
5. Caitlín Matthews, *In Search of Woman's Passionate Soul* (Rockport, ME: Element Books, 1997), passim, especially 180.
6. Thomas Moore, *The Soul of Sex: Cultivating Life as an Act of Love* (New York: HarperCollins, 1998), 232.
7. Fred Alan Wolf, in the film *What the Bleep Do We Know*, directed by William Arntz, Betsy Chasse, and Mark Vicente, 2004.
8. Morton T. Kelsey, *Companions on the Inner Way: The Art of Spiritual Guidance* (New York: Crossroad Publishing, 1983), 104.
9. Valerie Wilkinson, email to author, December 5, 2004.
10. Martin Buber, "Goblet of Grace," reprinted in *Parabola* 23, no. 2 (Summer 1998): 84.
11. Clifford Balenquah, conversation with author, Bacavi, Third Mesa, Arizona, March 18, 1987.
12. Candace Pert, *Molecules of Emotion* (New York: Touchstone, 1999), 137–39, 181–86.
13. Apuleius, *On the God of Socrates*, trans. Thomas Taylor (Edmonds, WA: Holmes Publishing, 2001), 23n.9.
14. Dennis Tedlock, ed., *Popul Vu: The Mayan Book of the Dawn of Life* (New York: Touchstone, 1985), 174. In his note about this passage Tedlock points out that it's more than emotional love and devotion Tohil wants, it's "the whole thing," the sacrifice of his worshipers' hearts (302).

CHAPTER 11. "YOUR FULLNESS IS MY DELIGHT"

1. Toni Morrison, *Beloved* (New York: Knopf, 1987), 59.
2. D. H. Lawrence, *The Rainbow* (London: Penguin, 1981), 137–39.
3. Diane Wolkstein and Samuel Noah Kramer, *Inanna: Queen of Heaven and Earth* (New York: Harper & Row, 1983), 40–41.
4. Wolkstein and Kramer, *Inanna: Queen of Heaven and Earth*, 154.
5. *New Oxford Annotated Bible with the Apocrypha*, ed. Herbert G. May and Bruce M. Metzger (New York: Oxford University Press, 1977), 817–18.

6. M. Esther Harding, *Woman's Mysteries Ancient and Modern* (New York: Harper & Row, 1971), 135–37.

7. Nancy Qualls-Corbett, *The Sacred Prostitute: Eternal Aspect of the Feminine* (Toronto: Inner City Books, 1988), 40.

8. D. M. Dooling, introduction, *Parabola* 7, no. 3 (Summer 1982): 2–3.

9. Steven Foster and Meredith Little, *The Trail to the Sacred Mountain: A Vision Quest Handbook for Adults* (Big Pine, CA: Lost Borders Press, 1984), 11. In this section of the handbook, Foster and Little suggest several questions that people can ask themselves as they determine what kind of ceremony best suits their needs.

10. Qualls-Corbett, *Sacred Prostitute*, 84, 86.

11. John P. Dourley, *Love, Celibacy and the Inner Marriage* (Toronto: Inner City Books, 1987), 8.

CHAPTER 12. HOW BIG LOVE CAN BE

1. P. L. Travers, *What the Bee Knows: Reflections on Myth, Symbol, and Story* (London: Penguin, 1993), 16.

2. John G. Neihardt, *Black Elk Speaks* (Lincoln: University of Nebraska Press, 1961), 165.

3. Erich Neumann, *Amor and Psyche* (New York: Bollingen Foundation, 1956), 140.

4. Frederick Buechner, *Wishful Thinking: A Theological ABC* (San Francisco: HarperCollins, 1993), 119.

5. Joanna Macy, *Despair and Personal Power in the Nuclear Age* (Baltimore: New Society, 1983), 23. Macy has written widely about and presents workshops and seminars worldwide on the subject of despair and empowerment.

6. Thomas Moore, *The Soul of Sex: Cultivating Life as an Act of Love* (New York: HarperCollins, 1998), 156.

7. Although Matthews is speaking here of the daimons of women, her comments are relevant to both men and women who are developing a relationship with the Beloved. Besides an obsession with the inner dialogue that excludes the outer world, other problems are neglect of the Beloved, "causing a build-up of dammed power"; total identification with one of the daimonic masks (the example Matthews gives is the businesswoman who models her behavior on that of the male executive), so that one sports a particular quality of the daimon rather than developing a balance of her own traits and gifts; giving power to the critical voice; or demanding, directly or indirectly, that real-life partners take on the qualities of the inner guide. All these problems reflect a life out of balance. See *In Search of Woman's Passionate Soul* (Rockport, ME: Element Books, 1997), 116–48.

8. Apuleius, *On the God of Socrates*, trans. Thomas Taylor (Edmonds, WA: Holmes Publishing, 2001), 14.

9. Morton T. Kelsey, *Companions on the Inner Way: The Art of Spiritual Guidance* (New York: Crossroad Publishing, 1983), 22–24.

10. Christmas Humphreys, *Buddhism* (Hammondsworth, Eng.: Penguin, 1967), 125. Humphreys points out that for Buddhists thoughts are actual forces in the world. A prayer, or sutra, is not just a recitation of words; it is a conveyer of potent psychic energy.

11. Vincent Rossi, "Original Sin," *Parabola* 8, no. 1 (Winter 1983): 17.

12. Steven Foster, with Meredith Little, *The Book of the Vision Quest* (Spokane, WA: Bear Tribe Publishing, 1987), 53–54.

13. Quoted in John P. Dourley, *Love, Celibacy and the Inner Marriage* (Toronto: Inner City Books, 1987), 35.

14. "The Beloved," retold by Zalman M. Schacter in *Parabola* 1, no. 1 (Winter 1976): 94–95.

CHAPTER 13. THE LOVER WHO CAME BY STAYING AWAY

1. Quoted in John P. Dourley, *Love, Celibacy and the Inner Marriage* (Toronto: Inner City Books, 1987), 37–38. Jung helped the woman to withdraw her projection on him, and to discover the divine within herself, a process that gave her new vigor and a sense of purpose. His amazement in the process is evident in his description of it, and he marvels about the "afflux of energy" that, freed from its former clinging to a human and outer object (himself), was transformed into a potent fuel for powering the self. The three quotes from Jung that I use here are ones Dourley attributes to *Symbols of Transformation*, 130; "On the Psychology of the Unconscious," *Two Essays in Analytical Psychology*, par. 214; and "Transformation Symbolism in the Mass," *Psychology and Religion*, par. 396.

2. Fred Alan Wolf, *The Spiritual Universe: One Physicist's Vision of Spirit, Soul, Matter, and Self* (Needham, MA: Moment Point Press, 1999), 170.

Ackerman, Diane. *Deep Play*. New York: Vintage Books, 1999.

———. *A Natural History of Love*. New York: Vintage Books, 1995.

———. *Origami Bridges: Poems*. New York: HarperCollins, 2002.

Akhmatova. Anna. "The Muse." *The Complete Poems*. Translated by Judith Hemschemeyer. Boston: Zephyr Press, 1992.

Apuleius. *On the God of Socrates*. Translated by Thomas Taylor. Edmonds, WA: Holmes Publishing, 2001.

Badiner, Alan Hunt, ed. *Dharma Gaia: A Harvest of Essays in Buddhism and Ecology*. Berkeley, CA: Parallax Press, 1990.

Baring, Anne, and Jules Cashford. *The Myth of the Goddess: Evolution of an Image*. New York: Penguin, 1993.

Barthes, Roland. *A Lover's Discourse: Fragments*. Translated by Richard Howard. New York: Hill and Wang, 1979.

"The Beloved." Retold by Zalman M. Schacter. *Parabola* 1, no. 1 (Winter 1976): 94–95.

Berenson-Perkins, Janet. *Kabbalah Decoder: Revealing the Messages of the Ancient Mystics*. Hauppauge, NY: Barron's Educational Series, 2000.

Bettelheim, Bruno. *The Uses of Enchantment: The Meaning and Importance of Fairy Tales*. New York: Vintage Books, 1977.

Bly, Robert. *A Little Book on the Human Shadow*. San Francisco: Harper & Row, 1988.

———, ed. *The Soul Is Here for Its Own Joy*. Hopewell, NJ: Ecco Press, 1995.

Brensinger, Elizabeth. *Earth Dreams*. New Tripoli, PA: Red Road Press, 2002.

Brown, Molly Young. *Growing Whole*. Center City, MN: Hazelden Educational Materials, 1993.

Buber, Martin. "Goblet of Grace." *Parabola* 23, no. 2 (Summer 1998): 81–84.

Buechner, Frederick. *Wishful Thinking: A Theological ABC*. San Francisco: HarperCollins, 1993.

Calasso, Roberto. *Ka: Stories of the Mind and Gods of India*. Translated by Tim Parks. New York: Vintage Books, 1999.

———. *The Marriage of Cadmus and Harmony*. Translated by Tim Parks. New York: Vintage Books, 1993.

Caldecott, Moyra. *Women in Celtic Myth: Tales of Extraordinary Women from the Ancient Celtic Tradition*. Rochester, VT: Destiny Books, 1988.

Campbell, Joseph. *The Hero with a Thousand Faces*. Princeton: Princeton University Press, 1968.

———. *The Masks of God: Primitive Mythology*. New York: Penguin, 1984.

Camus, Albert. *Lyrical and Critical Essays*. Edited by Philip Thody. Translated by Ellen Conroy Kennedy. New York: Vintage Books, 1968.

Carson, Rachel. *The Sense of Wonder*. New York: Harper & Row, 1956.

Chekhov, Anton. *The Unknown Chekhov: Stories & Other Writings*. Translated by Avrahm Yarmolinsky. New York: Ecco Press, 1987.

Cragg, Kenneth. *The Call of the Minaret*. New York: Oxford University Press, 1964.

Danielou, Alain. *The Hindu Temple: Deification of Eroticism*. Rochester, VT: Inner Traditions, 2001.

Dante Alighieri. *Purgatorio*. Translated by W. S. Merwin. New York: Alfred A. Knopf, 2000.

De Troyes, Chrétien. "The Story of the Grail (Perceval)." In *Arthurian Romances*. London: Penguin, 1991.

Donne, John. *The Complete English Poems*. New York: Penguin, 1986.

Dooling, D. M., introduction. *Parabola* 7, no. 3 (Summer 1982): 2–3.

Dostoyevsky, Fyodor. "The Eternal Husband." In *Three Short Novels of Dostoyevesky*. Translated by Constance Garrett. Edited by Avrahm Yarmolinsky. Garden City, NY: Anchor Books, 1960.

Dourley, John P. *Love, Celibacy and the Inner Marriage*. Toronto: Inner City Books, 1987.

Drengston, Alan, and Yuichi Inoue. *The Deep Ecology Movement: An Introductory Anthology*. Berkeley, CA: North Atlantic Books, 1995.

Duerr, Hans Peter. *Dreamtime: Concerning the Boundary between Wilderness and Civilization*. Translated by Felicitas Goodman. Oxford: Basil Blackwell, 1985.

Eisler, Riane. *Sacred Pleasure: Sex, Myth, and the Politics of the Body*. San Francisco: HarperCollins, 1996.

Eliade, Mircea. *Myth and Reality*. Translated by Willard R. Trask. New York: Harper & Row, 1963.

―――. *The Sacred and the Profane: The Nature of Religion*. Translated by Willard Trask. New York: Harcourt Brace Jovanovich, 1987.

Eliot, Alexander. *The Universal Myths: Heroes, Gods, Tricksters and Others*. New York: Truman Talley Books/Meridien, 1999.

Erdoes, Richard, and Alfonso Ortiz, eds. *American Indian Myths and Legends*. New York: Pantheon Books, 1984.

Ernst, Carl W. *Sufism*. Boston: Shambhala, 1997.

Eshelman, Clayton. *Juniper Fuse: Upper Paleolithic Imagination and the Construction of the Underworld*. Middletown, CT: Wesleyan University Press, 2003.

Foster, Steven, with Meredith Little. *The Book of the Vision Quest*. Spokane, WA: Bear Tribe Publishing, 1987.

―――. *The Roaring of the Sacred River*. New York: Prentice Hall, 1989.

―――. *The Trail to the Sacred Mountain: A Vision Quest Handbook for Adults*. Big Pine, CA: Lost Borders, 1984.

Fowler, Barbara Hughes, trans. *Love Lyrics of Ancient Egypt*. Chapel Hill: University of North Carolina Press, 1994.

Frankl, Viktor. *Man's Search for Meaning*. Boston: Beacon Press, 1992.

Freeman, Mara. "The Wide-Spun Moment." *Parabola* 23, no. 2 (Summer 1998): 29–35.

Fuller, Margaret. "Woman in the Nineteenth Century." In *The Woman and the Myth: Margaret Fuller's Life and Writings*. Edited by Bell Gale Chevigny. Old Westbury, NY: Feminist Press, 1968.

Gallegos, Eligio Stephen. *The Personal Totem Pole Process*. Velarde, NM: Moon Bear Press, 1996.

Gardner, John, and John Maier, trans. *The Epic of Gilgamesh*. New York: Vintage Books, 1985.

Gaunt, Simon, and Sarah Kay, eds. *The Troubadours: An Introduction*. Cambridge: Cambridge University Press, 1999.

Gertrude of Helfta. *The Herald of Divine Love*. New York: Paulist Press, 1993.

Goldin, Frederick. *The Mirror of Narcissus in the Courtly Love Lyric*. Ithaca: Cornell University Press, 1967.

Gore, Al. *Earth in the Balance: Ecology and the Human Spirit*. New York: Penguin, 1993.

Graves, Robert. *The White Goddess*. New York: Farrar, Straus and Giroux, 1978.

Hamill, Sam, ed. *The Erotic Spirit*. Boston: Shambhala, 1996.

Harding, M. Esther. *Woman's Mysteries Ancient and Modern*. New York: Harper & Row, 1971.

Heaney, Marie. *Over Nine Waves: A Book of Irish Legends*. London: Faber and Faber, 1994.

Hillman, James. *Anima: An Anatomy of a Personified Notion*. Woodstock, CT: Spring Publications, 1985.

———. *Loose Ends*. Dallas, TX: Spring Publications, 1975.

———. *The Soul's Code: In Search of Character and Calling*. New York: Warner Books, 1996.

Hirshfield, Jane, ed. *Women in Praise of the Sacred*. New York: HarperCollins, 1995.

Holl, Adolf. *The Left Hand of God: A Biography of the Holy Spirit*. New York: Image Books, 1996.

Houston, Jean. *The Search for the Beloved: Journeys in Mythology and Sacred Psychology*. New York: Tarcher/Putnam, 1987.

Humphreys, Christmas. *Buddhism*. Hammondsworth, Eng.: Penguin, 1967.

Ibn Hazm. *The Ring of the Dove: A Treatise on the Art and Practice of Arab Love*. Translated by A. J. Arberry. London: Luzac Oriental, 1994.

James, William. *The Varieties of Religious Experience*. 1902. Reprint, New York: New American Library, 1958.

Jaynes, Julian. *The Origin of Consciousness in the Breakdown of the Bicameral Mind*. Boston: Houghton Mifflin, 1976.

Johnson, Robert A. *Ecstasy: Understanding the Psychology of Joy*. San Francisco: HarperCollins, 1987.

———. *Owning Your Own Shadow: Understanding the Dark Side of the Psyche*. San Francisco: HarperCollins, 1993.

———. *We: Understanding the Psychology of Romantic Love*. San Francisco: HarperCollins, 1983.

Johnson, Trebbe. "The Monster of Grim Prospects." *Parabola* 23, no. 3 (Fall 1998): 6–13.

———. "Wedding Night with the God." *Parabola* 29, no. 1 (Spring 2004): 83–89.

Jung, C. J. *Memories, Dreams, Reflections*. Translated by Richard and Clara Winston. New York: Vintage Books, 1965.

———. *On the Nature of the Psyche*. Translated by R. F. C. Hull. Princeton: Princeton University Press, 1969.

Jung, Emma. *Animus and Anima*. Woodstock, CT: Spring Publications, 1957.

Kabir. *The Kabir Book: Forty-Four of the Ecstatic Poems of Kabir*. Versions by Robert Bly. Boston: Beacon Press, 1977.

Keller, Evelyn Fox. *A Feeling for the Organism: The Life and Work of Barbara McClintock*. San Francisco: Freeman, 1983.

Kelsey, Morton T. *Companions on the Inner Way: The Art of Spiritual Guidance*. New York: Crossroad Publishing, 1983.

Khan, Hazrat Inayat. *The Heart of Sufism*. Boston: Shambhala, 1999.

Lao-tzu. *The Way of Life*. Translated by Witter Brynner. New York: Berkley Publishing Group, 1972.

Lawrence, D. H. *The Rainbow*. London: Penguin, 1981.

Lewis, Samuel L. *Sufi Vision and Initiation: Meetings with Remarkable Beings*. San Francisco: Sufi Islamia/Prophecy Publications, 1986.

Macy, Joanna. *Despair and Personal Power in the Nuclear Age*. Baltimore: New Society Publishers, 1983.

————. *World as Lover, World as Self*. Berkeley, CA: Parallax Press, 1991.

Matthews, Caitlín. *In Search of Woman's Passionate Soul*. Rockport, ME: Element Books, 1997.

Matthiessen, Peter. *Nine-Headed Dragon River: Zen Journals 1969–1982*. Boston: Shambhala, 1986.

May, Rollo. *Love and Will*. New York: Dell, 1969.

Merwin, W. S. *The Mays of Ventadorn*. Washington, D.C.: National Geographic Directions, 2002.

Metzner, Ralph. *The Well of Remembrance: Rediscovering the Earth Wisdom Myths of Northern Europe*. Boston: Shambhala, 1994.

Moore, Thomas. *The Soul of Sex: Cultivating Life as an Act of Love*. New York: HarperCollins, 1998.

Morrison, Toni. *Beloved*. New York: Knopf, 1987.

Neihardt, John G. *Black Elk Speaks*. Lincoln: University of Nebraska Press, 1961.

Neumann, Erich. *Amor and Psyche*. New York: Bollingen Foundation, 1956.

Nouwen, Henri J. M. *Life of the Beloved*. New York: Crossroad Publishing Company, 1992.

Nurbakhsh, Dr. Javad. *Sufi Women*. New York: Khaniqah-Nimatullahi Publications, 1983.

Oelschlaeger, Max. *The Idea of Wilderness*. New Haven: Yale University Press, 1991.

Ortega y Gasset, José. *On Love*. New York: New American Library, 1976.

Otto, Walter F. *Dionysus: Myth and Cult*. Translated by Robert B. Palmer. Bloomington and Indianapolis: Indiana University Press, 1965.

Pagels, Elaine. *The Gnostic Gospels*. New York: Random House, 1979.

Pert, Candace. *Molecules of Emotion*. New York: Touchstone, 1999.

Pizan, Christine de. *The Book of the Duke of True Lovers*. Translated by Thelma S. Fenster. New York: Persea Books, 1991.

————. *Writings.* Selected and edited by Charity Cannon Willard. New York: Persea Books, 1994.

Plath, Sylvia. *Letters Home: Correspondence 1950–1963.* Edited by Aurelia Schober Plath. New York: Bantam Books, 1977.

Plato. "The Symposium." *Great Dialogues of Plato.* Translated by W. H. D. Rouse. New York: New American Library, 1956.

Plotinus. *The Enneads.* Translated by Stephen McKenna. London: Penguin, 1991.

Plotkin, Bill. *Soulcraft: Crossing into the Mysteries of Nature and Psyche.* Novato, CA: New World Library, 2003.

Qualls-Corbett, Nancy. *The Sacred Prostitute: Eternal Aspect of the Feminine.* Toronto: Inner City Books, 1988.

Rosenthal, Laurence. "Confronting the 'Next Impossible': Musical Studies with Nadia Boulanger." *Parabola* 14, no. 1 (Spring 1989): 78–83.

Rosenzweig, Franz. "The Lover of God, the Love of Man." *Parabola* 20, no. 4 (Winter 1995): 63–65.

Rossi, Vincent. "Original Sin." *Parabola* 8, no. 1 (Winter 1983): 12–21.

Rothenberg, Jerome. *Shaking the Pumpkin: Traditional Poetry of the Indian North Americas.* New York: Alfred van der Marck Editions, 1986.

Rousseau, Jean-Jacques. *Confessions.* Translated by Angela Scholar. New York: Oxford University Press, 2000.

Rumi, Jelalludin. *The Soul of Rumi.* Translated by Coleman Barks. San Francisco: HarperCollins, 2001.

Sandford, Christopher. *Clapton: Edge of Darkness.* New York: Da Capo Press, 1999.

Schama, Simon. *Landscape and Memory.* New York: Vintage Books, 1996.

Skutch, Alexander F. *The Minds of Birds.* College Station: Texas A & M University Press, 1996.

Smith, Huston. *The World's Religions.* San Francisco: HarperCollins, 1991.

Suzuki, D. T. *Essays in Zen Buddhism.* New York: Grove Press, 1961.

Swan, James. *Sacred Places: How the Living Earth Seeks Our Friendship.* Santa Fe: Bear & Company Publishing, 1990.

Swimme, Brian. *The Universe Is a Green Dragon.* Santa Fe: Bear & Company, 1984.

Tagore, Rabindranath. *Later Poems of Rabindranath Tagore.* Translated by Aurobindo Bose. New York: Minerva Press, 1974.

Tedlock, Dennis, ed. *Popul Vu: The Mayan Book of the Dawn of Life.* New York: Touchstone, 1985.

Teresa of Avila. *The Life of Teresa of Jesus: The Autobiography of St. Teresa of Avila.* Translated by E. Allison Peers. Garden City, NY: Image Books, 1960.

Travers, P. L. *What the Bee Knows: Reflections on Myth, Symbol, and Story*. London: Penguin, 1993.

Tweedie, Irina. *Daughter of Fire: A Diary of a Spiritual Training with a Sufi Master*. Nevada City, CA: Dolphin Publishing, 1986.

Von Franz, Marie-Louise. "Daimons and the Inner Companion." *Parabola* 16, no. 4 (Fall 1991): 36–44.

Walker, Barbara G. *The Woman's Encyclopedia of Myths and Secrets*. New York, HarperCollins, 1983.

Warner, Marina. *Alone of All Her Sex: The Myth and Cult of the Virgin Mary*. New York: Vintage Books, 1976.

————. *Fantastic Metamorphoses, Other Worlds*. Oxford: Oxford University Press, 2002.

Willard, Nancy. *Testimony of the Invisible Man: William Carlos Williams, Francis Ponge, Rainer Maria Rilke, Pablo Neruda*. Columbia: University of Missouri Press, 1970.

Williams, Charles. *The Figure of Beatrice: A Study in Dante*. London: Faber and Faber, 1958.

Williams, David. *A Naturalist's Guide to Canyon Country*. Helena, MT: Falcon Publishing, 2000.

Wolf, Fred Alan. *The Spiritual Universe: One Physicist's Vision of Spirit, Soul, Matter, and Self*. Needham, MA: Moment Point Press, 1999.

Wolkstein, Diane. *The First Love Stories*. New York: HarperCollins, 1991.

Wolkstein, Diane, and Samuel Noah Kramer. *Inanna: Queen of Heaven and Earth*. New York: Harper & Row, 1983.

Woodman, Marion. *The Pregnant Virgin: A Process of Psychological Transformation*. Toronto: Inner City Books, 1985.

Yeats, William Butler. *Selected Poems and Two Plays*. Edited by M. L. Rosenthal. New York: Collier Books, 1969.

Yutang, Lin, ed. *The Wisdom of China and India*. New York: Modern Library, 1942.

Zolbrod, Paul G. *Diné bahane': The Navajo Creation Story*. Albuquerque: University of New Mexico Press, 1985.

Zolla, Elemire. *Archetypes: The Persistence of Unifying Patterns*. New York: Harcourt Brace Jovanovich, 1981.

Zweig, Connie, and Jeremy Abrams, eds. *Meeting the Shadow: The Hidden Power of the Dark Side of Human Nature*. New York: Tarcher/Putnam, 1991.

Trebbe Johnson is the director of Vision Arrow, an organization offering journeys to explore wildness and allurement in nature and self. She leads vision quests, workshops, and ceremonies worldwide. Her writings about myth, nature, and spirit have appeared in many media, from her narrative poem "The Fruit of Eve," which received a Poetry Society of America award; to her Telly Award–winning video "Only One Earth," produced for the United Nations celebration of Earth Day; to "Yards," her essay about the wilderness in suburbia, for which she received a Pushcart Prize honorable mention. A passionate explorer of both inner and outer nature, Trebbe has camped alone in the Arctic wilderness, studied classical Indian dance, and co-guided a camel caravan with the Tuareg people in the Sahara Desert. She lives with her husband, Andrew Gardner, a potter and rustic furniture maker, in rural northeastern Pennsylvania.

www.visionarrow.com
www.trebbejohnson.com

green press INITIATIVE

NEW WORLD LIBRARY is committed to preserving ancient forests and natural resources. We printed this title on Transcontinental's Enviro Edition 100 Natural recycled paper, which is made of 100 percent postconsumer waste and processed chlorine free.

Using this paper instead of virgin fiber for the first printing of this book saved:

• 89 trees (40 feet in height and 6 to 8 inches in diameter)
• 37,722 gallons of water
• 16,280 kilowatt hours of electricity
• 8,170 net greenhouse gases
• 4,159 pounds of solid waste

We are a member of the Green Press Initiative — a nonprofit program supporting publishers in using fiber that is not sourced from ancient or endangered forests. For more information, visit www.greenpressinitiative.org.